ƒP

THE
IMMIGRANT
ADVANTAGE

What We Can Learn from
Newcomers to America about
Health, Happiness, and Hope

CLAUDIA KOLKER

Free Press

New York   London   Toronto   Sydney   New Delhi

f**P**

Free Press
A Division of Simon & Schuster, Inc.
1230 Avenue of the Americas
New York, NY 10020

First Free Press hardcover edition October 2011

For information about special discounts for bulk purchases, please contact Simon
& Schuster Special Sales at 1-866-506-1949 or business@simonandschuster.com.

The Simon & Schuster Speakers Bureau can bring authors to your live event. For
more information or to book an event contact the Simon & Schuster Speakers
Bureau at 1-866-248-3049 or visit our website at www.simonspeakers.com.

Manufactured in the United States of America

10   9   8   7   6   5   4   3   2   1

Library of Congress Cataloging-in-Publication Data

Kolker, Claudia.
The immigrant advantage: what we can learn from newcomers to
America about health, happiness, and hope /
Claudia Kolker.
p. cm.
1. Immigrants—United States—Social life and customs—21st century.
2. Immigrants—United States—Social conditions. I. Title.
JV6456.K65 2011
305.9'069120973—dc22   2011004498

ISBN 978-1-4165-8683-8

For Marielena and Jonas Kolker

CONTENTS

THE
IMMIGRANT
ADVANTAGE

Embarking

*P*HO FOR LUNCH again?" my office mate asked. Maybe it was the vapor of beef broth, star anise, and garlic I trailed every time I ate this addictive Vietnamese soup. Connoisseurs, I knew, actually judged pho as much by its scent as by its flavor. I didn't mind a bit of aroma.

I had started a new beat for the *Houston Chronicle*, on immigrants' lives. My stories bubbled first from ethnic newspapers, day-labor sites, and talking to sources as often as I could over pho. But eventually, my best ideas flowed from friends—friends like my Vietnamese-language tutor, Ngoc Le.

Teaching me Vietnamese was probably the only task Ngoc ever left incomplete. After tutoring me for years until my schedule made it futile, she turned to schooling me in Vietnamese culture. It was her true calling. Ngoc had a genius for skating between worlds. She'd come to the United States in the 1960s, not as a refugee but as a graduate student, and married a Vietnamese student who would become a doctor. Years later she divorced, with no regrets, scandalizing her Vietnamese peers. Now the same ladies she'd horrified called Ngoc for lunch. They wanted to learn how her three kids—hip and delightful: I knew them—had all earned college scholarships.

"It's like fruit trees. You feed and you prune every day," Ngoc told me one day over lunch. But the truth was that she had cherry-picked, brilliantly, from Vietnamese and American traditions to raise them. There was Asian-style pressure: "You can be anything you want—a doctor or lawyer," she told them. But there was also the American notion of well-roundedness: Ngoc made her kids learn Spanish and sent them to volunteer in Latin America.

Her approach to money was a similar hybrid. Once I recommended a movie, and she replied, "I don't go to movies."

"Never?"

"Never," she said. "I see videos. I prefer to spend my money on more important things."

That night I repeated the conversation to my husband, Mike. We couldn't see it: Why the scrimping? Ngoc had a job, benefits. She was not prone to self-abnegation. A few weeks earlier she'd shown up at tutoring with a smile full of metal. "Braces," she said demurely.

As I mulled it, though, I found something provocative about Ngoc's example—the idea that some of the expenses I took for granted could, possibly, be lived without.

It became a household joke. "Live like an immigrant," Mike said when we wavered between takeout or making pasta. Every once in a while we'd go with the pasta.

The enormous distinction between us and Vietnamese immigrants, of course, was that we had never known insecurity. A few years later, though, I did become acquainted with uncertainty. I was pregnant and suddenly aware that every decision Mike and I made about our time, our money, and our environment would bear consequences for our children. Yet the resources we had—by choice, I reminded myself—differed a lot from those I'd grown up with, and vaguely assumed would have on hand when I had kids of my own.

So I began paying closer attention to successful immigrants. I was newly impressed by the parents of a Vietnamese boy who drove an hour to my house so I could tutor him—although he already was an honor student. I asked my older but still able-bodied Trinidadian friend, Shirley, why her son pestered her to move cross-country to live near him. And I thought again about Ngoc's careful frugalities.

For about two years, if you met me at a party and were discernibly of foreign birth, you ran a strong risk of getting The Question. "What's the smartest habit that people from your country bring here?"

Most people had ready answers. "Not airing dirty laundry in public," a Vietnamese friend said. "And sending checks to our parents."

"Parties with the whole family," a Filipina replied.

"Hospitality," said a friend who'd lived in Lebanon.

It took a while for me to refine the query. I was looking for practices that could be split from their surrounding cultural systems and copied. Practices that other Americans—like me—could adapt for ourselves.

Good practices.

"In Mexico, the youngest daughter traditionally never marries and spends her life keeping house for her parents," my mom offered before I (the youngest daughter) cleared that point up.

Some of the most compelling ideas I heard were religious. I especially admired Muslim burial, which, instead of filling the earth with formaldehyde and concrete, inters the dead in a plain piece of cloth. In death there is no rich or poor, the saying goes. Muslims say goodbye, not with top-of-the line casket hardware, but by lovingly handwashing the body.

Like its Jewish counterpart, this desert custom dovetails beautifully with Americans' reawakened interest in sustainability and the environment. But it is a religious rite, and the customs I was interested in had to stand on their own, independent of the faith or even the culture that created them. Customs like Vietnamese money clubs.

Do you know eleven people you'd trust with half your earnings each month, sure they would hand it back the instant you asked? It's not an American custom to rely this way on others, crossing the borders between friendship and finance, social nicety and real need. For the most part, we don't have to. But Hen Le, a fifty-seven-year-old Vietnamese refugee living in Houston, showed me that sometimes the un-American way can bring us what we want most.

Le needed $16,000 fast, and had no obvious way to get it. Ten years after arriving in the United States as a refugee, he didn't have the collateral to get a loan from a bank. And with his meager weekly pay as a mechanic, Hen could never save quickly enough to catch a sudden, gleaming opportunity—the chance to build a repair shop on a cheap patch of land, and for the first time in his life be his own boss.

But Le possessed something many other Americans do not: eleven friends—not intimates, but members of his peer group—whom he was willing to entrust with half his salary each month. And these acquaintances shared a tradition: a kind of club, with which ordinary Vietnamese have leveraged friendships into buying power for nearly one thousand years.

This book is about Hen Le's club, and a half dozen other ingenious customs that immigrants have carried here from around the world. Understandably, the newcomers rarely talk about these practices with outsiders, and I found that few researchers had closely studied them. These are folk customs, after all, practiced quietly in kitchens and living rooms. Honed over centuries, tailored to human needs and quirks, the customs described in this book brilliantly solve conundrums many Americans face every day.

Taken together, these customs also illuminate a riddle that epidemiologists have studied for decades. It's called the immigrant paradox: the evidence that immigrants, even those from poor, violent lands who live hard lives in the United States, tend to be physically and mentally healthier than the rest of us.

The term first appeared as the "epidemiological paradox," in a groundbreaking 1986 report showing that Latinos in the Southwest lived as long as non-Hispanic whites. Later studies showed Latinos

actually live *longer*—especially immigrants. The findings were baffling, because Latinos are burdened with all kinds of health risks: less
education, lower income, more obesity than native-born whites. But
the research holds true today. In 2010, the Centers for Disease Control reported that Latinos, about half of whom are foreign-born, now
live two and a half years longer than non-Hispanic whites. They live
nearly eight years longer than African Americans.

West Indians, South Asians, East Asians, and recently arrived Africans have the same edge. Across the board, America's immigrants typically live longer than those of us who are native-born. They give birth
to healthier babies. Even their psyches may be more resilient. According to a recent series in the *American Journal of Public Health,* 48 percent of Americans of all ethnic backgrounds will experience a mental
disorder during their lives, whether depression, substance abuse, or
alcohol abuse. Asian, Latino, and Caribbean immigrants show varying
rates of mental illness, but consistently reported fewer overall mental
problems than the native-born.

What can explain this? Selection, we know, is the biggest piece in
this puzzle. It takes a sound mind, and a strong body, to leave one life
behind and wrest a new one from an often unfriendly culture. If you
come here legally, the U.S. government requires a health exam. If you
cross without documentation, the desert, human predators, and hunger provide one free of charge.

Regardless how they get here, people who immigrate also tend to be
optimistic and committed to improving their lives, and both correlate
with health. But selection doesn't fully account for the health paradox in
all its forms and nationalities. Especially among Mexicans, the paradox
"violates one of the most predictable patterns we see in most parts of
the world and for most diseases," Dr. Paul Simon, a physician with the
Los Angeles County Public Health Department, says. "Poorer health
outcomes are generally seen in groups at the lower end of the socioeconomic scale. The question is, what are immigrants doing right?"

Behavior, many researchers think, is the other main puzzle piece. Immigrants smoke and drink less, breast-feed more, and their kids more often grow up with both parents. More subtly, the circuitry of their personal lives looks different. Today's non-European immigrants come from societies that still rely on dense social and religious networks. They belong to close-knit, extended families. And often, because circumstances force them to, they put off individual gratification to strive for communal goals. The traditions described in this book show some of these social circuits in action. They are practical, focused actions with specific goals. But as the circuits light up, they also form an intangible buffer against some of the risks that come with being an immigrant. Such circuitry, it turns out, can protect the rest of us too.

For almost as long as I've been a reporter, I've written about immigrants. Their stories energize me. I've learned how much will it takes to carry on life after trauma. I've seen the daring needed to work without speaking your boss's language. And I've witnessed desperate battles, often lost, to preserve families that were the only reason to leave home in the first place.

I first got an inkling of those passions during the 1980s, as a high school student in Washington, D.C. The now-fashionable Adams Morgan neighborhood was dingy and dodgy, a first stop for the city's incoming Africans and Central Americans. Strolling to a restaurant there one Saturday morning, I spied something odd. A wiry Latino man lay fast asleep near the curb in dusty jeans, leather tool belt, and boots. He obviously wasn't a panhandler. Yet just as clearly, he was a stranger. People got drunk and passed out in D.C. every day, but not often on big thoroughfares after a hard day of work.

A decade later, as a freelance writer in San Salvador, I learned who this man, like thousands of others who appeared in the city at that time, probably was. My high school days coincided with the start of El Salvador's grisly twelve-year civil war. Hundreds of thousands of Salvadorans streamed into the United States illegally, fleeing death squads, guerrilla recruiters, or memories of their own murdered families. Many headed to Washington because its construction work paid especially well.

I had moved to Central America on impulse. After college, I worked at a news service a few years, then went to graduate school in New York. I left mid-semester to volunteer with a pioneering woman doctor working in El Salvador. Refusing to affiliate with left or right, she ran a clinic that taught campesinos basic medical skills, and had somehow kept it running throughout the war. Vaguely, I figured I would go on to pursue public health.

Instead I stumbled onto foreign freelancing. I knew fairly little about the war that was ending when I arrived, but I knew it had traumatized every person I met. As the clinic workers and patients told me what they survived, the unfurling peace process transfixed me. How could former enemies share this small country? How could anyone function after twelve years of death squads and sons dead on roadsides?

I began writing about what I saw for a few U.S. papers. The *Houston Chronicle,* in particular, wanted more. "We have a huge number of Salvadorans here," the foreign editor said over the phone. "They want to know if there are jobs. If it's safe to go back."

For the next four years, I freelanced all over Central America and the Caribbean, stitching together assignments from the *Chronicle, The Economist, The Boston Globe,* and a half dozen others. The experience would tint my view of the simplest features in my own life: the worth of a dollar, the privilege of an intact house. Not long after I arrived in El Salvador, my photographer boyfriend Mike drove me to a guerrilla camp. It looked like a scene out of Robin Hood. In a forest speckled with small huts and tents, green-clad guerrillas slipped silently between the trees. One, a sturdy teenage girl with sleeves rolled to her biceps, was pointed out as a lethal shot during ambushes.

What do you want to do after so many years as a fighter? I asked her.

She wanted to get married and be a mom.

A few years later, before moving back to the United States, I began joining Mike to work in Port-au-Prince, Haiti. A grueling embargo was underway, an attempt to force out the general who ousted President Jean-Bertrand Aristide. Outside a shuttered baseball bat factory, a crowd of workers surrounded me. They were tense with hunger and rage, and had two completely logical questions.

"How will your writing help us?" and "When will we be able to work?"

As a lot of us do, I'd grown up acutely aware how much I owed to being American. My insouciance about the future. My unhindered education. The chutzpah to go, as a single woman, anywhere that I pleased. Uneasily, I started to daydream about waking up one day as the same person, but in a new country, faced with the kind of obstacles I made my living describing.

When I moved to Houston in the mid-1990s, and landed a real, full-time job at the *Chronicle,* the city was hurtling through one of the fastest demographic changes any U.S. metropolis had ever seen. A formerly white town run by white men, Houston today has no one ethnic majority. And uniquely, perhaps, among America's big, melting pot cities, it is home to large communities of all four major U.S. ethnic groups. The faces I noticed in places like Hermann Park, near downtown, reflected that distinctive mix of Latinos, Asians, African Americans, and Anglos.

As a majority-minority city, though, it won't be special for long. In about thirty years, thanks mainly to immigrants and their children, the rest of America will look much like Houston. Living here,

I quickly saw, was like taking a round-the-world balloon tour of the countries that were now reshaping the United States.

My fascination with immigrants' lives also stemmed from my own family experience. My dad's family hasn't strayed far from the Eastern Seaboard since 1889, when they arrived from Ukraine. Like most Eastern European Jews, my older relatives showed zero nostalgia for the old country. When my dad took our tiny, refined Aunt Rebecca to hear a klezmer band, he loved it, as he did mariachi and union songs from the thirties. "That's nice," she said. "For those people."

My mother, though, comes from wandering folk. Born and raised in Mexico City, she is what's called a *chilanga,* with all the cosmopolitan attitude Americans expect from New Yorkers. But her parents themselves were immigrants to Mexico: my grandfather from Honduras and my grandmother, Concepción, from Nicaragua. My grandmother's parents were industrious people in a brutal society. Her father, a small landowner, planted orange trees in a ring around their house to encircle his family in blossoms. But when he visited my grandmother, Concepción, at school, she felt ashamed of his farmer's clothes and leather sandals.

A few years later, Concepción won a scholarship to medical school in the city of León. The townsfolk there came unglued. A woman! Studying naked men! Women hurled dishwater at her on the street. So with 100 pesos in her pocket, she left for medical school in Mexico, where public education was free and women professionals well accepted. She was Nicaragua's first woman doctor, but Mexico was her home.

Migration, however, works in mysterious ways. At the close of World War II, as concentration camps were liberated, Concepción applied to the UN's relief team for displaced persons. A Bolivian adviser mentioned her request to Nelson Rockefeller, who invited her to join the U.S. contingent. In one of the odder turns of Latin/U.S. history, the country girl from Nicaragua was made a captain in the U.S. Army.

My mother, meanwhile, was at a Quaker school in Philadelphia.

When a teacher secured her a U.S. college scholarship, she assumed it was a brief sojourn before graduate school back in Mexico. Then, in botany class at the University of Maryland, she met a handsome fellow from Baltimore.

Which is how I came to grow up Jewish and Mexican in the Maryland suburbs and think little of it. True, all four of us kids learned Spanish, and ate tortillas before you could buy them at Safeway. For Jewish holidays we drove to Baltimore, where we were doted on by stylish aunts. But the true depth of my ethnic awareness was better measured in fourth-grade music class, when I chose the hand-carved maracas because, well, I was Mexican. I clashed them like cymbals until they nearly splintered, displaying what I considered my inborn Latin beat.

Yet our household rhythms really were foreign in some more subtle ways. It used to aggrieve me that we never got TV dinners or Danish-Go-Rounds. Friends, meanwhile, were enthralled by the long sit-down dinners that we shared every night and needed permission to skip. But that's just how Mexicans organize family life. Americans, of course, had organized their lives exactly the same way, just a generation before.

Of all the ethnic groups in America, only Native Americans saw this continent immigrant-free. In 1776, 70 percent of white settlers were from Britain, with others coming from Spain, Holland, and France. One-third of Americans at that time were African slaves.

From 1820 through 1925, close to 36 million more Europeans arrived. A wave came from Ireland, peaking during the potato famine. Germans and Scandinavians arrived next. Some Chinese, Japanese, and Mexicans also came in the nineteenth and early twentieth centuries. But between roughly 1880 and 1920, with nearly 15 million newcomers, mostly Italians, Slavs, Greeks, or Jews, Americans lashed out. The 1924 National Origins Quota Act banned almost all Southern and Eastern Europeans, not to mention Asians and other nonwhites, from entry. By 1960, in a country founded by immigrants, less than 6 percent of Americans were foreign-born.

In 1965, Congress finally scrapped the quotas, making family links and special skills central to gaining a visa. The number of newcomers who have responded to this policy is without precedent. Today, more than 37 million immigrants live in this country, an estimated 11 million of those without authorization. The numbers may seem overwhelming—but the actual percentage of our current population that is foreign-born hovers at about 13 percent, lower than it was a hundred years ago.

What *is* truly historic is how different these newcomers are from one another. Thanks to the twists of U.S. policy, they step ashore with the most varied educational and economic résumés of any generation of immigrants before them. Mexicans, as you might guess, are the most numerous, the poorest, and the most likely to be undocumented. That's largely because, shortly before Congress ended quotas, it also put the kibosh on a program welcoming unskilled Mexican workers. The move inadvertently launched the torrent of illegal migration we see today. Since the jobs still beckoned, workers kept coming. But ever-tightening border enforcement now discouraged the newcomers from leaving. It was a radical change from the circular flow of generations past, when as many as 85 percent of undocumented arrivals were offset by other Mexicans heading home.

Yet, contrary to stereotype, Mexican immigrants are roughly as educated as the Poles and Italians of a hundred years ago. What's changed is the dwindling of blue-collar jobs that once pushed European immigrants forward—and the new weight of nonlegal status, which hampers the advance of many immigrants, especially Latinos, today.

Asians and Africans, meanwhile, walk off their planes with top-notch credentials. Banned from the United States for so long, most have no family to join here. So most Nigerians, Koreans, Chinese, and Indians who get visas today are distinguished by their schooling and affluence. Jamaicans, meanwhile, who prior to 1965 could enter as British subjects, arrive today with more family links and slightly less education—typically high school.

Of all the educated immigrants, Nigerians stand at the top of the heap. Many were young men who came for college during the oil-rich 1970s and stayed when political chaos erupted at home. Now, according to 2006 census estimates, 37 percent of Nigerian immigrants have bachelor's degrees, 17 percent hold master's, and 4 percent are PhDs. That's compared to the 19 percent of U.S. whites with bachelor's, 8 percent with master's, and one percent with a PhD.

In 1975, another tide of immigrants swept in. It was a massive, emotionally battered surge of displaced Vietnamese. Driven by the fall of Saigon, they would become the biggest refugee wave in U.S. history. First came the skilled, educated class who had cooperated with the United States, then more than one million migrants from all over Indochina. Hmong tribespeople, Vietnamese boat people, and survivors of Cambodia's killing fields, this second wave varied in wealth and schooling. The past status of each—as for Mexicans, Koreans, Indians, Nigerians, and Jamaicans—would greatly inform their progress in the United States.

There was little, in other words, that I could generalize about the immigrants now recasting the U.S. population, and even more sharply redefining Houston. Little, except that regardless of education and wealth, each needed to sort through the customs from their past lives, keeping only those that would help them thrive in America.

I set out to explore the customs in this book because the more I learned about them, the more I realized they addressed some puzzle of American life I had seen myself. Who doesn't want to rein in impulse purchasing? Or serve a healthy, fresh-cooked family dinner for the price of a meal at McDonald's? Who wouldn't long for assurance that her next date won't be mad, dangerous, or totally unsuitable? Who wouldn't want to help a new mother walloped with sadness?

But can those of us who are not from the cultures that gave rise to these practices really take them as our own? It's one thing to develop an appreciation for someone else's traditions. It's another matter entirely to pluck them up and take them home like shiny coins. Would they keep their currency if I wasn't a Bengali student or a Mexican waitress?

The truth is that it's American tradition to copy the neighbors. The Pilgrims lived through their first starving winters by emulating Native American planting and fishing. In the mid–nineteenth century, an American cowboy in Colorado so admired the Mexican vaqueros' wide-brimmed hats that he paid Stetson to craft one for him. The Mexicans deemed his knockoff *tan galan,* "so gallant," a label that evolved into the "ten gallon" hat.

It was the Germans who pioneered early childhood education here, doggedly building kindergartens every time they cleared land for a settlement. They also cultivated a passion for vigorous outdoor games on Sundays, enraging the Puritan neighbors, who found the practice blasphemous. But eventually it became an American religious rite of its own.

Italian Americans, meanwhile, suffered so terribly in their first years here that many returned to Italy. Those who stayed were hectored to abandon their diet. Italian cuisine, the social reformers warned, was "of poor nutritive quality, [its] spices allegedly favored alcoholism, and shopping for expensive imported products in neighborhood independent stores was . . . wasteful." The Italians paid no attention, of course, and ordinary Americans learned to love their food too.

Without knowing it, we even live in each other's houses. Roam any street in the South and you'll find shadows thrown from West African villages, folklorist John Michael Vlach claims. These shadows spring from a housing design that spread from New Orleans, which in the early nineteenth century was about one-third white, one-third slave, and one-third former slaves from Haiti. The free Haitians built themselves houses like those back in Africa, three or four rooms long, with a deep roof slanting over a porch. These so-called shotgun houses, Vlach says, gave Americans their first glimpse of a structure that now defines community life across the country: the Southern front porch.

A lot of our mainstream customs, in fact, spring from the margins. Almost always, cuisine takes the first leap. Soul food, bagels, salsa, pizza, and fried rice all gained entree into American homes long before their creators did. Then again, most European groups we call mainstream were marginal themselves at some point. Early colonists especially despised the unlettered Scotch-Irish, who settled Appalachia and the South during the eighteenth century. Yet the rednecks, as they were called even then, left their footprints far outside the South. Their backwoods "familiarity" and "lack of deference to age, wealth, birth and breeding" repelled other colonial Europeans. But a couple of centuries later, the casual manners of figures from Chuck Yeager to Bill Clinton characterize Americans to the rest of the world.

Strangely, the most crucial trait the Scotch-Irish brought may have been their openness to foreign ways. It's a bit counterintuitive, considering their obsessive clan ethic; this was the community that spawned the Hatfields and the McCoys. But roaming northern Ireland, northern England, and Scotland for hundreds of years, they learned to copy any survival skills that seemed to work. When they got to the New World, the Scotch-Irish successfully fought their way onto Indian land—by adapting the natives' own war and wilderness customs. Ethnic hostility, in other words, has never necessarily dampened American respect for a good idea.

But to fully understand the customs I was exploring—and to see how they might be worked into other Americans' lives—I had to see them in action. So I visited immigrant enclaves all around the country. I snooped and I loitered, questioning the incredibly hospitable residents about how these beloved customs are actually lived. And always I asked about their dark sides. "Don't idealize," a college sociology professor had warned.

My first stop was a Houston savings club. I wanted to parse why this ancient, precapitalist system still thrived a hemisphere and a millennium away from its source. I was astonished at the range of people these clubs attract. There were re-education camp survivors, former army officers, comfortable professionals like my friend Ngoc, and workers like Hen Le, still grasping for the middle class. Decade after decade, something about savings clubs kept drawing these Vietnamese in.

My next stop was Akron, Ohio, unlikely epicenter of a Mexican rite that may reduce postpartum depression, and, without a doubt, makes new mothers better rested. Trailing health workers, dropping in on households, and meeting the opinionated family that ran La Flor restaurant, I eventually wondered why this practice wasn't taught alongside Lamaze.

It took longer to sell me on the South Asian style of courtship. To test the idea, I traveled to a Pakistani sweet shop in Queens, a hip Hoboken diner, and a Columbia University dorm room, listening to love stories. But it was only when an Indian friend sent me to her cousin in Nashville, a woman with good reason to believe in this courtship tradition, that I started to believe too.

Even if you find the perfect mate, challenges still lie ahead. You may well have children—and sooner or later have to educate them. Thus I headed to Los Angeles, where immigrants from Korea have pretty much mastered the U.S. public school system. The tools they bring for this task are mind-boggling: churches that dole out college guidance, newspapers with weekly guides on everything from school districts to acing the SATs. But even non-Asians can copy one of their most common techniques. To learn how it worked, I lurked around the Park La Brea pool to meet Korean students, and visited traditional "study places" in Los Angeles and the San Fernando Valley. Then I tried the system out on my kids.

Jamaicans, meanwhile, achieve several modern American goals with one very Old World approach: They live with their parents. Preoccupied with independence, I expected this to be the least adaptable custom I studied. Yet not only did it seem to work, the West Indians I knew seemed to *enjoy* it. So I called the Jamaica Organization of New Jersey, which arranged for me to spend three days living with a gregarious math teacher, her mother, and various members of their beguiling family.

Back in Houston, *pho* still on my mind, I tried out a Vietnamese technique for getting family dinner on the table each night. It got onto my table, all right—in four courses, freshly cooked, for less than ten dollars total.

Today, more than a year after embarking on these experiments, I am a convert. Many of these practices are so elegant and efficient at reaching American goals, I believe, newcomers need to hang on to them.

And the rest of us should consider trying them out for ourselves.

Not all imported traditions make sense. Some, such as honor killings, the caste system, and female circumcision, are abhorrent. Others, while charming on the surface, nevertheless rely on hierarchies we've discarded, systems in which divorce is unheard of and women and children have no choice but submission.

But the best of these imports, such as the ones in this book, do not spring from anyone's loss of power. To the contrary: For little or no cost, usually marked by some sort of party, they magnify the power of anyone who adopts them. They fortify our most portable resource— our conduct. And they harness core instincts like reciprocity, the need for approval, love of laughter.

Ingenious as they may be, I realized, most of these traditions aren't really foreign at all. They are masterfully refined variations on classic American good sense. Meant to promote thrift, community, and individual backbone, versions of these customs lie packed away in every American's family history. Adapting the best habits of first-generation immigrants, I think, can help us recall our own.

This book is for anybody who senses something off-kilter about our daily life, and wants practical ideas to regain footing. It is not about immigration policy. Nor does it analyze what immigrants do or don't take from our economy. It is about the immigrants who are already here, and what they can teach us. For the hundreds of thousands of newcomers who land here each year, success hinges on one factor: how well they learn to be American. For the rest of us, who know our good fortune but still struggle to find love, keep families close, and rein in runaway consumption, the challenge is different. We need to learn how to live like immigrants.

1

How to Save:

The Vietnamese Money Club

Pay first and then get what you have paid for.

—VIETNAMESE PROVERB

FROM THE CORNER of a banquet table strewn with empty dishes, I watched large-denomination bills change hands. A Vietnamese man in a porkpie hat strolled from seat to seat. Smiling, he leaned toward one guest, then another, clasping shoulders and collecting.

Three crisp hundreds from a skinny man with glasses.

Six fifties from a chic matron in gray pumps.

Altogether more than fifty people crowded at the tables in the Houston restaurant. All had come from Vietnam, and all had known each other more than thirty years, since first arriving, penniless, after Saigon's fall. Their faces rounder now, their bellies gently paunched, they plucked morsels of fried squid and catfish off lazy Susans. When the man in the hat came round to take their cash, they each embraced him.

This could easily be dues time at a class reunion or Rotary dinner. But something unusual was happening with all that money. Instead of tucking it into a box or money pouch, Cao Do, the man in the hat, slipped the bills into an envelope. He passed it to the oldest woman at the table. Putting down her chopsticks, she licked a forefinger and counted. Then she opened her handbag and dropped the cash into it.

I was witnessing a *hui.* Pronounced to rhyme with "boy," it is a centuries-old Vietnamese tradition that harnesses peer pressure to force its members to save. A bit book club, a bit Weight Watchers, the hui hinges on one transaction.

Every month, cash in hand, members meet to contribute their dues. And each month a different player takes that lump sum home, interest-free. In Vietnam those dues might be pitifully small, the equivalent of one or two dollars. High rollers, businessmen who don't talk to people like me, deal in the tens of thousands.

The guests at Cao Do's table that day contributed $300 each. It was the pool of all their cash that the woman with the chopsticks stuffed in her purse as I watched. After paying dutifully to the hui for months, she had reached her turn to collect.

Though everyone calls them by different names—Cambodians have *tontines,* Mexicans *tandas,* and Nigerians *esusus*—rotating loan clubs exist in nearly every traditional culture. In each system, peer pressure interwoven with social pleasure compels people to save what they otherwise might spend. The same forces, transformed into a fear of humiliation, discourage them from defaulting.

Among Asians, money clubs date back at least to the thirteenth century; one Japanese document cites a hui-like club that operated in 1275. Nearly a millennium later, the parched economic landscape that gave birth to huis still prevails in much of the world. For small-time merchants and farmers who don't have access to modern banks, and whose only other options are loan sharks or a jar buried in the garden, money clubs, along with jewelry and land, are still the safest methods to raise or store wealth.

But money clubs have also played a considerable role in the U.S. economy. Japanese and Chinese immigrants relied on them heavily to build businesses in the nineteenth century; in 1988, *Time* reported that Korean immigrants had used clubs called *kyes* to raise up to $10 million for houses and small businesses in the San Francisco Bay area. Eleven years later, another survey calculated that 80 percent of Korean households in the United States still took part in a kye, and that around Washington, D.C., kyes held approximately $100 million at any one time.

In the three decades since they arrived here, America's estimated 1.1 million Vietnamese immigrants have deployed thousands of huis in the same way, launching businesses here and providing for families left behind in Vietnam. Huis helped seed Houston's seemingly magical burgeoning of tiny nail salons, convenience stores, and pocket-size restaurants within months of their owners' arrival—often in blasted neighborhoods where other poor residents found jobs and business ownership out of reach. Fifty miles away, on the Gulf of Mexico, money clubs with payouts from hundreds of dollars to $20,000 or more allowed refugees to buy boats and gain a foothold in the shrimping industry.

Until recently, Western scholars wrote about huis and other rotating credit groups with a certain dismissiveness. They were the last-ditch tool of the very poor, they said. And, indeed, Muhammad Yunus borrowed from the revolving loan tradition in developing the Grameen Bank, insisting that its microloans would more likely be repaid if guaranteed by a peer group.

But the money club mechanism is more commonly a tool for the stable and aspirational. After all, you need some sort of surplus before you can join. In Houston, most Vietnamese refugees had to wait a few years to emerge from dire poverty before they could join. Today, Cao Do's hui includes military officers, engineers, and business owners who use banks and credit cards as well.

I can't say I ever worried about finding a safe place for my wealth. But I had been hearing about huis, and the lore surrounding them, since first arriving in Houston. A hui, my Vietnamese friends would tell me, is much more than a poor man's substitute for a bank. It alters behavior, they claimed. And it somehow manages to make frugality fun.

It's 1:00 p.m. on the second Saturday of the month: the day after payday, and two weeks before the next bills arrive. Time again for the hui.

Freshly lipsticked, ties straight, Cao Do's friends file into the banquet room. Kim Son restaurant sits in a strip mall, but its foyer recalls the Library of Congress. It's a fitting look for this seat of communal power.

Houston boosters, not just the Vietnamese ones, sometimes boast about Kim Son's success as if it were a municipal achievement. In a way it is. When Son La arrived here as a refugee in 1975, he found a subtropical climate that felt like Vietnam. He also found a state economy unfettered by state income tax and a distinctly Houstonian willingness to ignore social origins. That is, if you could get rich.

Almost everybody who moved to the city in those days had done so for jobs. For a man like La, Houston offered promising ground. Starting with a pocket-size soup joint, La and his family slowly turned Kim Son into a mainstream dining empire. Their secret was pampering the Texan palate. Houstonians, they found, appreciated jalapeños and cilantro. But they wanted their food clearly identifiable, light on the fish sauce, and free at all times of fat globules, exoskeletons, and eyeballs.

Once La got the hang of these predilections, Houston fell in love with his cooking. It's common now to pop into a Kim Son at lunch and see Latinos, blacks, and sixth-generation Texans happily wrapping their spring rolls in lettuce. As their fortune grew, the Las built another restaurant, and another. Finally they built the *pièce de résistance*—the marble and red velvet palace where Cao Do's friends meet for their hui.

As Do's guests settle in at their tables, waiters begin ferrying rice, soft drinks, and platter after platter of garlicky catfish and squid. Twenty years after starting this club, Do's friends have finally mustered the financial security for nice meals out. Accordingly, each month's winners—there are always two—agree to buy the Kim Son lunch for everyone. Also by consensus, the club no longer pays out anyone in the first month; instead, the players bank the money in an emergency account. Last year they used it to help a member pay for his wife's funeral. Other groups donate one month's winnings to a charity.

These are common money club variations, but the xeroxed sheet that Do now hands to each table was his own innovation. It's a copied image of a Texas Powerball ticket. Vietnamese tend to relish gambling, and this hui decided to spend a few dollars from the communal fund on playing the lottery. The smidgen of extra risk reflects their trust in Do.

Do is sixty-six, medium height, but seems younger and much taller thanks to a very round, almost pumpkinish head. He is dressed a little more casually than his guests, in an elegant charcoal jersey shirt, sleek loafers, and the porkpie lid. He has the smile and antic grace of a Rat Packer, and I like him right away.

"Without Do, we always say, we wouldn't do this," says the slender woman who is translating for us. Do, joining us at an empty seat, smiles modestly. It's clear the tribute delights him. "Where did you learn your management skills?" I ask. "Boy Scouts," he replies. "And, when I became an adult, the Vietnamese navy." Displacement and language barriers sidetracked those talents. In this country, Do is two years from his pension as a custodian for a public school district.

Do's money club has been running continuously for twenty years, but its focus has changed enormously. "We'd just arrived, we didn't have anything. We needed new cars, deposits for houses," he says. "That's why we started it—we needed the money." Do's original cofounder, an old friend from the military, was the one who launched the group. He needed to raise money fast for a house deposit. Between them, he and Do recruited eighteen other families, all of them scrambling for a toehold in the new country.

Because, back then, no one had either money or leisure to spend a whole Saturday afternoon at a restaurant, the club members squeezed into each other's apartments. They switched places in the rotation often and graciously in those first years, accommodating their fellow refugees' fast-changing lives. Almost each month, someone would ask to collect, to buy suddenly available shop space or finance a wedding for a child who assumed, unlike her parents, that Houston was her permanent home.

As more refugees found their footing, the hui grew fast: from two dozen, to three dozen, to fifty families. People joined now for the fun of it, lured by friends, and friends of friends. They ventured out to Kim Son, and resolved to raise monthly dues from $200 to $300. For efficiency, Do came up with the idea of splitting the group in two, to keep the cycle from dragging out fifty months. Finally, in a sign of the members' new financial stability, they decided to add an extra $15 to their monthly payment, money they'd never recoup. It would go instead to a general fund for charity, emergencies—and more parties.

Now that most are in their sixties and seventies, few really want to talk about work, or trying to buy a car, or scaring up a house payment. Instead they chatter about pleasures: favorite old foods and places in Vietnam, or the entertainment at their upcoming New Year's celebration here at Kim Son.

"This is just like our club now," Do says. "We meet together to have friends to invite to weddings, to help when we have problems." Even their problems are different now—like other Americans, the hui members have to struggle not to fritter away what they have.

"Some people cannot save," Do adds. "This makes you do it."

*   *   *

Hen Le needed $16,000 in cash and had run out of places to find it.

When I first met fifty-seven-year-old Le at the money club, he was turned out like the other guests: closely shaven, in a beautifully tailored European-style suit and discreet tie. Yet Le looked subtly unlike his peers, more broad-shouldered, athletic, forearms rounded with muscle. He resembled a bond trader who invests in spinning classes, massage, and a trainer. What Le's physique really reflected was more than thirty years of manual labor. He had joined the money club to stop being someone else's employee and launch his own business.

Le grew up well-to-do in Tay Ninh Province, South Vietnam, where his father owned a regional bus service. Ambitious, Le studied agriculture and landed a scholarship to earn an MA in the United States, but was vanquished by the English requirement and in the end couldn't go.

"Are you kidding?" I said. "Your English is perfect."

"It is now," he said, shrugging.

One year after his failed move to America, Vietnam fell to the Communists and Le got out on a military ship.

"I followed the stream of people," he said. Arriving in Houston, Le worked twelve years for a mechanic before a well-to-do woman friend offered to partner with him in an auto shop. As Le tells it, she didn't like it when he married someone else three years later. They dissolved the business. With the $22,000 from the settlement, Le grabbed a bargain parcel of land outside Houston. He vowed it was time to work for himself.

Halfway through the process, the well ran dry. Though he owned the property, Le still needed to construct the building and buy machinery. He borrowed $40,000 from friends and former neighbors in Vietnam, many of whom didn't charge interest. "They'll lend to you now—you'll lend to them one day," Le shrugged. Another $20,000 went onto credit cards, some nimbly swapped every six months—

zero-interest accounts—and some at steep interest. But the mix of individual and corporate loans still didn't cover Le's needs. The business was slipping out of his hands. And that is when the hui lifted him onto its strong, supple back.

Several years before he'd begun building, Le and his wife signed on with three separate money clubs, at $200 apiece. They knew they would need lump sums of cash. Between all three clubs, two of which extended several years, Le theoretically could get access to $16,000, with no interest, no balloon payment, and no collateral required beyond his good name.

But you can't build a mechanic's shop with three chunks of money scattered over three years. So when the time came to build, Le exercised the hui's ancient friendship clause. He asked to change his place in the rotation. Le wanted all three of his shares, from all three clubs, in the same month. The players were glad to comply.

Everyone knew this was what huis were for.

To the entrepreneur who wants to collect early, a money club creates capital. For the prudent or the impulsive, collecting late gently enforces savings. But money clubs also help members unexpectedly tapped on the shoulder by some stroke of luck, whether a car accident, a death—or an opportunity. That understanding is what makes a hui distinct from, and in certain moments even more powerful than, a savings account or a bank loan.

"That's why it's called a friendship loan," Le said.

A few months after visiting Cao Do's club, I drove to the outskirts of Houston to see what Le had done with his loan. When I pulled into the shop, he was sitting alone in front of a worn turquoise-colored counter. A plastic bottle filled with green tea sat nearby. On a wall-mounted TV screen, a Vietnamese youth and a little girl in traditional clothes were scrambling up a mountain away from pursuers.

Le tipped back in his chair.

He was still fit and good-looking, with the casual manners of someone twenty years younger. But he sounded weary as he described the years since he'd gathered his loans. Though he had owed as much as 20 percent interest on his credit cards, he completed all his hui payments first, within twenty-five months. Next he paid off his friends.

"But why?" I asked, surprised. Wouldn't it make more sense to pay off the cards, with their compounding interest? Le tapped both hands to his chest. "They trust me to loan me money. Why wouldn't I pay them first?"

A call lit up his cell phone, and Le stepped into the workshop to talk. I waved my thanks and slipped out. My car waited amid the herd of bashed junkers, near a white sign that had taken thirty years of work and friendship to hoist: **Hen Le Auto Shop**

"A hui works because the friends are always connected by one person who's going to be accountable," fifty-three-year-old Dan Nguyen told me one autumn day. We were ensconced in the back room of her business, Astro Dry Clean, in a strip mall in southwest Houston. Dan (it's pronounced "Yan") led a money club. In fact, as is common, several members of her group also belonged, paying a separate set of dues, to Cao Do's club.

Dan's group was just a few years old, and she'd handpicked every member. She'd grown up in this work. As a little girl, she'd lived for months at a time with her grandmother, a formidable businesswoman who, among other enterprises, ran a hui. Once a month, she dispatched little Dan to the market to collect members' money, which she stuffed into a black drawstring purse she hid in her shirt.

In her schoolgirl shorts and Dutch-boy haircut, eight-year-old Dan was a natural manager. So forty years later, when she decided to launch her own money club in Houston, she chose her players as carefully as she would ripe tomatoes. In the week before every meeting, she methodically called all thirty-five players to remind them—

and to discreetly ask about any personal problems that might impede payment. As long as they were honest about it, Dan would cover for them. Without exception, Dan told me, she always knew she'd get paid.

Shame, after all, is the cement that keeps money clubs solid.

"Huis are all based on trust and saving face," says John Sibley Butler, a University of Texas sociologist who studies immigrant entrepreneurs. "You just don't default. In the United States, it used to be to file bankruptcy, you'd be ashamed. But our whole banking system is based on the idea that you can bail out of loans and default."

Yet surely, I told Dan, hui members default too—especially since the system traditionally doesn't permit IOUs.

I was considering my own experiences only that month, when an outrageous parking ticket, a ceiling pipe vomiting water onto my carpet, and an emergency dental bill all converged. What if I hadn't been able to cover all that with a card? What if I'd needed to withdraw every penny before the hui?

This, after all, is how more than 60 percent of bankruptcies begin: not as the aftermath of some prolonged spending binge, but in the form of swift, unexpected debt following an illness or accident. No one is immune to such avalanches, but especially not first-generation immigrants who may barely speak English.

"What if *you* had all those expenses?" I asked. "All at one time? And you just couldn't pull together the cash for your hui?"

Dan looked at me quizzically. She straightened a plastic tube of almond cookies so it lined up with a tin of ginger candy. Finally she said, "I would still pay."

"But," I persisted, "what if there were just no cash, because you'd spent it on other needs?"

"Well," Dan said slowly, "Asian people usually have a little money put aside for emergencies."

And emergencies, Dan knew well, spare no one.

Years before she became a dry cleaner, Dan was a brainy college girl who planned to teach English. Then the Communists took over in Vietnam, and Dan and her husband, with their two-year-old girl, had to flee in a wooden rowboat. A typhoon nearly obliterated them. "I held my daughter so tight, so tight," Dan whispered, clutching her arms as she remembered.

But they made it to Hong Kong, and a friendly couple in Louisiana offered to sponsor them in the United States. The refugees lived with the Americans for two weeks before striking off on their own. Thirty years later, Dan saw her benefactors again. Hurricane Katrina had engulfed New Orleans, and the now elderly couple drove all night to Dan's house, where she gratefully offered them shelter.

Other Vietnamese shared Dan's perspective. Raised in a culture of perpetual crisis, in which banks and institutions tended to be the first casualties, even Vietnamese who are just scraping by try not to spend their last dollar. Once they reach the middle class the mind-set remains.

I could see Dan wrestling to come up with a scenario in which she couldn't meet her commitments.

"I'm the leader. If I didn't have it, I guess I would borrow it," she finally said. "But only from someone outside the hui."

It seemed hard for her even to utter these words aloud.

Nevertheless, there are absconders. Tellingly, the clubs they defraud are usually giant, impersonal webs that fund major enterprises—and lack the personal relationships of small, self-help clubs like Dan's. One of the most spectacular crack-ups occurred in 1979, in Hawaii, where a money club organizer defaulted on $16 million he owed to 1,100 players. Some victims had been ponying up $200,000 every month, according to UCLA sociologist Ivan Light.

At the lower altitudes, where most Vietnamese play, only one person I met could name a cheating case. "People who default tend to be people who are cut off, somehow, with few family links," the woman told me. In the case she had heard of, the defrauder was a widow with an adult son. They seemed responsible enough until one night they just didn't show up. They were never seen in Houston again.

But hui players do break a sweat trying to meet their obligations. In the desperate first years after landfall in America, meat and fish might disappear from dinner as the meeting approached, Dan recalled. An urgent light bill might go unpaid. Siblings, children, resident uncles, and grandparents would turn out their pockets to ensure the hui debt was paid.

Lose your car, and you're stuck in the house. Declare Chapter 7, your credit is ruined for years. But you can work your way back, and Americans do so all the time.

Cheat your money club, though, and you betray the very friends who have helped you. Not only your "face" but your right to be trusted has been ruined. And the repercussions never have an expiration date.

The next winner of Cao Do's hui didn't bother to attend. It was Dan's twenty-eight-year-old daughter Minh, the two-year-old who was nearly swept away in the typhoon. Now a high school English teacher with a Houston drawl, Minh was saving for a wedding. Unlike her mother's austere existence, Minh's life was pure American mayhem: work, exercise classes, beach vacations. She didn't want to hobnob at Kim Son, Minh told me over the phone. She just wanted the money.

"My mother talked me into it," Minh said. "I did it to save for the wedding. She told me how I could save $200 a month, in a pot with everybody else. So I joined the hui in February, and I'm getting married in December. In just nine months I'll have gotten access to $7,000."

Her fiancé found the hui appalling. "He can't see the reason for it," Minh said cheerfully. "He kept saying, 'We should take out a loan.' But he was born in this country. He took out loans for college and for dental school—it's a way of life for him. For me, loans are to be avoided at all costs."

But why? Weren't huis loans as well?

The difference, Minh said, was the larger philosophy a hui represented. She had seen her mother's extreme responsibility growing up. She now wanted to add it to her own repertoire. She especially liked how she could start repaying months before using the money.

Minh also saved in a school retirement plan. But the hui's cash-only policy, and the specter of disgrace in front of her mother's friends, guaranteed she would spend within her means. Most Americans shrink from mixing their friends and their money, for good reason: any dispute metastasizes into a double loss. But I'd never seen hui players show any qualms. The dread of shaming themselves is so potent, it seems, they are confident their fellow players feel the same.

On the day of her wedding, Minh wore a scarlet *ao dai* and silk crown. A dozen groomsmen dressed in emerald, turquoise, and amethyst lined up in the driveway, waiting to give her dowry boxes of tea and jewelry. That night, under Kim Son's gold-trimmed ceiling, Dan held a reception for three hundred guests. It was a night she had dreamed of for years. The daughter she had clung to so tightly at sea was safe, happy, and, despite a spectacular wedding, free of debt.

Half a lifetime after moving here, even well-to-do Vietnamese often feel in their bones that fate is cruelly capricious. The wheel-like cosmology of Asian religions, and Vietnam's relentless calamities, have done their part to shape this. So has the shock of being a refugee in a new country. It may take that level of trauma to create the intense frugality common among Vietnamese immigrants.

That was the first reaction of sociologist Rubén Rumbaut, a gregarious University of California expert on U.S. immigration. Rumbaut has studied Vietnamese immigrants since 1975, and still keeps in touch with the first families he interviewed. He remembers the exact birth weight of the girl for whom he was named godparent. A former exile himself, he came here as a boy when his family fled Cuba and feels a kinship with the Vietnamese.

When I asked Rumbaut in 2007 if he thought Americans could, or would want to, set up money clubs, he was dubious. "When you are an immigrant and have lost everything—and let me tell you I have been there and done that—you learn very quickly to focus," Rumbaut said. Pinching pennies on the small, consistent scale encouraged by a hui might be "almost mission impossible," he speculated, if you had grown up in late-twentieth-century America.

Many Vietnamese, young and old, that I quizzed at the time pretty much agreed. It's not only the thrift, they said. Mingling personal relationships with finance is foreign here. Investment clubs, which surged a few decades ago, really hinged on a different idea: a wish to profit by pooling intellectual resources. We Americans talk about the things we've bought, or dream of buying. But there is still something taboo for many of us about exposing how much—or, really, how little—money is in our hands. It's even more rare to admit we may need help controlling it.

But then saving and spending have long been complicated notions for Americans. To the Puritans, your material good fortune was granted, not earned. A strong spine or a sprouting barley patch merely signaled God's preexisting goodwill, not any reward for your work or piety. Visible misfortune, in the form of poverty or illness, indicated divine disfavor.

Born in the twilight of the Puritan era, Benjamin Franklin brashly rejected this view. In phenomenally popular books, such as *Poor Richard's Almanack,* he celebrated thrift and hard work precisely because almost anyone who employed them could carve earthly good fortune out for himself. After his death, this new sense of empowerment broadened into one of entitlement. Profiting from the continent's dizzying bounty—the acreage, the trees, the game, and the fertile soil—

was a divine right. Codified and politicized, the idea expanded into the notion of manifest destiny.

Ever since, through booms, depressions, wars, and superpower-dom, these crosswinds of belief about what we deserve, and how we should steward it, have continued to whirl. Even before the economic downturn, some Americans were trying to rethink their spending habits. Launched in 1973, Debtors Anonymous harnesses some of the same forces a hui does. Members want to control their financial habits, and hope the mixed support and pressure from their peers will help them. Even closer in spirit are the cheerful Internet blogs whose authors narrate their wayward spending impulses—and hope an audience will keep them in check. One blogger was digging out of more than $38,000 in debt just as the recession hit. Sounding like a flustered hostess before a dinner party, she told the *New York Times* she dreaded letting her online visitors down.

"I've been wanting one of those LCD TVs for quite a while now," she told the paper, "but every time I see them, I think about having to come on the blog and say I bought it."

The distinction is that both Debtors Anonymous and spending blogs start with dysfunction. A hui, by contrast, is premised on functionality and the wish to maintain it. Yet using peer pressure to bring out the best, rather than simply bandage the worst, in our financial selves is a deep-rooted U.S. tradition. In the early 1900s, San Francisco financier A. P. Giannini formed the Bank of Italy to lend to fellow Italian immigrants. In those days, Italians were often rejected as laborers because they were so emaciated. Giannini understood that these men were nearly starving themselves out of devotion to their extended families, whom they were supporting both here and in the Italian countryside. He loaned to them based on what he knew of their individual habits and on their families' reputations. His instincts proved right: the skinny immigrants paid off the great majority of their loans, and Giannini's business became the Bank of America.

More recently still, African American housewives in the Deep South conducted money clubs exactly like huis in all but name. "My grandmother was part of a housewives' savings club—that was what it was called," Sylvea Hollis, then a doctoral student in American history at the University of Iowa, told me.

Hollis specializes in the study of black fraternal organizations and mutual aid societies—powerful, secretive clubs in which black men paid dues and amassed sometimes substantial sums of money. They deployed it for businesses, charity, and legal representation in an era when white institutions ignored African Americans or actively tried to exploit them.

The housewives' club, however, worked differently. It was a classic rotating credit association, in which, every other week, members paid a small sum that they could get back one time in a large payoff. Hollis, a little girl in the 1980s, would watch curiously as her grandmother's friends came to the house, impeccably dressed in hats and Sunday dresses. Her grandfather was a repairman who made a lot of his money doing odd jobs. Her grandmother was a domestic worker.

The other women in the club were also housekeepers, launderers, or hardworking homemakers who raised gardens and needed to marshal all their wits to keep their children fed. Hollis would watch the ladies file in, polite and formal as if attending a tea party.

"There wasn't Robert's Rules of Order, but there was a ritual," she said. "They'd have a hostess—they would sit down around the table and serve the tea or lemonade."

And then they did something more typical of Americans a half-century later. One by one, each woman described how the past two weeks had gone for her economically: her small household triumphs, her surprise expenses, how her meager budget had fared overall. It was an ongoing support group, a regular shot of courage to face a lifetime of struggle.

When the time came to pay their share—and they were small

sums, Hollis said—the hostess primly wrote each woman a receipt. The money went for household expenses, never whims or indulgences. Like a traditional hui, the housewives' savings club was serious behavior modification, only dressed up as a party.

I wanted that for myself.

In December 2007, I was pretty good at living simply, thanks to years of self-employment. I had no wish or need to starve myself of purchases that made me happy. Yet I felt nagged by a persistent blob of brainless spending. It was like a dieter's five pounds. I couldn't say that it threatened my health, but because I didn't actively want or even remember what I had bought, the steady, unnecessary spending stung my self-respect. What vexed me most were two expenditures I seemed to make almost every day: a Starbucks chai and a $10 salad mixed by a cheerful lady in a toque.

These weren't mad binges. I could afford them, too, having recently started a job on the *Chronicle* editorial board after several years freelancing. Mike and I were expecting twins, and I was delighted at the new income and benefits. It felt good, after tapping on a laptop in coffee shops, to totter around an office again in pencil skirts and collect a salary.

Under these circumstances, an overpriced tea or box of salad should not have represented much drama. But the two snacks felt emblematic of other, similarly wasteful purchases and of the joyless state in which I made them. I stepped out for salad and $4 tea, not when I needed these foods, but when I was bored and couldn't bear looking at a beige, featureless office one minute more.

To buy these items, I'd plunge into the Tunnel, the swarming subterranean shopping mall that shields Houston's white-collar workers from the summer sun. Buying tea there was a lovely transaction—like getting a present. The cashier's kind smile, the fragrant milk, the human-like warmth of the cardboard cup made me cheerful. A pitiful way to reaffirm life, I acknowledge. But there it was.

And in the aggregate, as financial columnists always tell us, I knew those few bucks could go far. I couldn't help thinking about what they might buy for someone like the mother I once saw in a stifling Port-au-Prince shack, heaving irons from red-hot coals to press her son's school shirt. It was just that marching through the day, trying to remember this hypothetical use for small change, was hard.

A lot of my friends felt the same way.

"It seems I waste $200 a month on stupid things," a coworker said. This equaled my own calculations exactly. I wondered if it was coincidence that that was a popular sum for recreational huis in Houston.

Which led to an obvious thought.

Maybe I should start a money club.

And so began a slow, cautious campaign to sell the idea to friends. I picked and chose whom to ask, as I'd learned from Dan and Hen and Cao Do. The members might have any number of motives, but I had to be sure whichever motive they had would endure for twelve months. I mainly asked journalists: I shared a building with hundreds of them. And reporters, I also figured, worry a lot about the link between their words and their names. This seemed a promising trait.

"At least journalists have a code," my friend Sarah said. She wanted in. Twenty-six and new to the paper, she was currently spending (as I did at her age) almost everything she earned.

"I need to do this," she said. "I have to save more money."

A friend who grew up in wartime England considered the plan.

"But not for the money part," she said. "What would be fun would be seeing the friendships develop, and watching people help each other." Her thrifty mother would have loved the idea, she told me. But she felt no need for it.

My friend Elena Vega, an interpreter from Mexico City, signed on enthusiastically. She had just finished a marathon and had a soft spot for self-improvement projects.

Unlike Mike.

"Absolutely not," he said. "Why would I give my hard-earned money to other people?"

But it wasn't hard to rally a dozen friends who saw the logic. Alien as a money club first sounds, in our regulated financial system, its fundamental goals actually translate perfectly in this culture. Fiscal discipline. Human connection. Even risk-taking, I told myself, is an integral part of American tradition. But I kept that part strictly in check: the dues would be $200, no more than I already squandered each month.

I scheduled our first meeting for the middle of the month, as I'd learned from Cao Do: just around payday, two weeks before the next bills came due. The full cycle took just over a year, and ended just as I finished researching the other practices on my list. Like any immigrant, I had embarked on the money club with optimism and resolve, but had no clue about what lay ahead.

I'll tell you at the end of the book how it worked.

2

How to Mother a Mother:

The Mexican *Cuarentena*

The Accidental Cuarentena

My husband Mike is the kind of person on whose shoulder tiny babies melt to sleep. I'm a different case. Before I had kids of my own, I could swear my presence made babies cry. Toddlers and older kids, I could relate to: there were a million things to talk about, and I appreciated how frank they were about their views. But I'd never even held a newborn.

So in the spring of 2003, when I learned I'd be giving birth to not one, but two babies, Mike's stepmother handed me the phone number of a woman I barely knew. It was her niece, the recent mother of twin infants. I was thrilled. Before I called, I lined up a legal pad and three pencils as if for the SATs.

I trusted Theresa at once. She was smart and irreverent, and her advice was succinct.

"Get help," she said. "Before the babies are born, line up six weeks' worth of people to come stay with you. They need to be people you're totally comfortable with. We had three relatives come stay with us for two weeks each."

Six weeks of guests? With tiny, shrieking newborns, and me exhausted, maybe miserable? This was the opposite of how I planned to launch family life. For years I'd heard and read about the chaotic first weeks with a newborn. "Crazy" and "overwhelmed" echoed through these accounts like a gong. As a casual hostess at best, I had zero interest in amplifying that stress with guests for whom I'd have to bathe, wear clothes, and entertain.

"They're not guests," Theresa said. "They are going to cook, shop, and answer your phone. They are going to take care of *you.*"

Cowed by my lack of baby skills, in the end I did exactly as Theresa instructed. It was about the best advice I'd ever gotten. Only three years later, during a wintry week in Ohio, did I realize this counsel was more than just good luck. Theresa had given me the outline of a *cuarentena:* an ancient set of postpartum rituals still practiced with religious intensity by migrants from rural Mexico. The cuarentena is a folk custom, handed down for centuries by people with no other resources. It's meant to protect the lives of newborn babies and, even more urgently, their mothers. While it is practiced throughout Mexico, it's no coincidence that the cuarentena thrives most fully today in Chiapas, the poorest state in Mexico, with the highest rate of infant mortality.

Yet I soon saw why migrants in Ohio swear by cuarentenas, too, and why even affluent cultures around the world still practice variations on it. For the poorest of the poor, the six weeks of a cuarentena may be a family's only weapon against infection and other deadly threats to a new mother. But a cuarentena can also buffer against postpartum depression, which plagues mothers and babies in wealthy cultures as well. For most women, a cuarentena can do what many Americans are taught to think is impossible. It can make the first weeks with a baby a dream.

Chiapas to Akron

The dented door swung open the moment I knocked. Inside I saw an orderly oasis, toasty warm and perfumed with the scent of cooking fruit. Ushering me forward was a rosy-skinned woman in her late twenties. Her hair was sleeked in a ponytail fastened with a silk carnation. She wore a fresh-laundered cotton sweater with pink sequins on the collar. It took a couple of seconds before I registered that the soft cotton stole resting on her neck was a small human. The woman was Anarosa Alvarez, and the bundle was her eight-week-old baby, Diana.

Anarosa sat placidly on the couch and motioned for me to join her. Like parlors I'd seen in Chiapas, her little living room was nearly bare. But the apartment walls were cobbled with mementos: wedding photos, family groupings, images of Anarosa's two-year-old son, Daniel, in an outsize three-piece suit. In the bedroom, I could see a teddy bear collection strung like Christmas lights. Meanwhile, the intoxicating smell filtered from the apartment's other side. I sniffed the air like a beagle.

"That's Carmen, my sister-in-law, cooking," Anarosa smiled. "She's making me a snack."

Until two weeks ago, Carmen had cooked far more than snacks. As Anarosa's closest female relative in Akron, she presided over every day of her sister-in-law's cuarentena. It was a given that Carmen would care for baby Diana. That was probably the easy part. A healthy baby, after all, mainly needs feeding, changing, and comforting. But a full cuarentena means nurturing the mother as if she herself were a newborn. That requires cooking special foods, shopping, cleaning, and gently, persistently policing her moods as she adjusts to motherhood.

The idea of a postpartum rest is actually more common than we realize. Except for in North America, most cultures still set aside a period in which a mother recovers, bonds with her baby, and gets special care. The length of time can vary: Chinese women lounge in seclusion for thirty days, while the Onitsha women of Nigeria relax with their babies for three months. From South Asia to the Philippines, the Middle East to South America, new mothers and their babies rest for forty days.

Why forty? The number has trailed mystical associations behind it for millennia. To the Babylonians, forty days was the worrisome time period during which the Pleiades star cluster vanished from sight and the skies belched forth their annual onslaught of rain. The notions of deluge, endurance, and testing continued to attach to the number forty in the Old and New Testaments, Islam, and Buddhism. Think of Noah coasting the flood, Israelites roaming Sinai, Jesus fasting in the wild. The Prophet Muhammad and Buddha both were said to have reached spiritual turning points at forty years of age.

Throughout civilization, in other words, forty has marked an interval of flow from one spiritual state to another. But the cosmic meaning likely endured because forty also echoes the rhythms of our bodies. Ancient peoples knew they could expect to live about forty years. Observing the cyclical changes of heavens and hormones, they understood that a baby's gestation lasts forty weeks. And a new mother's womb, they must have known, returns to its shape and position in about forty days.

Growing up in Chiapas, Anarosa learned from her family that the forty days after birth are critical. During that time period, they say, both a woman's body and her inner life force grow perilously "cold." Those who love her need to avoid chilling her vulnerable system with the wrong foods, even emotions (in Chiapas, anger is frosty). Most importantly, a new mother requires peace. Tiresome acquaintances are banned. Only the mother's dearest friends and female relatives may see her.

Sex is forbidden.

So is getting out of bed.

For six weeks, therefore, Anarosa, an impoverished mother of two who worked in a lightbulb factory, spent not one moment cooking. She didn't wash her own clothes, rinse the dishes, dress her son, or so much as touch a broom or vacuum cleaner.

During the cuarentena, others did it all for her.

Birth in La Chamba

Almost forty years ago, a young anthropologist named Laurence Kruckman arrived in a remote Colombian lowland village called La Chamba. Hidden in the humid deep valleys of the Andes, La Chamba was inhabited by subsistence farmers who grew corn and beans and rarely saw money. Kruckman, a sandy-haired postdoctoral student from Southern Illinois University, planned to study the effect of modernization on La Chamba's villagers.

It was on a visit home to Chicago, though, that Kruckman witnessed the most radical—and terrifying—change he'd ever seen in another person. Two friends, new to the city, had just had a baby. Seemingly without warning, the young woman plunged into a postpartum psychosis. Frantically researching her condition, Kruckman found little guidance. The journals offered almost nothing about psychosis, which is extremely rare. But they also had little to say about far more common postpartum disorders: the mild "baby blues" that hit as many as 80 percent of American women, and postpartum depression, experienced by as many as 20 percent.

With medical care, Kruckman's friend slowly regained her health. But after that visit home, his priorities changed. Returning to Colombia, he began studying the weeks after childbirth. What he found there was baffling. In La Chamba and the other villages he visited, women all knew that three days after giving birth they might fleetingly feel anxious or sad. But after almost eight years, Kruckman came to a puzzling conclusion: rural Latinas apparently didn't experience postpartum depression at all.

The few ethnographers looking at these questions shared Kruckman's findings. Women in preindustrial societies that are based on strong kin and community ties report little or no PPD as we understand it. Infant mortality, yes—at rates of 25 percent or more in the poorest places. Womanhood in itself, Kruckman knew, was often a brutal experience in these hardscrabble societies.

What could be the explanation? There's still no consensus. We still don't fully know why some women suffer postpartum illness and others don't. Endocrinologists do know that the weeks after childbirth are times of seismic hormonal activity. In the three days after childbirth, pregnancy hormones bottom out, and prolactin, which enables breastfeeding, spikes. These changes are so predictable that the English dub the resulting three-day mood swings the "seventy-second hour depression."

There's also a fairly reliable list of risk factors for postpartum depression. Family history of depression. A geographical move in the preceding year. Conflict with spouse or between a new mother and her own mother. Other factors include too little household help, economic stress, and isolation. Sleep deprivation, doctors know from experience, is one of the most common triggers.

What is not known, Kruckman told me the winter that I met Anarosa, is how and when these risk factors will result in depression.

Places like La Chamba could offer one clue. Mothers there, like women in Chiapas, often lived without electricity, running water, or doctors, unprotected from sickness or natural disaster. What they had, though, was a ritual, one that Kruckman believes buffered them from the anxiety and serious depression that so many American women face after giving birth.

It lasts forty days. *La cuarentena*—the gentle quarantine.

Anarosa's Cuarentena

In the foggy Chiapas highlands, where Anarosa had her first child, a new mother is treated like royalty. While she was pregnant, Anarosa shouldered her many chores. She had to, she'd say—they were share-croppers, her husband toiled all day long on the soil, and someone had to keep the house going. But as soon as she gave birth, in the mud hut that smelled of wood smoke and clay, the pampering started. She was allowed to shuffle from the family cot to a hammock, and eventually around the room. But on most days, she could take not even one step in the yard.

The world, however, filed in to see her.

Taking turns, Anarosa's best friends, including Carmen, popped in every few hours to spell the main caretaker, Ana's mother, and quietly amuse the new mother. No one expected anything from her, though. New mothers aren't supposed to talk too much—it could swell their abdomens. Playfully, Anarosa's young friends coaxed her to eat: broth, a tortilla, herb tea. Banned were chilling foods like pork, beans, lemons, and avocado.

Every few weeks, another visitor ducked into the dim house: the massage specialist. With the greatest care, the old woman rolled Anarosa to one side and pressed the tired muscles of her hips, back, and belly. Then she tightly wrapped her waist with a rebozo, a vivid, all-purpose shawl, to make her post-baby stomach flat and strong.

The only time Anarosa took the wrap off was on sauna day. Three times or more after having a baby, even the poorest woman in Chiapas stretches her legs, rolls out of bed, and heads out the door. She's expected at the steam bath, a small adobe hut found in every village or family compound in the region. Inside, the sauna mistress, and perhaps a friend or two, wait in the cozy gloom. *Whoosh.* Water dippers over warm rocks. Eucalyptus and other herbs deliciously perfume the steam. For the next half hour, as someone else minds the baby, it's

Anarosa's right—her *duty*—to bathe in the vapor and giggle as her best friend and the sauna mistress swap dirty jokes.

The cuarentena worked a bit differently in Ohio. Two years after arriving in Akron, snow was falling, and Anarosa dutifully snuggled in bed with her baby. Carmen, who lived in the apartment upstairs, crept in every morning at nine to bring Anarosa cornflakes and milk. There were no aromatherapy baths, no parade of old friends. Nevertheless, Anarosa smiled dreamily as she recounted that time.

"What word would you use to describe those first weeks?" I asked her.

"Relaxing," she answered at once.

Carmen—stout, without makeup, dressed in men's gym shorts—plopped down on the couch to tell the rest of the story. During the first twenty days, she said, when Anarosa's husband worked, Carmen managed the cuarentena single-handed.

"I barely slept," Carmen said. "I'd get home from the factory at two in the morning and then I'd come here."

"Sometimes she'd get home at three if she couldn't get a ride," Anarosa amended. "She looked tired."

Every morning, for forty days, it was the same. First, Carmen cleaned the little apartment. Then she woke and dressed two-year-old Daniel. Finally she moved on to the heavy lifting: cooking lunch for Anarosa's husband, her own husband, and two or three other laborers whose day began before dawn.

For the weeks she took care of Anarosa, Carmen assumed not only her sister-in-law's duties, but many of the anxieties of a new mother too.

"What did you do all the time you were resting?" I asked Anarosa. "What did you think about?"

"I don't really remember," she said. "I thought about the baby. I watched novelas, which I never do normally—I'm always in too much of a hurry."

"*I* didn't watch any novelas," Carmen said shortly. "I didn't have time."

Worn out as she was, Carmen carefully tended to Anarosa's emotions. When she came in each morning, she'd settle on the end of the bed and the two friends would chat. They murmured about the baby, the snow, Carmen's job.

"I always felt so confident, because I had someone I trusted to take care of the baby if I rested," Anarosa said.

But the truth is that Carmen, who didn't have children, was frequently terrified. In Chiapas she'd been a foot soldier, not a captain. Secretly, she called her mother back home to ask what to cook. And once, when Anarosa readied for a rare trip out of the house for a checkup, she asked Carmen to change the baby while she dressed.

"I was scared," Carmen said. "I was afraid I would break her little legs. I had to call the doctor to ask how to do it."

But she never let on. As a result, Anarosa's biggest postpartum complaint was being forbidden from cleaning up after Daniel.

"But—didn't you feel guilty?" I asked. The women looked briefly at each other.

"She knew I would be there," Carmen said. "She didn't have to ask."

"It was understood that she'd help out," Anarosa said, nodding. "And she knew I would help her."

Love and Purslane

The young Mexican man crouched by the highway and clicked open his knife. It was summer, around 4:00 a.m., and the truckloads of workers who had migrated here from Guanajuato and Chiapas and León would soon be rumbling past. The dirt of Painesville, Ohio, can grow almost anything from vegetables and roses to pine trees destined for lawns across the country. Nearly twenty years earlier, the Mexican workers who came here seasonally to work in the nurseries began finding border crossings tougher, but that the money they earned during growing season could sustain them all year long. They brought their wives and settled. Now Painesville schools, about fifty miles from Akron, are more than 25 percent Latino.

Leaning groundward, the young man peered at a frail-looking plant with fleshy leaves. It was purslane, or, in Spanish, *verdolagas,* one of the most common weeds in North America. It grows in sidewalk crevices and along highways. If you buy the cultivated specimen from a garden shop, the flowers are quite pretty: shell-like pinks and ivories, like cactus blooms. Generally, though, wild purslane is ignored.

Nicking the shallow root with his knife, the young man gave the plant a shake and tossed it into a plastic bag. Then he climbed into his truck and left for work.

That night, when he got home, he pulled the purslane from its bag. Stripping the leaves with two fingers, he tossed them into a pot of chicken soup he'd started that morning. Then he carried a bowl to the sofa, where his wife and newborn baby had spent the day.

That bowl of soup represents one facet of an apparent medical miracle. Against expectations, babies born to Mexican immigrants have better birth outcomes than those of American-born minorities. Even more astoundingly, these newborns are as healthy as those of native-born white American women—and sometimes healthier.

The amazing vigor of these babies with so many socioeconomic disadvantages persists even after birth. Through their first hour, week, and month of life, these babies are actually *10 percent* less likely to die than those born to non-Hispanic, white U.S. women.

The health of these babies at birth, and for the vulnerable weeks afterward, may be the most stunning example of the immigrant paradox. More than twenty years ago, sociologists Kyriakos Markides and Jeannine Coreil published a watershed report showing that Latinos, many of them immigrants, had markedly longer life expectancy—

and often better health—than the better-off, native-born Americans among whom they lived. In the years since, their work has been much studied, argued over, and developed. But study after study has confirmed the unusual early health of Mexican immigrants' babies.

Part of this, researchers concur, is due to behavior. Mexican-born women, we know, smoke less and consume much less alcohol than their white and African American counterparts. A study based on 568 low-income Mexican farm workers in California also found that women who came to the United States later in life had better health behaviors—including diet—during pregnancy and immediately after giving birth than those who'd spent more time here.

But they also have a tradition for being cared for *after* pregnancy. For more than three decades now, research has shown that social support correlates to fewer pregnancy complications. According to the study of California farm workers, the more social support the mothers-to-be received from loved ones, the better their prenatal diet was.

So it's logical that cuarentenas, which encourage mothers to eat well in the first months *after* having their babies, play a role in the immigrant paradox as well. By bolstering a mother emotionally and physically, a proper cuarentena strengthens her ability, in turn, to care for her newborn.

I had seen the emotional side of that nurturing in Anarosa's Akron living room. You can see some of its physical components by the highways, where the young laborer was harvesting roadside herbs for his wife. He may not have known it, but purslane is something of a wonder food. In a rhapsodic essay, gardening expert Joan Huyser-Honig writes, "Researchers have identified it as the richest source of omega-3 fatty acids . . . of any vegetable yet examined. A simple serving of fresh purslane leaves (a little less than a cup) provides the minimum daily requirement of alpha-linoleic acid, a type of omega-3 fatty acid."

A building block for developing brains and eyes, omega-3s are also popular as a first-line therapy for mild depression. The most common way to get them is by slurping fish oil or popping prenatal vitamins.

Or you can find them free, by the roadside, in a clump of purslane.

Men Taking Care of Women

The Mexicans I met in Ohio clung to the cuarentena as best they remembered it. But in less than two decades, they had also tailored it to their new circumstances. Most dramatically, men now often take the place of faraway mothers and sisters.

"I didn't see this in Latin America," confessed Kate Masley, a medical anthropologist at Cleveland State University. After studying the cuarentena in Honduras, Masley spent a year learning how Mexican women practice it in northeastern Ohio. In both places, Masley found, mothers sum up the cuarentena with a common refrain.

"We take care of ourselves," they say.

But it's only in the United States, Masley said, that men take care of them too.

It is a question of necessity. Mexican women who migrate here as adults tend to come alone or with their husbands and children. Few are lucky enough, like Anarosa, to have a female relative who can make the journey with them. So husbands have to take on some postnatal duties—at times, all of them.

"I'm good at cleaning a house," announced Juan Alberto Ramirez, who was mopping the floor at Restaurant La Flor in Painesville. He couldn't have been more than twenty. And frankly, he looked to me like a slacker, with his absurd, elflike beanie and decorative gold teeth. So I was quite surprised when he volunteered that he had a baby at home and knew what a cuarentena was. Not only that, he had cooked and cleaned for his wife for the entire forty days.

Later that afternoon, Juan's brother-in-law Esteban dropped in and revealed that he, too, was something of a domestic god. Odd as it would be in Mexico, he took on all the housework after the birth of each of his children.

"In Mexico," he said, "they'd call you *mandilón* [henpecked].

"Even here, there was a case when I was out in front of the house sweeping, and a woman said, 'How strange. I've never seen a man with a broom.' But the house has to get clean. It doesn't matter where you are. I think doing that work is a matter of respect of a man for a woman."

That role reversal takes place elsewhere in the country too, a pair of researchers discovered in a rare study of cuarentenas in Texas' Hidalgo County.

"Husbands who seldom did housework inside the home became responsible for sweeping, lugging the laundry to the laundromat, and washing the floor," the team found. "During the forty days, the father was [also] taught infant care by his wife or partner."

Allowing the mother to rest and focus on her baby was a priority among the twenty-four families studied. In these highly traditional homes women did close to 100 percent of the household labor through their ninth month of pregnancy, but in the forty days after the babies came, the women did only one-third of their usual chores.

That is what happened to Adriana, a homemaker I met through workers at Restaurant La Flor in Painesville. Adriana was a solidly built, carefully made-up young woman in her twenties with a six-month-old son. She spoke English easily, after attending high school here with her six sisters.

"My husband never liked to wash dishes or clean the bathroom," she said. "But my mother-in-law, who also lives here, told him, 'You have to help. You have to do it for forty days.'"

And he obeyed. A compulsive housekeeper, Adriana could barely stand it. I looked around her Painesville apartment and immediately envisioned her on the couch, consumed with annoyance. Now that she was back on her feet, nothing was out of place. A crystalline fish tank burbled, the carpet was recently vacuumed, even the plant on the TV had been dusted. For forty days, Adriana's husband fruitlessly attempted to meet this standard, and it drove him and his wife batty.

Yet they both stuck to the cuarentena. In the night he got up and gave the baby his bottles; by day, doggedly, he did his best to tidy under his wife's dissatisfied gaze.

And at least three times a day, he brought her warm *atole*. An iconic Mesoamerican comfort drink made from roasted corn and thickened with milk and sugar, it is the staple food of the cuarentena. It's believed essential to make mother's milk plentiful. So much of the cuarentena revolves around mother's milk, in fact, that I started to wonder if that's why this custom has hung on so long.

Before having kids, I can't say I thought much about breast-feeding. I just knew I should do it. But in fact, it can be tricky. As many mothers can attest, feeding a baby this way requires peace. It also involves practical guidance.

And yet in the United States a new mother has to cross her fingers that the helper she's found will be not only instructive, but kind. The pricey consultant supplied by my maternity hospital was neither. I asked her advice when I realized breast-feeding two babies, exclusively, for a full year would mean just a few minutes of sleep every three hours, for months. "Then that's what you'll do," she snapped. (Reader, I didn't.)

Women who practice the cuarentena, by contrast—women who've grown up caring for infant relatives—nevertheless take it for granted that they'll have guidance. This may have been the one cuarentena task that Adriana's husband couldn't quite master. Instead her mother and sisters took the day off work and drove in from a distant town to give advice. That's what a cuarentena is for, after all.

"The cuarentena is to take care of yourself after childbirth, to repose," Adriana told me. "And someone is teaching you to breast-feed."

This may be the best example of why cuarentena logic translates so well to this culture. Whether in a Chiapas village or in Manhattan, a new mother's emotions and her baby's physical health are tightly entwined. Making breast-feeding tranquil is an efficient way to attend to both.

Comfort Food from the Gods

Two weeks later, back in the subtropical green of Houston, I got a taste of atole. I'd been walking through my neighborhood, wondering why every person I'd asked about the cuarentena had sworn by this stuff. Of all the ancient recipes that have vanished in the mists of time, why had this one made its way to Akron, Ohio? Looking up, I found myself in front of La Guadalupana Bakery and a potential answer. Wedged next to the Time Food Mart (Beer/Lottery Tickets/Groceries), the bakery is famous for its authentic Mexican cuisine. No Tex-Mex chimichangas here. But its cinnamon-scented coffee and green enchiladas are irresistible. And sure enough, they serve atole.

"Natural Gatorade," author Daphne Miller has called this drink. A slow-releasing source of glycogen, this virtuous drink offers complex carbohydrates, trace minerals, and a bit of pep thanks to raw sugar. It's a direct legacy of the pre-Columbian cultures that revered corn. Part of atole's mystique today surely springs from the sense that this food was a gift from the gods.

When my to-go cup finally arrived, I took a taste. It was sweet, and drinking it felt festive and wholesome at the same time, like sipping Guinness. What surprised me was how long it took to serve it. The cook later told me that atole takes about half an hour to simmer and needs to be slowly reheated on the stovetop with extra milk each time it's served.

Like heating a bottle for a baby, I thought. This practice— "mothering the mother," as anthropologist Dana Raphael dubbed it—

existed long before the women's movement. It's based on something even more primal: the desperate importance of mothers for the tribe's survival. In the traditional cultures that practice some form of postpartum ritual, it's in the interests not only of the immediate family, but the community, that a woman emerge from childbirth physically and emotionally strong. The cuarentena, with its seriousness about food and its ban on multitasking, acknowledges how much energy this recuperation takes.

Scratching out enough to eat, thankfully, is not a problem for most mothers in this country. But carving out the time and attention to adjust to motherhood may be harder here than in the Chiapas highlands.

The federal Family and Medical Leave Act, established under the Clinton administration, made history when it guaranteed U.S. men and women 12 weeks of unpaid leave time without penalty. In practice, though, many of us don't feel we can financially or professionally afford it. According to one study, even mothers with fully paid leave took only an average of 10.5 weeks with their babies. Those without paid leave marched back to work after 6.6 weeks.

Six weeks, of course, about equals the length of a cuarentena. But it's safe to guess that not a lot of the women who took that time devoted it to resting, eating nourishing foods cooked by others, and indulging in saunas.

And other U.S. women take less time than that. Raphael, a pioneering breast-feeding advocate, argues that many American women focus on recuperating—and getting to know their babies—for only two weeks: the same chunk of time the workplace commonly allots for vacations or giving notice.

This standardized dose of personal time even shapes our thinking about how our bodies work. Lina, a Colombian graduate student at the University of Texas, and her husband planned a week off for both of them after she gave birth to her first child. Based on what she'd seen here, Lina thought this sounded about right. Luckily, a male adviser who had children "looked at me like I was crazy," Lina said. "This is a baby," he told her. "You'll be gone until next semester."

One of my best friends, formidable in her professional life, found herself cooking dinner for her mother the day after having a baby. I've heard of others who sat through dinner parties thrown by well-meaning parents or felt obligated to host unwanted guests days after giving birth.

"Why not refuse?" I asked each time I heard one of these stories. But the answer was the same: twenty-four hours after being in labor, most women don't have the energy to wrest control from people who are less than attuned to their needs.

Plus, we are tough. At the age when my mother's generation was swooning over Sweet Sixteens, my friends and I were being urged to "Be! Aggressive!" by field hockey coaches. I was personally impressed by my sixth-grade reading of *The Good Earth,* where the Chinese heroine O-Lan gives birth, stoically and rather swiftly, in a rice field before matter-of-factly getting back to work. But in demolishing the idea that our bodies are frail, we've overcorrected. O-Lan may have given birth on her own without a tea break. But elsewhere in China, new mothers "do the month," resting in a lounge chair by the fire.

Visitors from other countries, in fact, often find our post-baby customs horrifying. Paola, an ad executive from Colombia, told me her mother was so shocked by Paola's postpartum ordeal that she begged her to come home—to Cali, then murder capital of the world. At least there, with her first baby, Paola had been able to rest for forty days straight. Friends brought movies and novels, or showed up simply to watch TV with her. It was, at times, boring, Paola recalled. Boring—and soothing.

Here, though, where she had her second baby, Paola was so worried about making money that she returned to work after two weeks.

"I'd go out for a sales call," she said, "and pull over and cry and cry and cry. I was so exhausted. I would think, I have a little baby and I don't even have time for her."

It was a terrible depression, and it took a full year for her to recover. Looking back, a cuarentena might have cost less.

Quarantine

"I saw a cuarentena gone bad," an interpreter friend told me one day at lunch. She'd just been called into a mental hospital, where a suicidal young mother from El Salvador had arrived. Alone except for her husband and sister-in-law, the woman had been duly confined to her house for forty days. But through her sister-in-law's misguided advice, the young mother was fed nothing but corn tortillas.

Unable to speak English, trapped in her house, the woman tried to kill herself. When I heard the story, I recalled something an Ohio health worker had told me. Women who came here as children, and only remembered bits of the cuarentena's rules, seemed at greater risk of postpartum depression. Without family and friends carefully organized to support them, they were not sheltered by a cuarentena. They were captive to it.

That happened to Miriam, a young waitress at La Flor.

It was lunchtime, my last day in Ohio. Oblivious to the patrons filing in to eat, she tucked her pen behind her ear and furrowed a pierced brow remembering.

"I was alone all day," she said. "It's difficult, because you can't do a lot during those forty days, and I couldn't see my mother and my sisters because they lived far away."

Miriam didn't have a car, and the main thing her husband remembered of a cuarentena was that she should stay home resting. But everyone she knew was working, not just one but two or three jobs. Her husband loved her, but his factory job ended at midnight.

Miriam was not experiencing a cuarentena. This was solitary confinement. Finally, her mother staged an intervention. She couldn't visit Miriam herself—she lived too far away and had a houseful of small children. But it was unnatural, unsafe, she declared, for her daughter to be alone. So she, Miriam's husband, and her older brother devised a plan: a drive-by cuarentena. Every morning, Miriam's husband drove her and their newborn an hour across town and left them at Miriam's mother's. It was crowded there, not tranquil exactly, but it was a home. It was buoyant with the kind of companionship even the poorest mother could expect back in Guerrero, Mexico. Miriam loved it.

"The rest of the forty days were fun," she chirped, reclaiming her pen. "It wasn't boring, because I had to get to know the baby."

In their first days of motherhood, it was as if Miriam and the woman from El Salvador were trying to cook from a half-remembered recipe. Only Miriam's mother recalled the key ingredients. The truth is that the components for a traditional cuarentena in this country don't exist. Mexican or not, few of us have the lifestyle and extended family to provide forty days of uninterrupted team care.

So Miriam's mother updated the recipe.

American Cuarentena

It was only a series of flukes—expecting twins, ignorance about newborns, and a stranger's advice—that freed me from much of the typical American postpartum ordeal. Instructed by Theresa, I stumbled into my own cuarentena.

The first few days, I outsourced with a baby nurse. I couldn't quite imagine how you were supposed to change two infants or get them to stop crying at the same time. Expertise was what I wanted, and during the four days and three nights she stayed with us, Shirley Perez comfortably assumed the role of mentor.

She arrived at the house like Mary Poppins, carrying a big mesh bag of home-cooked rum cakes, Trinidadian green sauce, and tamarind candy from her mail-order food business. She had spent much of her life caring for newborn twins, and the families she worked with invariably begged her to stay on when the children got older. She always declined. Too much running around.

My first night home from the hospital, she cooked us a soothing dinner of Trinidadian chicken and that green sauce, and smiled but shook her head when I asked for the recipe. She gave me bay-leaf tea and taught Mike to bathe the girls. Often, on dark afternoons when the girls were napping, I found myself creeping down to the living room, where Shirley sat reading, just to be near her. That was the most important thing. She was company.

I liked the feeling that there were rules to follow in that period, that observing them somehow was auspicious, a kind of barter for extra protection of my little ones. I also liked feeling that someone who knew me, my husband, and the babies was monitoring our well-being in those first clueless days, proffering time-tested guidelines and, in her understated way, confirming that we were doing a good job.

After Shirley left, Mike and I took a few days with our daughters to parent alone. He was a natural, of course. Until quite late in the twentieth century, even in this country, a baby's arrival would be more of a family affair—or, to be precise, a women's affair. The father tended to be odd man out. But like a lot of men his age, Mike was fully on board as a *comadre*, to play with a Spanish expression: a co-mother. And of all the social innovations of twenty-first-century Western society, this was surely one of the finest.

We did exhale with relief, though, when the next wave of cavalry came. Our friend Spike, we'd decided before the babies were born, was the lowest-maintenance helper we could have in those nervous first weeks. Spike, who has long chestnut hair and a tattoo of a cow on her bicep, had single-handedly raised a strapping teenage son named Henry Mowgli while supporting herself as a writer. Blowing into town from Austin with a bag of groceries and two tiny Kurt Cobain caps, she cooked big meals and praised the babies' deportment. Of paramount value in a cuarentena helper, she disappeared gracefully for hours to work on her novel.

Day 25, a week after Spike, my sister, Luisa, arrived. Because she lived in New Mexico, she had spent less time in our household than Spike, but because she knew me so well she knew exactly how to make me happy. There were clean, healthy meals from Whole Foods. There was a freesia on the table. And three weeks in, there were also, on occasion, two angry babies shrieking inexplicably. Yet Luisa's presence, somehow, dulled that truth.

One night Anna was yelling so loudly that adult speech couldn't be heard. After a respectful interval, Luisa finally mouthed, "Shall I?" Whisking her away to the third floor, she got her to stop crying by perching her on a pile of cushions. Luisa snapped a picture commemorating the moment: Anna, beatific as the Panchen Lama, on a silk throne. It eased me to know that my girls' happiness could lie in someone else's hands.

My mother, Marielena, came next. It will be noted that the grandmothers, though they were there for the birth, weren't the first caretakers. It was definitely noted by them. But the genius of Theresa's advice, I now realized, was the deft way it modernized an ancient formula. Choose the people you want around you in the order that works best, I had learned.

Those who worship in my mother's cult know that certain situations bring out her brilliance. Teaching a seminar on *Don Quixote*. Making friends via hand signals with a teenage girl in Ramallah. Persuading small children they are significant and understood.

With natural disasters, she is at her absolute best. Just a few months later, with Hurricane Rita bearing down, she would climb into the car with the babies and me and swap driving shifts on a seven-hour trip to San Antonio. But the babies' arrival wasn't a natural disaster, simply a momentous change that I wanted a grasp on before she arrived. By the time her plane landed in Houston, I was ready to enjoy her. She had done a magnificent job as a mother, and I fully planned to copy it.

Mike, though, had some adjusting to do.

He almost collapsed one night when Marielena marched down the stairs with an infant firmly wedged under each arm.

"Put them down!" he barked.

"Mike, I raised four children and I never dropped any of them," she retorted, and proceeded on.

But the only child-care difference I had with her concerned my poor, depressed beagle. One night I asked if my mother could walk her. Marielena ignored me. I asked again.

"I want to spend time with the girls," she said.

"You said you were coming to help," I pouted. "And that's the one thing I really need."

Annoyed, she pulled down the leash and stalked out with the dog.

An hour later she returned in bright spirits.

"I found a house I'm going to buy down the street," she announced.

I smiled. Now, this was a cuarentena gone right. I had been asking her to move to Houston for years, but before the girls came she wouldn't hear of it. After six weeks of help, Mike and I knew what we were doing, or at least were trying to do. I didn't need any more care. But the girls needed a grandmother, and at this, I knew, Marielena was brilliant.

Rest. Guidance. Companionship.

In my own happenstance cuarentena, these three ingredients turned a potentially stressful time into something strengthening. It's a complicated mix to get right if you're winging it, though. That's why ritual, even if it involves a ban on sweeping, can do so much.

In most places where a cuarentena is observed, birth is a religious event, a crossing from the spirit realm to our own. For anyone, giving birth is an existential change. A cuarentena, or something like it, acknowledges that you're still the person you once were, but confusion, even fleeting sadness, is natural.

You don't have to be from Chiapas to see how rest, guidance, and companionship can turn a potentially punishing experience into a kind of sanctuary. I could hardly call my first few weeks as a mother a classic cuarentena. And yet thanks to good advice, I rested far longer that I might have and recruited far more help than I ever would have thought I needed.

Finding peace during a baby's first forty days, it turns out, is not just a matter of luck.

3

How to Court:

South Asian Assisted Marriage

Twenty-eight-year-old Reena scanned T.G.I. Friday's for a man she had never met. She still couldn't believe it had come to this. Reena was a vivacious businesswoman, entrancingly pretty. She had found her last boyfriend perfectly well, thank you, with no one's help. But in the end, that's what made this evening a necessity.

There was a practical reason Reena was here.

For three and a half years, during college in South Carolina, Reena had dated that previous boyfriend. He seemed perfect, wooing her with the persistence of a film hero. Their families even came from the same area in India. It seemed inevitable to Reena they would marry—seemed so right up to the month before graduation, when he called to say they were through. Later, a mutual friend told Reena her boyfriend had worried because their families belonged to different subgroups of the same caste. He supposedly feared that if his parents disapproved, they might pass their fortune to his younger brother.

Which was why Reena was at this T.G.I. Friday's in Columbia, South Carolina, on a Saturday night. Date night. Dates, though, imply fun, playing the field, gradually deciding if there's enough spark to speak of the future. This was no date. Reena was here to audition husbands from a candidate pool supplied by her mother.

*   *   *

The idea of marrying someone picked by one's parents strikes most of us as unthinkable. Counting the reasons is like lining modern American values up on an abacus. First, of course, there's no romance in it. From childhood we are regaled with, groomed for, and promised romance. In a secular society, lightning-strike love may be the last miracle most people still expect. Who would forgo this magical birthright for a chance to interview applicants prescreened by Mom? It's the difference between stumbling on a wild apple tree in the woods and waiting at the breakfast table for Chex.

We also question whether a parent can be trusted to find the right partner for a child. American parents and children routinely spar over politics, dress, and career; seeing eye-to-eye about whom to love seems out of the question. And there's something outright improper to us about the notion of a mother scouting brides for her grown son. Marriage, as we understand it, is the most intimate bond possible between adults, fused by sexual chemistry outsiders can't guess at. No one, we say, knows what goes on in a marriage. For a parent to be the first one to envision this, and accordingly choose a child's spouse . . . Ick.

That was pretty much Reena's view for most of her childhood. After all, she was born here, and though her family is Hindu, she grew up attending Baptist schools in Houston.

"I'd like to think of my upbringing as half and half. Our parents raised us with the traditional Indian values: family, academics above everything," Reena told me. "But I was very against meeting guys the way my parents met."

Her father attended university in swinging London during the 1960s, but he returned to his family's village during vacation with one goal: to marry. All his British roommates were dating, but Indian custom forbade him to do so. He was lonely. The moment the brilliant young bachelor arrived in his father's hometown near Mumbai, a procession of hopeful parents filed to the house with their single daughters. The bachelor liked Reena's mother the best, and she liked him too. So two weeks later they married and left for London.

Reena's mission at T.G.I. Friday's differed fundamentally from her father's in India. To her own surprise, she was embarking on an assisted marriage—a newly popular South Asian courtship process that is neither traditional arranged marriage nor American dating, but a hybrid of both. It's a team effort to find love, in which parents, older siblings, or family friends known as "aunties" methodically collect and screen prospects.

Naturally, these referrals reflect the screeners' own tastes. And, likewise, some families lean, hard, on their child to choose a favored contender. But in a complete departure from arranged marriage through the ages, the decision to wed belongs to the young people alone.

Only a few decades old, assisted marriage is now common in middle-class Indian, Pakistani, and South Asian communities in the United States. No statistics chart the number of those who use it, but it's clearly been influenced by economic gains in South Asia and the Westernization of second-generation immigrants here.

Many of these young South Asians have no interest in participating in an arranged marriage. They're products of American culture, sophisticated, educated, and often (though they let their parents think otherwise) sexually experienced. Even so, they often retain one traditional South Asian value. Courtship, they believe, is not a lark.

It's a hunt for a spouse.

It wasn't that Reena had lost interest in romance, then, or that she'd decided to go back to tradition. Arranged marriage, after all, was not a tradition that she had witnessed firsthand. No: like many Americans her age, especially women, Reena no longer found dating scintillating.

She found it dispiriting and dull. She wanted to invest her energy in one person.

"All right," she told her mother one day. "You can start faxing me names."

"Do it," Ayesha, a young Pakistani-American editor, urged over french fries at a Hoboken, New Jersey, diner. "It's free! And you'll see how many people out there are willing to get married."

Ayesha was pushing me to try Shaadi.com, the enormous matrimonial website distinguished from Western online dating enterprises by two traits: it caters to Indians, Pakistanis, and other South Asians, and its sole objective is to get them married.

Daters need not apply.

I had met Ayesha to learn more about courtship trends among *desis,* the nickname used by young Indians, Pakistanis, Bangladeshis, and Sri Lankans who live in the West. A bubbly woman with brown eyes and golden skin, Ayesha was the cofounder of *Bibi* magazine, a giddy social and marriage bible for South Asians in the United States. Inspired by *Latina* (its editor and Ayesha shared a dentist), *Bibi* was an unabashed bonbon.

To understand younger South Asians, Ayesha explained, you need to start with their parents.

"Marriage is still the be-all and end-all" for that older generation, she said. It's the pass to adulthood, the mark of a functioning community member. "No wife, no life," as Indians say. Younger South Asians tend to share that notion, but the route they want to take, and the type of candidates they will consider, are both new.

Fifty years ago, "South Asians" as a group didn't exist. Indians, Pakistanis, and Sri Lankans rarely strayed from their own villages, much less interacted socially with other cultures. Then the 1965 immigration law uncorked a vast wave of migration from the subcontinent.

Indians alone are now the fifth-biggest immigrant group in the United States. Though it wasn't accurate, American bureaucrats and political activists gave all the newcomers one name: South Asians. The alchemy of immigration turned this made-up identity into reality, and immigrants from the region now use it themselves. Their children, who sometimes intermarry, are *Bibi's* main readers.

"We look kind of the same, we can understand each other," Ayesha told me. "It's like putting spices in food. They all blend."

Bibi, which in 2007 went from print to online, indulges this audience with a visual explosion of golden saris, crimson veils, and glittering bangles. The content, though, can be serious. A much-talked-about survey in 2002 revealed that most respondents had had sex before marriage. A few years later, *Bibi* ran a controversial piece on rising rates of South Asian divorce, until recently a taboo topic.

It's a subject Ayesha knows well. Much as she believes in marriage, she was the first Pakistani woman that she knew to get a divorce. And she thought she had chosen so well. Born and educated mostly in New York, Ayesha also lived in Saudi Arabia, Canada, and Pakistan. Her parents were cosmopolitan, observant Muslims who let her marry whomever she wanted. Although she waited until her late twenties, she delighted everyone when she chose a good-hearted guy whose family shared her parents' values.

No one was as surprised as Ayesha and her husband when it didn't work out.

"We were both very committed to the idea of marriage," she explained as we ate. "But he thought he wanted someone more Western than he really did. I thought I wanted someone more traditional than I really did. We were both wrong."

She sighed.

"When you've been divorced in my community, not too many people want to marry you again. At least, that's how it used to be," she said. "Luckily, people are getting more easygoing."

But the experience didn't leave her angry, Ayesha said. It just reinforced her belief that no path to marriage is foolproof—and that assisted marriage is as likely to work as any.

When arranged marriage surfaces in American headlines, it is usually in reference to some kind of atrocity. It is not an unfair portrayal. Extremely poor and religiously orthodox societies from China to the Middle East consider their children property to employ or marry off as desperation demands. Girls suffer the most. In the developing world, complications from pregnancy and childbirth are the leading cause of death for girls between 15 and 19.

But middle-class families who have more choices often arrange marriages in a different spirit. They still want to preserve or improve their standard of living. But these parents also have the luxury of seeking happiness for their child. So as their kids approach college age in Bangalore or Karachi, mothers and fathers sound the alert. It's time to start dealing in biodata, the South Asian term for brief résumés listing a young person's main marriageable traits.

In crafting ads for newspaper matrimonial sections, parents may boil down the biofacts to just a few words: caste, religion, degrees earned, occupation. For women, if applicable, the ads promise "homeliness"—the talent for cleaning and cooking to a mother-in-law's standards. A "wheatish complexion" advertises coveted lighter skin. And "no dowry requested" signals disdain for the custom that causes thousands of murders each year when Indian or Pakistani in-laws deem a new bride insufficiently lucrative.

Their real work starts when a promising response comes in. Parents marshal neighbors, religious leaders, and village gossips for useful intelligence. Does the family have a good name? Is it financially stable? Have any members suffered infertility or divorce? (If so, points off for the candidate.) Digging deeper, a good parent tries to suss out if the mother-in-law is a tyrant, or the bride's father hides a mean streak.

Finally, the prospective in-laws—en masse—come to tea.

"In Pakistani culture, the guy goes to the girl's house," Ayesha told me. "In Sikh culture, it's vice versa. Everyone in the family has their pet questions." Everyone except the marriage candidates, that is. In traditional families, the girl displays her social skills by serving tea and sweetmeats adorned with sugar or edible silver. The boy, including Ayesha's brother during his own courtship, may not address her. If all the parents agree, the young people marry. If not, the process starts over.

But in the last thirty years, both on the subcontinent and in the United States, this system has changed. Educated, financially strong young women demand a say in their future. And because young people in the States frequently move to new places for jobs, parents realize couples must depend on each other emotionally as they never would have in a traditional extended family.

Western-style dating, with its emphasis on chemistry, might seem the most obvious path under these modern terms. There's just one problem. As Americans who are educated, choosy, and haven't found a mate can attest, our system for finding love can be a tad inefficient. Assisted marriage provides one solution. When it works, it blends the Western belief in individual freedom with the South Asian conviction that parents are a valuable resource in the quest for a mate. Yearning to marry, in this system, isn't a mark of neediness. It's a mature and admirable desire.

What a contradiction to most trend stories about single Americans: students so immersed in hookup culture they can't form relationships, cohabitation eclipsing marriage, commitment-phobic, Peter Pan men moving back home. To glimpse South Asians' seriousness about marriage, I decided to take Ayesha's advice and visit Shaadi.com. I was curious, in particular, about what sort of men would enter this market, where all the deals are for keeps.

Logging on, I found an image of a stunning Indian couple embracing under a mountain; their wedding date appeared in a caption below. Signing up for a profile, as Ayesha promised, couldn't be easier. Female, Communications Industry, and Houston were simple. Age forty-three. Astrological sign? Gemini. Food preferences and religion appeared on a menu: "Semi-veg" fit about right. It was pleasant to find that, in addition to tabs for Hindu, Jain, Muslim, Zoroastrian, and Sikh, Shaadi also offered the more generic "Spiritual" option, and "No Religion" at all. It even gave a space to label oneself. "1. Traditional. 2. Moderate. 3. Liberal." Option 3, please.

All that remained was filling the small box for Personal Profile. "I am a writer who likes to travel and is interested in meeting someone who is secular, tolerant, and curious about other cultures," I typed. Not exactly Mata Hari, but I wanted to see if anyone (else) might consider marrying the real me.

Twenty-four hours later, at a friend's cabin in Pennsylvania, I turned on my laptop and a throng of e-mails fairly leaped out. Twenty or thirty more crowded in every few days for several weeks, until I either exhausted the pool or my inaction suggested I'd married or died. The decency of my suitors moved me. "I like your attitude and would like to correspond further," wrote Omar, a fifty-five-year-old engineer, secular and Muslim, from Silicon Valley. "I share your goals of social tolerance and harmony," said Kumar, fifty, a civil servant in Minnesota. Most winning was Subash, a mechanical engineer in L.A.

"Are you sure you're not a journalist doing research? I'll take a chance anyway. I like your views and think we would have a lot to talk about."

I thought we might too, but for obvious reasons a correspondence was not to be.

*　　*　　*

Before the twentieth century, most couples in the United States met through a diluted form of assisted marriage. Real arrangements never got much traction here, but until the 1920s, families, especially mothers, actively took part in courting. Wooing was literally "calling": a visit to the girl's home at her mother's invitation.

In Puritan New England, young people could grab a little privacy even in snug family parlors, with the use of a "courting stick." A long wooden tube with ear trumpets at both ends, it allowed the couple to whisper nothings from opposite sides of the hearth while between them the girl's family safely clacked needles and perused Scripture.

By the mid-nineteenth century, middle-class girls could ask their mothers to initiate calls. While parents naturally wielded veto power, girls could collaborate with them to indicate the boys they wished to pursue. This power faded at the start of the twentieth century when affordable cars and supermarkets reinvented many of our social mores.

Group outings and home visits transformed into one-on-one "dates." Then, in the prosperous midcentury years, Americans shifted "their attention partially from thinking about how to work and earn to pondering how to spend and consume," wrote sociologist Martin King Whyte in a 1992 study on dating and marriage satisfaction. Whyte went on to note, "The assumptions involved in shopping around and test driving various cars or buying and tasting Wheaties, Cheerios and Froot Loops were transferred to popular thinking about how to select a spouse."

With more leisure, prosperity, and education than ever before, Americans for the first time in history could marry strictly for love. But the long-idealized romantic marriage was hard to sustain. By the 1970s, when no-fault divorce became possible, marriages were dissolving in record numbers. Free to "shop" for our partners as much as we pleased, we somehow weren't making choices that stuck.

Dating, it may be, *doesn't work.* Sure, it may be entertaining. The joys and humiliations broaden perspective. But the "marketplace viewpoint" that comparison shopping helps us choose the best partner doesn't necessarily hold up. According to Whyte, a survey of 459 Detroit women between eighteen and seventy-five revealed that "Women who had married their first sweethearts . . . were just as likely to have enduring and satisfying marriages as women who had married only after considering many alternatives. Similarly, women who had married after only a brief acquaintance were no more (nor less) likely to have a successful marriage than those who knew their husbands-to-be for years." There was "no clear difference between the marriages of women who were virgins at marriage and those who had had a variety of sexual partners and who had lived together with their husbands before the wedding."

Whyte's findings were more than twenty years old, but I hadn't seen them refuted. Fascinated, I shared them with several Indian Americans close to my age.

"I totally believe them," said a thirty-three-year-old hospital administrator in Manhattan, who had recently asked her parents to send her marriage candidates. "I would be able to commit rather quickly if the person I met had a lot of the things I am looking for."

She was willing, she said, because she had seen so many good marriages among her parents' peers and so few among the parents of her American friends. *Those marriages just look happy from the outside,* I thought. It must be easy to get along, after all, if both partners agree the wife must submit to the husband. It turns out, though, that a considerable number of educated South Asian women have spoken their minds on the record about this topic. And they don't sound submissive at all.

One of the best known is Renu Khator, president of the University of Houston, married for three decades to a man picked by her parents.

In interviews, Khator often credits her husband for pushing her to earn a doctorate in the United States.

"This may sound crazy," a C-SPAN interviewer asked Khator in 2008, "but did you ever fall in love with him?"

"Yes, I am very much in love with him even today," Khator replied. "And I did fall in love with him very quickly because if you meet him he's just a wonderful man."

A few research teams have even tried to quantify the satisfaction of arranged marriages versus "love" marriages. In one study of twenty-eight Indian arranged marriages, twenty-five Indian love marriages, and thirty-one Americans who'd found each other in our normal, haphazard way, Indian women in arranged marriages rated the highest scores in marital satisfaction.

Another study traced the emotional arc of the two types of marriage over a decade. While partners in love matches reported their feelings ebbed over that time, the arranged couples said their feelings grew. At about the five-year mark, the arranged couples' love surpassed that of the love matches, and it continued to increase in the years that followed.

Reena, in a long skirt, boots, and jaunty red poncho, ventured into the restaurant. She was looking for the son of her mother's best friend, who was visiting from New Jersey. Though it didn't mean much to Reena, he was, by South Asian standards, the perfect catch: a newly minted doctor, in town to interview for a residency.

"I'll meet him for dinner," Reena told her mother, after giving his biodata a glance. But he needed to at least call first, she insisted. How else would she know how to recognize him?

His answer, when they talked, took Reena aback.

"I look like a Greek god," he told her.

Hmm. He was either very cocky or very funny. Or, possibly, very good-looking.

Then she found him in the foyer of T.G.I. Friday's—pudgy and bespectacled. Adonis he was not. He wasn't much of a wit either.

"Do you want Oysters Rockefeller?" he inquired suggestively. "It's an aphrodisiac, you know."

"I was like—Oh God! Just let me eat my dinner!" Reena recalled. Then, at one horrid moment over the chicken Parmesan, the doctor fixed his eyes on Reena's and popped the question.

"What is your parents' income level?"

"What?"

"Would you say high income, middle income, low income?"

"Middle income," Reena instantly shot back.

"My parents are pretty well-to-do," she told me later. "I wasn't going to let him know that, obviously. I want someone to want me for myself."

As soon as the plates were cleared, she left for the ladies' room. When she came back, the Greek god was gone.

At least he'd paid up. Hideous as the episode was, Reena didn't fault her parents. That was what these meetings were for—to see how the human behind the biodata measured up. Parents and friends could provide contacts and screen them for family background. But it was up to the candidates themselves to gauge chemistry, the variable that makes assisted marriage more than a glorified business deal.

Not everybody needs a mate, and countless couples would be happier if they'd never reproduced. But the revolutionary Western idea that women, in particular, can be complete without mates has spawned its own problems. Chief among them: longing to settle down with a spouse sometimes comes off as vaguely shameful.

In her picaresque memoir *Marrying Anita*, Indian American journalist Anita Jain describes trying to wriggle free of that stigma. "We wonder what's wrong with us," Jain writes, "when really we should wonder whether there isn't a better way of doing things." Knowing that people who love you think your wish for a life partner is laudable, and in fact want to help, erases that shame. The unsentimentality of the process can actually put people at ease.

"Currently, there is one person my parents have found for me," the hospital administrator e-mailed at lunchtime from her office. Her parents located him through friends, and after seeing his biodata, she agreed to meet him. It went well, and now a third date was approaching. If he didn't pursue her, she insisted, she wouldn't take it to heart: "It's probably because his family made him call me, and he really has a girlfriend."

Greek god notwithstanding, one of the more appealing features of assisted marriage is the consideration you must show all contenders. Protocol demands that either party, or both, report to their parents if they're not interested. Empty promises "to call" don't wash. Too many people are watching, worried about their reputations, to allow improper behavior. And your parents will do the dirty work for you.

"Oh, there are all kinds of ways to say you're not interested," Reena told me with a laugh. "Your parents just say they've decided you should finish your studies first."

It seems a humane contrast to the behavioral jungle that daters face on sites such as Match.com. With some 15 million members to consider, newcomers are left to their own devices. They must sift liars, adulterers, and predators from serious seekers of love. Women, especially, can come away humiliated. "It's like a huge candy shop for men," one friend complained. "The selection is endless, and constantly changing. Why would anyone commit himself to one woman when there are thousands of other possibilities who might be better?"

Unfiltered as it is, the process can also be frightening. "I've been doing the evening check-in for a girlfriend in her thirties who's online dating," a coworker told me. "She's being methodical, meeting people in a coffee shop three or four nights a week. But yesterday she said, 'You know, nobody knows any of these men that I'm meeting. I could be out with a violent rapist, and have no idea.'"

Families on an assisted marriage campaign narrow the choices to a more accountable pool. And even though the rules are restrictive—you must be serious about marriage, and sex with a prospect is strictly off limits—they help to ensure a certain level of decent treatment. Especially if you have been seared by regular dating, those rules may suddenly seem a tradition worth keeping.

"No more doctors. If I'm going to go through with this process, I need someone I have something to talk about with," Reena announced to her mother shortly after the Greek god debacle. "Find me a business-man."

There is nothing mystical about the goals of traditional arranged marriage. Loving parents want their child to have a strong, happy union, but historically, arranged marriage in South Asia is about preserving family and caste status. In Pakistan and India, a bridegroom from the same village—or even better, the same block—is still considered ideal. Among Indians in the United States, caste, the intricate social system based on ancestral occupations, matters not at all to some families, and very, very much to others.

That was certainly the case with Reena's college boyfriend. They both came from similar backgrounds in the state of Gujarat. But apparently, for his family, that was insufficient. Reena was not of the right social group, and moreover, the community she was from was too liberal. "His community expects more from a daughter-in-law. They're very strict," Reena said. "You don't speak your mind, you can't just say, 'No, I don't want to go to this dinner party' to your mother-in-law."

Now that Reena was back in the marriage pool, her parents were trying to be reasonable. Nonnegotiables: a sound education, a decent income, and Indian cultural values. Caste counted for little. Even so, Reena was traditional enough to prefer a South Asian groom, sooner rather than later. Among South Asians, a woman's marriageability traditionally expires when she turns twenty-five. She becomes what some call a Christmas cake—past the sell-by date. Setting to work with all her business training, Reena read, considered, and meticulously cross-indexed the references that her parents faxed over.

"I went though numerous, numerous guys they sent," Reena said. "I'd look at their pictures. Talk to the guy. If we got along, we'd try to meet. Some, though, weren't willing to fly to South Carolina."

But if Reena was patient, her mother was nonplussed. What was taking so long? About a year into the search, the mother unburdened herself to an old friend in Charlotte, who had some helpful news. She had just talked to an acquaintance anxious about the same thing. "'Her twenty-seven-year-old son hasn't settled down yet,'" Reena mimicked the complaining mother. "'He could even end up with a white girl.'"

Phone numbers were quickly exchanged, but this time, because the personal connections were so close and the parents' desperation level code red, no biodata, photographs, or even online correspondence changed hands. Reena took in her mother's phone message with little emotion. She'd just moved to Atlanta for work, and the guy was just one more name on a very long matrimonial to-do list.

After several months, though, when he called, Reena agreed to meet for dinner.

The fellow who knocked on her door was no oil painting. His name was Rajesh. He was a little shorter than average, with a stolid face that looked uneasy cracking a smile. In every way, he seemed the opposite of vivid Reena. When they sat down to dinner at a Cheese-cake Factory—"These encounters are so close to business meetings, there's no point in going someplace atmospheric," Reena said—she noticed with vexation that he rejected any dish containing seafood. Reena and her family were bons vivants, foodies who shopped, traveled, and sampled new cuisines whenever they could.

Picky, she thought disapprovingly.

Promisingly, though, Rajesh liked business. He managed a wire factory, he explained, a friend's start-up that specialized in custom-made cable connectors for all sorts of computers. He wasn't a high roller, exactly, but Reena liked his ambition to own a firm one day. She, too, dreamed of buying and selling and building projects from the ground up. He listened to Reena's plans attentively.

"He was kind of reserved. I'm more of a talker. But we had a really good conversation together," Reena said. Then, after dinner, he took her to play video games, which Reena loved. Rajesh competed fiercely with her and didn't hesitate to win at every game. Then he surprised her by proposing they go salsa dancing.

"He knew how to salsa dance?" I asked.

"No!" she said. "He knew that I loved to. It's kind of unusual—most guys would be pretty inhibited about that, wouldn't they?"

Out on the floor, an overenthusiastic dancer shoved Reena in the hip, but Rajesh caught her firmly. He opened doors as they left. He took her to an Italian café for dessert.

She said, "I don't really like dessert. But I'll watch you."

Late in the evening, after 1:00 a.m., Rajesh saw Reena home and began the long drive to his family's house back in Nashville. He'd been up since dawn, Reena knew, and had worked a full day before meeting her in Atlanta. She called him on his cell as he drove off. "I'm going to talk to you," she announced, "because I know you'll be sleepy."

They talked and talked until he finally reached his street and Reena said, "I'll let you go now."

"No," he said. "Please keep talking."

She'd met the one.

Just before Sunday dinner at my mother's house, I grabbed a thin book I thought would intrigue her. *First Comes Marriage,* it was titled, *Modern Relationship Advice from the Wisdom of Arranged Marriages.* The unscientific treatise offered author Reva Seth's conclusions about matrimony after interviewing more than three hundred South Asian women with arranged marriages in Canada, the United States, the United Kingdom, and Europe. Not that Seth was one of these women. A Canadian citizen in her thirties, she has a law degree and a husband she met across a crowded room at a party. Helpfully, the book's promotional material included photos of the regal, raven-haired Seth and her suave business consultant husband.

I thought my mother, a great champion of romance, would be fascinated by this hybrid approach to love. But when I slid the book to her across the dinner table, her jaw tightened.

"You're not interested?" I asked.

"I don't think anyone," she said, "should be involved in a marriage except the two people themselves."

I shouldn't have been surprised. Growing up, we're taught that true love travels on wings of fate, overcomes any obstacle, and is the most transformative emotion we will ever experience. Fairy tales introduce the belief; films reinforce it. And for some people—like my mother and father—love really did happen that way.

When they met in botany class at the University of Maryland, my dad, Jonas, was just sixteen, having skipped several grades. My mother was there on a scholarship while my grandmother trained nearby for the U.S. relief effort in Europe. When the young man with the five o'clock shadow that made him look older caught my mother's eye, they fell in love. "I met the man I'm going to marry," she told her roommate.

Some of the Jewish girls didn't like it a bit. They coaxed the Dean of Women to report the romance to my mother's uncle (not her mother). With luck, they seemed to think, the family in Mexico would make them break up. The uncle wrote back that in Mexico, people were allowed to fall in love with whomever they chose.

But my father's parents were even more averse to the match than the coeds, refusing to pay for his medical school if the romance continued. In confusion but not anger, Jonas headed to premed courses in Baltimore, and Marielena returned to Mexico to start graduate school. Then, a year later one of them wrote to the other—my mother can't remember which one. They reunited, traveling every few months by bus between Baltimore and Mexico City to see each other. Seven years after that first meeting in botany, they got married.

And here is where the story becomes, to me, truly romantic—and where it digresses from South Asian and other conventional wisdom about the importance of shared backgrounds, common ethnicity, or supportive in-laws. Although my mother never converted to Judaism, my father's parents converted to her emotionally. As soon as she joined the family, they treated her as a beloved daughter. Marielena loved them back extravagantly, learning the Passover Haggadah and coddling my paternal aunts and grandmother for the rest of their lives. The final frontier was crossed when I was in elementary school. Leaving their four kids with the two grandmothers, my parents went on vacation in Europe. When they returned home, slightly nervous, after two weeks, they found the two women had become bosom friends.

"Your children are growing up without beliefs," my atheist Mexican grandmother told my dumbfounded parents. "I think you should send them to Hebrew school."

Despite their biodata, in other words, Marielena and Jonas found enough in common to fall in love, vanquish family disapproval, and enjoy more than forty years of marriage. No wonder my mother believes in romance. I do too—but I think you have to be ridiculously lucky to find it.

When I first met Mike in San Salvador, I was standing by the coffee machine at the Associated Press office, waiting for a friend. I fell for him a week later, in the Reuters office in the same building. While examining wire copy as it unfurled from the printer, I heard a ceiling tile clatter down. A cloud of plaster dust and two long legs followed.

"Fixed the air-conditioning duct," a Texan voice announced. Then two feet hit hit the floor.

What are the odds? I could never have met this man by reading a fax in Washington, D.C. On the other hand, how many people can expect true love to fall from the ceiling?

"What surprises me," memoirist Jain writes, "is how much [the U.S.] system leaves to chance encounter, to a kind of fate or fortune. For a decidedly unmystical society that seems to have the answer for everything else—the best medical care, cutting-edge technology, superhighways, and space shuttles—it seems odd that people are left to their own resources, casting around for another lonely soul, for what arguably is the most important decision of their lives."

My mother was right, I told myself after dinner that Sunday night. Love can't be predicted or engineered.

All the more reason to consider any possibility while you are looking.

Now a married woman, Reena met me on a drizzly spring night at a Sleep Inn motel in Nashville. She and Rajesh own the place together. Though the foundation of Indian social life is a cup of milky, cardamom-infused chai, the Sleep Inn's beverage menu was wanly American. Leading me through a cramped, fluorescent-lit lobby, Reena seated us in the breakfast nook and reached over the mini-Cheerios to pour coffee.

After that first, revelatory evening when they competed at video games and danced salsa, Reena and Rajesh knew the people who'd matched them up had succeeded. So the couple responded in a fashion that itself is part of the American assisted marriage system: they hid their feelings from the matchmakers. No matter that Rajesh soon began driving from Nashville to Atlanta to spend every weekend with Reena. To their parents, for more than six months, the pair said nothing.

"We wanted it on our own terms," Reena told me, and I later found out this is so common in assisted marriage it's almost an unwritten protocol.

If their families had divined that the two had "chemistry," not to mention were actually immersed in a romance, everyone involved would have pressured them to marry *tout de suite*. Why wait? The whole point, from some parents' view, is to identify eligible candidates, put them together, and if they see promise in each other, marry them off as soon as a spectacular wedding can be organized. But Reena, like many Indians who ask their families' help, was Westernized enough to feel that even falling in love, which she had, did not necessitate instant marriage. Cautious, she even went on a few dates with other men after meeting Rajesh.

"Just in case. It was all happening so fast."

Nevertheless, a few months later, on a four-week family trip to India, she didn't object when her mother insisted on buying an entire, hallucinogenically ornate bridal trousseau. For "someday."

By the time she returned to Atlanta, Reena was so desperate to talk to Rajesh she knew she had to be in his life permanently. He felt the same, and soon after, when they went for dinner at Nashville's lavish Opryland Hotel, he got down on one knee and proposed.

At this point in the story, Rajesh, whom I'd just met for a moment on my way in, appeared in the breakfast nook. His stolid face lacked expression.

"Reena?" he said. "The entire staff is listening to you."

Her eyes widened. "They are?"

She and I exchanged alarmed smiles, trying to recall exactly what details she had supplied about her pre-courtship dating days. Rajesh stood by the door, his mouth pressed in an irritable zipper.

"Yes. They're all out there by the reception. I told you to use the conference room." Then he disappeared.

"Is he going to be angry later?" I whispered as Reena and I sheepishly crept upstairs. "Not at all," she said. "That's it. We spat all the time, and then it's over. I mean, we're pretty much together 24/7."

Sure enough, a few minutes later Rajesh joined us, declaring himself done with work for the day and open to any question about love, dating, and Indian tradition that I had. Before my eyes, even as he physically disappeared into a mauve couch the exact shade of his button-down shirt, I saw Rajesh transform from the taciturn guy who first showed up at Reena's door into the kind, noble hero she wanted to marry. No biodata could ever predict it. Apart from their shared passion for business, there was not much confluence in their tastes (she: romantic comedies, he: action films) or even their interests (he: personnel management, she: salsa). As for lower income, middle income, upper income, the question never came up.

When they met, Reena was working for an international freight company, longing to start her own business. Rajesh was managing that warehouse, talking about becoming his own boss. After they were married, Reena found out it wasn't just talk. Her husband had actually bought the wire factory while they were dating. Now he is president, she is vice president, and with the proceeds of that business they bought the lot next door and the Sleep Inn.

"I tease him—I didn't know he was rich!" Reena said. "I thought he was a middle manager on $40,000 and I married him for love."

Love, made possible by the methodical and unsentimental meddling of their South Asian parents.

Night arrived, bouncing the conference room's fluorescent light against the dark picture window. My coffee was cold. I knew I was keeping Reena and Rajesh at work while their girls waited across town with grandparents. But I tarried. Reena had been right: she loved nothing better than chatting, and she was delicious to hear, garnishing her stories with droll little impressions and disarming self-analysis. Rajesh listened carefully as we wandered from divorce to generational differences to how we planned to educate our little girls.

So I pressed on. Could assisted marriage work for non-Indians too?

Oh yes, Reena said. So many of her non-Indian girlfriends were struggling now. One had asked her about it.

Rajesh agreed. The problem, I remarked, was how to transplant this totally foreign notion to a different culture.

"Marketing!" Rajesh said promptly. "My thinking is you'd have to show people the numbers, show them it works. Like on eBay. How many positive comments? How many negatives?

"It's different," he went on, "without the extended family networks, and castes, and geographical links that Indians have. So you'd just have to put yourself out there. Call your buddies, your buddies' wives. And you have to be specific in what you're asking for. 'Send me candidates who are educated. Not crazy.' For Americans it has to be spelled out. It doesn't for Indians. You just can't be ashamed—that's the biggest thing."

It's hard to imagine a twenty-seven-year-old software engineer calling his frat brother's wife for marriage referrals. But if they work, what's to prevent such requests from becoming normal, just as online dating has in less than a decade?

The auntie paradigm, it occurred to me, might translate most easily to this culture. So many of us leave home in our late teens, and so many of our families are fraught or dysfunctional, that by the time we look for life partners ten or twenty years later, friends often take on the emotional function that families once did. Describing assisted marriage to my own friends, though, I was surprised at how swiftly they approved the idea of help—coming from anyone.

"Wouldn't it just save a lot of time and trouble?" said one married friend.

"Actually, my mother did introduce me to my fiancé," wrote another, with whom I'd just gotten back in touch. I couldn't believe it. She'd always gone for poets and human rights activists, ideally Latin American. Her mother, a conservative New England schoolteacher, had urged her to consider bankers and estate attorneys. But when my friend, nearing forty, finally moved home, her mother launched the Meet a Man in Massachusetts campaign.

"She just felt that I wasn't being serious enough about finding a life partner," my friend explained. "And it's true, I probably wasn't. I guess I was just enjoying my relationships for what they were."

She did want kids, though, and gamely met with the men her mother referred to her. With the last, a civil rights lawyer, she fell in love.

My lesbian friend Carlotta declared assisted marriage so sensible she wanted to try it herself—with one caveat. "I'm ready to find someone serious," she said. "Only get me a wife. No husbands, please."

A flaxen-haired tomboy, Carlotta was my neighbor for two years in Houston, where she never seemed to have problems finding romance. But recently she'd left for a new job in a Colorado town that markedly lacked life partner material. Assisted marriage, while it couldn't lead to matrimony (at least in most states), nonetheless seemed an alternative to gay bars or dating sites, Carlotta told me.

"Come on," she urged. "It's a perfect way to see if this whole system works."

I'd need biodata, I said.

"This is so fun," she promptly e-mailed.

Age: 30
Female
Raised in Oklahoma and Tennessee
Graduated from small liberal arts college
Owner of a sweet mutt named Huck
Agnostic
Capricorn
A swimmer

She added just one personal note before including her work history: "I love the Kingston Trio and am currently constructing my first piñata."

I had a bias against young marriage—and to me, thirty seemed young. But I loved the idea of advocating for my friend in this serious matter of finding a mate. Plus, finding candidates would be a walk in the park. I'd been to lots of parties with Carlotta, and boys and girls both fancied her without even knowing her sterling character. As a marriage-assisting auntie, I'd simply harness the power of the Internet and start sending her names.

I don't know what I was thinking.

First, I'd underestimated how much time it took to explain that I was screening for a spouse, not merely dates. Spelling it out filled unacceptable tracts of e-mail space. And since none of my friends had ever gotten this kind of request, I needed to convey that Carlotta was self-assured and not tragic; bored with dating, not desperate. I also realized I needed to cull my targets, from the e-blast I'd planned, to a half-dozen consiglieri—the same trusted group I'd ask to assist a marriage for me.

Finally, I felt oddly protective. Something about exposing a friend's (well-disguised) persona and her (perfectly ordinary) hopes to the world was unsettling. I knew this reflected my own idiosyncrasy: unlike Carlotta, I shrank from blogging and social networking. In the end, though, it wasn't scruples that thwarted my mission. After corralling a few friends, sending biodata, and receiving hearty promises to forward my e-mail, there was radio silence.

"She sounds a bit too young and pretty," someone apologized in the lone reply. Six months later it was manifest: I'd failed. I didn't have remotely the time or social contacts this job really needed. But what I really lacked was the anxious urgency of a mother or an auntie. I just wasn't worried enough about Carlotta's future. I knew she'd lead a fine life, wife or no wife.

"I'm sorry," I said.

"No problem," she answered, amused. She'd just met someone on her own.

Americans might do ourselves, and certainly our kids, a favor if we rethought some of our tenets on love. That it manifests itself only in thunderbolts, for example, or that a soul mate is a sort of clone who shares our every whim. Above all, that love and happy marriage can occur only if you don't need them.

In the South Asian view, "shared background"—shorthand for religion, caste, income, and aspirations—makes up the basic equipment any couple needs for a chance at happiness. Though they've smudged them a bit, Reena and many of her peers still agreed with those principles. Reena cared about caste only insofar as it corresponded to shared experience ("Find me a businessman"). And while she married for love, the kind that keeps you on a cell phone for six hours on a rainy drive through Tennessee, she did choose a man who, literally and figuratively, speaks her family's language.

Even if it's a language that neither Rajesh nor Reena speaks to each other. "Face it—we're not transmitting much Indianness to our kids," Rajesh said to Reena, shrugging. "We grew up watching American TV. We went to American schools."

Would he teach his girls about assisted marriage? I asked.

"I wouldn't offer," Rajesh said thoughtfully. "I wouldn't want to alienate them."

What if they asked?

"Sure. It would be a mix."

"I'd help," Reena said without hesitation. She darted Rajesh a look. "I'd be subtle. But I would ask my friends, get names. Why not?"

4

How to Learn:
Korean and Chinese Afterschools

I T WAS ONE o'clock on a sultry Fourth of July in Southern California. At an hour and season when many teenagers were idling on
their couches, a dozen adolescents trudged out of a strip mall looking
like they'd just run an Ironman.

There was a Starbucks down the street; also a Chili's, a Burger King,
a gas station. Busy and bland in the bright sun, the strip looked inter-
changeable with countless others in the San Fernando Valley, advertis-
ing basic fuels to power through the day. The strip mall from which
the teens emerged, however, hawked something different.

Ivy After School. Eine Kleine Musik Klasse. Valley Newton SAT
Prep. A corkboard flapped with phone numbers for tutors.

The weary teenagers were finishing a class at Newton, one of California's hundreds of Korean *hagwons*: private, supplementary schools
that intensively teach one subject at a time to huge numbers of Asian
students. The word *hagwon* merely means "study place" in Korean, and
in some ways, hagwons resemble familiar outfits such as Sylvan Learning Center or Kaplan. All coach algebra and composition, decode the
mysteries of test-taking, and drill students to gain a few SAT points.

But hagwons, though they offer SAT prep, often offer far more.
Many of the students blinking in the sun outside Newton today had

been coming here three or five or even six days a week—winter, spring, and summer—since elementary school. They were not cramming. They were not dodging F's. They were harnessing a centuries-old Asian technique to reach a goal coveted by middle-class Americans.

They were getting a private-school caliber of instruction while attending public schools.

The higher standards start early. In the heart of Koreatown, Los Angeles's giant immigrant neighborhood, first-generation parents routinely work eighteen hours a day. Yet as soon as they can, even these newcomers scare up $250 to $400 a month for one of the several dozen Korean afterschools nearby. Mostly nonprofits based in Korean churches, they are essentially day cares, but with added focus on Korean language and culture. Throughout the city and suburbs, meanwhile, vans whisk thousands of Korean elementary students to informal, home-based afterschools. Often staffed by moonlighting teachers or graduate students, they ply the little ones with snacks, homework help—and math drills.

Further up the afterschool hierarchy loom hagwons like Newton. Unlike the humbler, homier afterschools, these for-profit hagwons laser in on one goal: excelling in American school. To grasp that prize, Korean, Vietnamese, and Chinese parents have signed up their kids at hagwons or similar, Chinese-run schools in constantly vaulting numbers for the past twenty years. Today, according to a Los Angeles study, over 50 percent of Korean youngsters surveyed had either gone to a hagwon or were attending one currently.

Like the great majority of middle-class Americans, the families of these kids can't muster $30,000 or so per child in tuition. But with Asian-style tutoring and hagwons, they have devised an elegant solution: they've built an entire complementary school system of their own.

*   *   *

"Not bad, not bad—you could do better," Kang Kim, Newton's owner, was murmuring as I inched past his students that July day. Inside the strip mall, Newton looked like a Third World travel agency. The walls were a dingy dough color, with dog-eared notices and calendars tacked here and there. In a small, windowless room, jammed with old-fashioned tablet chairs, a few students doubled over blue books. I squeezed into the cluttered foyer, which doubled as the office. Kim was going over a test with an anxious-looking girl.

"I'm sorry," she was saying as he tallied her score.

"No, no—it's just your psychological attitude," Kim told her. "You need to have confidence."

"I'll have to practice," the girl said. She looked distressed.

"You have to believe it," Kim said.

"Model minority" may sound positive, but the phrase infuriates many Asian Americans. Being born Asian, it implies, guarantees A's, obedience, and an inability to be harmed by racism, poverty, or rotten schools. In reality, the profile of an Asian student in this country varies wildly. It embraces the Taiwanese doctoral fellow in Boston, the Samoan dropout in Honolulu, and the rebellious Hmong girl in St. Paul whose parents can't read or write. Mashing together half a globe's worth of history and economics, the myth—not unlike similar stories about Jewish immigrants a century ago—pressures all these young Asians to meet one, higher-than-average standard of achievement. Those who don't are written off as outliers. Or worse, they are uncounted, unmentioned, not seen at all.

Yet the hated phrase contains one striking truth. Taken as a group, Asian Americans are less than 5 percent of the U.S. population. Nevertheless, they wring success from the public schools that fail so many others.

According to the National Assessment of Educational Progress, Asian American seniors have topped other students in math scores for years. In 2010, for the first time, they also exceeded them in reading. Nationally, Asian immigrants' children score higher on SATs than non-Asian kids the same age. And in 2000, more than half of Asian Americans between the ages of twenty-five and twenty-nine had a bachelor's degree, compared to about a third of white Americans the same age.

At Harvard, where almost 20 percent of the undergraduate student body in 2009 was Asian, one admissions reviewer was quietly told to hold Asian applicants to a higher standard because so many were contenders. No wonder the "model minority" label sticks.

"I hate to deal in, you know, stereotypes," a suburban math teacher in Houston faltered one day. I'd met her in line at a discount store, where she was buying little prizes for her students—fairy wings, coloring books—on her own dime. She was motherly-looking, quick to touch a shoulder, bubbling with stories about teaching fourth-graders. But when I asked if her Asian students had different study habits, she leaned toward me, uneasy.

"I think Asian kids are more intelligent," she said.

Really? She believed that?

"I know. Because every time I introduce a new math concept to my class, the Asian kids get it instantly," she said firmly. "It's as if they've always known it."

Actually, the Texas schoolteacher had intuited a truth. By the time a Korean student first sees long division at school, she might well get it instantly. When her teacher unpacks quadratic equations, she really seems as if she's always known it. Not because, as an Asian, she's innately good at math, but because she has already learned it at hagwon, the summer before.

*   *   *

Quitting time, Park La Brea pool, Los Angeles. It was 4:30 p.m. on Sunday, and Fourth of July weekend at that. But the parents of the wiggling young swimmers were determinedly rounding them up. Dinner had to be cooked and bedtime observed for the schedule of a Korean American schoolchild to proceed. And practically every child in the pool was Korean American. Even before moving to the United States, many Korean parents know to line up an apartment in this garden-filled, modestly priced complex zoned for one of the city's best elementary schools.

Alone of the youngsters climbing out of the pool, one boy and girl could be seen pleading their case with an adult, and then, overjoyed, scrambling back into the water. The indulgent "grown-up" was their uncle, fourteen-year-old Brian Park. He was tall for his age, with plaid shorts and a peach polo shirt that made him look from afar like someone's miniature dad.

When I shyly approached to ask about hagwons, he kicked aside a pile of bubblegum-colored Crocs so I could sit and hear him hold forth.

"Most Koreans I know go to afterschools," Brian said. "I started just after kindergarten, from three to six o'clock. It was every day. I hated it.

"I hated it," he repeated, "but it really helped my study skills. Can't say anything was wasted."

Brian was the oldest boy in a Korean family that migrated so his father could get an MBA. In the early days, when times were lean, his dad worked as a pool cleaner. Now, Brian said, the family was better off, owners of several dollar stores.

Yet even in those early years, Brian's parents hired tutors at home. "I was behind in kindergarten," he explained. Brian started doing well within a year, earning mostly A's for the rest of his school career. By grade school he was attending a traditional Korean hagwon; recently, he began to attend a Korean SAT prep/tutoring academy called A Plus

Math, twice a week. His grades were already good, he told me: this time he'd asked to be sent.

How is such a transformation possible? Why do children who start out hating hagwons grow into students who ask for more? To get to the answer, it's important to look at what a Korean afterschool program actually does.

Above all, a hagwon delivers time. Educators now agree that a moderate increase in hours of school can measurably boost grades and scores. One of the country's most renowned charter schools, KIPP (Knowledge Is Power Program), requires longer days—7:30 a.m. to 5:00 p.m.—and summer school, for precisely this reason. The program's cofounder, Mike Feinberg, told me that a typical public school has the kids about 1,100 to 1,200 hours a year. By contrast, "we give about 1,800 hours. If you want kids better at something you need to spend more time. It was common sense to us."

Even more powerful than the extra time, though, is how it is used. In 2006, the federal government hired a research firm called Mathematica to assess the $1 billion worth of ordinary public school afterschool programs for low-income kids. The results were horrifying. On most academic outcomes, "there were no differences between the treatment group students"—randomly assigned to afterschool programs—and the control group students, who didn't participate in them.

"Treatment group students scored no better on reading tests . . . and had similar grades in English, mathematics, science and social studies," the researchers wrote. "There were also no differences in time spent on homework, preparation for class, and absenteeism."

"However"—and this is where the findings got really depressing— "teachers reported lower levels of effort and achievement for treatment group students relative to control group students." In other words, this hugely costly national intervention actually corroded children's behavior. The kids who were randomly picked to take part in the afterschool programs acted up more than they would have if they hadn't been there.

The study also found that overall, the students in the afterschool programs spent as much time by themselves, unsupervised, as the children in the control group. Merely placing a child, some homework, and a caregiver in the same room, it became clear, did not automatically equal achievement.

Yet a few of those programs did succeed, and in 2009 another panel, this time hired by the U.S. Department of Education, set out to learn why. The panel members interviewed teachers, students, and program leaders. They read all of the literature. Borrowing a practice from medical research, they even rated the quality of evidence available for their findings.

In the end, they discovered the best afterschool programs work for the same bundle of reasons good schools work. Teaching has to be engaging—connected to real-life goals and experiences. Students' experiences in school have to buttress the learning process, not distract from it. But most critical of all, one panelist told me, is probably "dosage"—that is, attendance.

In the disastrous afterschool programs the panel studied, many students actually weren't *there.* Average attendance scraped at just 2.7 days a week. Obviously, a fourth grader who is not physically present isn't going to absorb fractions telepathically. But absenteeism is also a red flag signaling other problems that derail learning—such as transportation troubles, parental health problems or stress, and nontraditional work schedules.

Hagwons and Asian-style tutoring, on the other hand, can re-create the traits of the best schools. Built carefully around existing lesson plans, hagwons can also guarantee a motivated, decently behaved peer group. (Some researchers, in fact, think peer study does more for hagwon students than teachers do.) And attendance may be grudging— but it's excellent.

Finally, program evaluation is relentless. I once asked a Vietnamese high school student who tutored first graders if he enjoyed it. "It's incredibly stressful," he sighed. "Not the kids. Their parents. They'll fire you in a second if their kids' grades aren't good."

Hagwons also offer something intangible: a relationship with someone who cares deeply about your success. That was the lesson I learned from Nanci Zhang, a rambunctious and charming recent UCLA graduate. In public high school, Nanci had loved English and Spanish, but hated math and science. Instead of channeling her toward the humanities, her Beijing-born parents cultivated her lukewarm math skills with afterschool programs. Like Brian, she was grateful: in college, she had the skills to tackle both neurobiology and African American studies. When I met Nanci she was applying to AmeriCorps, the national service agency, and graduate school in public health. And what had made the difference, to her, were the relationships with her afterschool teachers and tutors.

"I think in the end we all want someone to care about us," Nanci said. "Having that one-on-one attention. You want to feel you're being cared about—by your parents, your teacher, the stranger who opens the door for you."

Throughout college, she'd earned her money tutoring. "I noticed when I talked to my kids, I leaned into them," Nanci said. "It meant, someone here wants you to succeed. I want you to do this well. See me next week and we'll see if this works. I don't think that would happen in a class of thirty.

"Tutoring," she added, "is like having a companion that excites you about learning things. I just wish I had had someone reading Betty Friedan with me in high school. A tutor lights a fire under your butt to go out and search for things you might like intellectually."

This is not a new idea: Before the arrival of universal education, tutors or visiting schoolmasters were often iconic figures in American communities, especially on the frontier. They stood for more than simply academics. Standard bearers of civilization, they not only cultivated their students' math and letters but also the moral development of their communities. Think of John Brooke, the threadbare but honorable tutor to Laurie in *Little Women*. When Brooke first proposes to Meg, the oldest March girl, her romantic-minded sisters can't stand the thought of her being whisked off to penury. But in the end, the family embraces him. The humble tutor, they see, embodies independence and integrity and loyalty, all the Yankee cultural values they revere most.

That personal investment is clearly the other key to supplementary schools' success. "The message," Nanci said, "was, 'This is what is in our power to do. Please let us do it.'"

The Maryland suburb where I grew up had superb public schools within walking distance. Ambling to Chevy Chase Elementary School on March mornings, I'd pass a grassy hill with words written in crocuses: AH SPRING OH SPRING. When I got to class, my teachers were lively, competent women who seemed to have all the time in the world.

Nevertheless, my parents moved me to a Quaker private school in sixth grade. Equally gentle, hippie-ish even in the lower grades, the school eventually became as intense as the Indy 500. "Compete with yourself," was how the Quakers put it, but it was competition all the same. It suited me perfectly.

Three things fueled my parents' decision to take me out of my perfectly good public school and place me in the private system. By fifth grade I was getting noticeably restless (a friend's mother had recently banned me for organizing a raw-egg-baseball game in their driveway). My mother revered the Quakers, having gone to a Friends school in Philadelphia. But the key factor was this: My parents could afford it. With some sacrifice, they were able to pay a tuition that would have been out of reach of most people, even our Chevy Chase neighbors.

Thirty years later, I live in a different part of the country, in very different circumstances. My dad was a physician; Mike and I are reporters. In the unlikely event that Quakers flood Houston and found a school, we'd need the mineral rights from our house to pay private school tuition. Our neighborhood, Montrose, is hardly Chevy Chase.

True, in the past decade Montrose has rocketed from edgy and cheap to hip and ridiculously inflated. The change is still underway, but clearly benefits the local grade school. A small 1920s building resembling the Alamo, the school is a magnet, which means it draws prosperous families from across the city who drop their kids off in Humvees, and Mexican immigrants in their white restaurant smocks who walk their kids to school from nearby apartments. About 15 percent are middle-class bohos like us, who moved into the neighborhood when we were childless and were amazed to see it grow child-friendly just in time for our kids. As the numbers of pushy middle-class parents rose, the school got better and better.

But I can't fool myself. Houston's Independent School District is, as the pre-K kids say, ginormous. Despite its magnet schools and charters, the district hemorrhages more than half of its students before graduation. Those who do graduate may or may not be able to add. The summer after Anna and Elena turned three, these statistics suddenly began to matter to me. We weren't going to be able to afford twelve years at a nurturing, nerdy little academy. Yet we couldn't just confidently send them ambling to public school as if it were 1975. I had no idea if the school we provided would be enough.

Enough for whom, exactly? Like a lot of middle-class Americans, I had a strong sense of what education should do. It was formed mostly of memories of my own schooling, which served me well, twined with a thick strand of anxiety about what my peers were up to.

Education, I thought, should train you to support yourself and do the work that you want to do. "Like a canoe," my friend Chris said. "A light vehicle that gets you to shore so you can run."

It should also teach concentration, I believed. It should foster critical thinking, fearlessness about new information, and most important, a relish for learning more.

And, I came to admit, it should allow you to feel as competent as the Joneses.

"We know how to count," Anna announced one morning in the kitchen. Our friend Nikki had stopped by for tea, and the girls were hovering adoringly at her shins like large gnats. "Onetwothreefourfiveseven," Anna said.

"Eight," Elena continued. "Nineteeneleventwelveeight."

"Better keep your day jobs," Nikki said cheerfully. I wasn't concerned: they'd shore up their numbers in a few months at preschool. Yet later that week, for the first time ever, I found myself wondering: Was I supposed to be teaching them more than I was?

I bet Nikki could count when she was three.

I began to think about friends with older kids, whose parenting I admired. Since this was Houston, the friends who came to mind were named Khuong, Le, and Aiyer. All, I thought, reassured, had sent their kids to Houston public schools. And all, I realized, had also sent them to tutors or afterschools.

There are limits to how closely most Americans can re-create an Asian afterschool experience. There are limits to how much we'd want to. It's all very well for me to compare education to a canoe. In countries such as South Korea, education has nothing to do with love of learning. It's an arms race.

According to Confucius, the ideal government is led by scholars. In the seventh century, following these teachings, China devised a punishingly hard civil service exam; Korea followed with a similar test a few centuries later. The plan was supposed to forge a meritocracy. But both in China and the cultures it shaped over the last millennium—Korea, Japan, Singapore, and Vietnam—the exam instead became the lone path for a whole family's economic advancement outside bribery, connections, or wealth. Pass the test, you could catapult upward. Fail, and you were condemned to life as a laborer.

Today, college entrance exams in Korea have a similar function. The intellectual paradise Confucius envisioned has become a grotesque test of endurance. "Sleep five hours, fail. Sleep four hours, pass," goes a famous chant. "If you don't do well on that college entrance test," a Chinese American woman told me, "you're basically going to peddle tea on the street for the rest of your life." In South Korea, parents often spend $25,000 a year, three years minimum, on cram school. Seoul's Gimpo International Airport has been known to ban landings and takeoffs while students are tested on listening comprehension.

The struggle may come to nothing. In Korea, only a fraction of the nation's graduates will gain space in one of the fifteen or so colleges that guarantee access to lucrative jobs. That desperate battle for admission, and the high chance of failure, may be the single biggest reason Koreans now migrate.

Nevertheless, first-generation Asian parents bring some of the hysteria with them. Esther, a student at the University of Southern California, began attending tutoring sessions in third grade. By junior high, in addition to public school and violin, her parents were sending her to daily afterschooling at a Korean hagwon. In high school, they added Saturday SAT prep as well. She didn't like it. In fifth grade, she started getting searing headaches. But Esther told no one. She was dogged, knowing her parents were working as hard as, or harder than, she was. The headaches grew unbearable until, in junior high, Esther's parents finally found out about them. Horrified, they shuttled her from emergency rooms to clinics to CAT scans and MRIs. Esther's symptoms, they learned, could be consistent with a brain tumor. But nothing showed up on tests.

Finally, when Esther was going into her senior year, a doctor made the diagnosis. Stress headaches.

"Rushing from one thing to another, we were taught—I don't want to say brainwashed—but we weren't really allowed to express our feelings," Esther told me. "If we disobeyed, we'd get the silent treatment. It felt terrible having them mad at us."

Esther's story terrified me. Yet there was something galvanizing about the Asian conviction that any child can do well in any subject, as long as she works hard enough, and something impressive about the way Brian had changed from a school-hating child to an ambitious fourteen-year-old. If Korean restaurant hostesses were acting on the belief that their kids' futures can be improved, I thought, I should start too. People with far fewer resources than I have habitually hold high standards for their kids. Perhaps, I felt, I should upgrade—slightly—my own.

I even shared a certain educational insecurity with immigrant parents. Many of them invest in English-language tutors because they can't speak or read the language themselves. My math skills, for no defensible reason, are as lame as if I'd come from a land with no written digits. But why shouldn't my girls be math whizzes? What if they could enter school, as so many Asian kids do, with the skills and certainty that math smarts are their birthright?

Some Indian friends swore by the Japanese-based Kumon academy, an Americanized version of a hagwon. They ferried their second grader there three times a week, and the boy was now doing seventh-grade math. Some people sent kids even younger. But Kumon was expensive, and we were already getting ready to shell out for Jewish preschool (Texas doesn't provide universal free pre-K).

I also realized that I was too American. Why would I hurl two four-year-olds into the icy sea of supplementary school before they'd even dipped a toe in pre-K? Put another way: This, thankfully, was not Korea. I didn't want my children to suffer from stress headaches, I didn't want them to spend the Fourth of July weekend in a strip mall. I just couldn't make myself believe that math classes for a pair of middle-class preschoolers would forge a difference in their destinies.

Then, a few months before the girls started preschool, I read about Growing Stars, a start-up company with a branch in San Francisco— and headquarters in southern India.

According to the newspaper story, English-speaking tutors with advanced degrees and excellent accents would coach your student in real time, communicating for free on Skype while scratching out figures and equations on a computer whiteboard.

For $15 an hour.

Mother got motivated. The price was catnip—who could resist at least trying? Growing Stars, too, was based in Kerala, a part of India I'd never set foot in, but found mesmerizing for its nearly 100 percent literacy, matriarchal tradition, and houseboats drifting through green canals. When we first talked to Tess, the girls' tutor, through my laptop, I felt like the batty Civil War veteran in Ray Bradbury's *Dandelion Wine*, calling Mexico to demand that his old friend stick the phone out the window and capture the din. As we cooled our heels waiting for initial hookup bugs to resolve, I would call out, for pedagogical reasons, of course, "Tess? Do you ever see elephants walking around near your house? Have you ever been on a houseboat?"

The girls were just glad to noodle on a backlit screen. But "Test," as they called her, was an impressive teacher. She'd been trained to teach older students, but she'd set up a curriculum for Anna and Elena, pretesting it on her own four-year-old, who sometimes volunteered answers faintly in the background. The classes were nothing more than I could have done: an hour's slog through a math workbook without fail each Saturday morning. But I wouldn't have done it. They wouldn't have sat through it.

Even with Tess, whose sultry, elegant voice charmed us all, the first sessions for each girl ended definitively after fifteen minutes. Class was over when Elena slithered to the floor like a discarded stocking, and when Anna inverted herself on my lap to type with her feet. Yet after four months, I could see that the girls' math skills and concentration had soared.

Propped up in my bed, equipped with large cups of frozen blueberries, they liked to take turns every fifteen or twenty minutes. They enjoyed cheating, mouthing answers to the girl on the hot seat like game show contestants. But they could also count by fives and by tens, write numbers up to a hundred, and tally up little five-stick bundles (admittedly, an arcane skill—perhaps more useful in India). One girl revealed a knack for pattern recognition; the other, by screwing up her eyes and cogitating fiercely, could see a whole number line in her head. Barely capable of either, I was thrilled. But I knew these were essentially party tricks.

What was real, and of real import, was how clearly my enthusiasm for this whole project fueled the girls. They basked in their newly discovered abilities; they paid attention because I spent a whole hour passionately paying attention beside them. I can't say for sure that this kind of tutoring, if I keep it up, will get them through the vast Texas school system and into college. But I'll certainly know I did all I could.

5

How to Shelter:

West Indian Multigenerational
Households

FOUR HOURS, AT $15 to $20 per hour. Add another hour and gas
mileage if the babysitter requires transportation. Call it a hundred
bucks, and that's not even calculating the main factor: do I trust this
person?

A tricky equation at best, deciding to take an evening out can be
even harder for a single parent. But it's one calculation that Sandra
Brown, a forty-four-year-old schoolteacher, does not have to make. A
tall, restless woman who favors gypsy bangles and jeweled flip-flops,
Sandra shares her small New Jersey house with her daughter, Lisa, and
her seventy-five-year-old mother, Monica.

I met Sandra for the first time when I showed up to live with her for
a long weekend. When I left, a little delirious from nonstop feasting
on beans, rice, oxtail, and jerk chicken, I realized that full houses are a
Jamaican tradition. Like other West Indians, they live with extended
family not just as a survival tool. They also do it to reach lofty economic goals. Partially as a result, West Indians boast one of the top
home ownership rates of any U.S. immigrant group. Between 2001
and 2008, 60 percent of Jamaican Americans owned homes, com-

pared with 54 percent of all other immigrants. Native-born Americans' home ownership rate was 70 percent.

Sandra's house in a marginal Orange neighborhood represented a triumph for her whole family. She and her older siblings grew up deep in the Jamaican countryside near Montego Bay, growing their own vegetables and climbing breadfruit trees to sell the produce at market.

Because the island offers so little chance for economic advancement, Jamaicans have migrated from the lush, economically paralyzed country in huge numbers for twenty-five years. Today, one-third of Jamaicans live outside Jamaica. When Sandra was twenty-one, her mother moved to New Jersey. Sandra soon joined her. Within one year of arriving, the two women bought this house in Orange together on their combined wages as a hotel kitchen worker and a live-in maid. Sandra's four siblings and a nephew came next. The seven shared the three-bedroom house for several years until each sibling had earned a community college degree. Today, Sandra and her mother are back on their own, but the brothers, sisters, nieces, and nephews still return for meals several times weekly.

The Sunday after I arrived, Sandra served such a feast for one of these sisters, her mother, her daughter, and me in her leaf-green dining room. Then, surveying the platters that had served the oxtails and rice, for once she left them on the table. She knew we'd clean up. She had been invited to a Haitian christening party with catering and live music. Despite the occasion, no children allowed.

Another single mother might have fretted. How long could she stay out? Could she justify six hours of child care, six hours away from her little one? Not Sandra. Her daughter was in fine hands indeed.

"Tookie, tookie, tookie," Sandra's mother sang in the living room. Clasping little Lisa's shoulders, Monica whirled her grandchild round in circles. "I'm just making play," Monica told me with a laugh. Lisa rubbed her cheek against her grandmother's, looking rapturous.

"She loves to be with my mother," Sandra said, climbing the narrow stairs. "When I'm home, Lisa sometimes pretends she doesn't care about her. But when I'm gone, she just loves her."

Lisa's father, a mechanic, used to live here, too. But three years ago Sandra asked him to move out. Oddly, the breakup didn't represent a great departure from Jamaican family tradition. West Indians, in the islands and here in the United States, have one of the world's highest rates of single-parent families. In the New York area, Harvard sociologist Mary Waters found in 2003, one-quarter of first-generation West Indian parents were divorced, separated, or widowed. Another 16 percent had never married at all.

Yet Jamaican kids may suffer relatively few lasting problems from growing up in one-parent households. The experience seemed to have fewer negative consequences for West Indian kids in New York than for native blacks and Puerto Ricans, according to Waters. The difference, she and her coauthors claim, may be the presence of extended family members such as grandmothers, who were more commonly part of the West Indian households.

Monica and Lisa's special simpatico had always given Sandra peace of mind. It also allowed her to spend less on higher-quality child care. Until recently, while Sandra headed to a second job at a community college, her mother would pick Lisa up from school. Now an arthritic knee has forced Monica to meet the little girl at the house, but the two still spend their afternoons together.

Though she didn't go out often, this evening Sandra could enjoy herself without worry. Child care, she had covered. And more. While multigenerational homes are most common among struggling immigrants, they offer developmental rewards affluent parents dream about. More advanced cognitive function? Check. Greater resilience from trauma? One-on-one adult attention? Check and check. More generations in the house can even boost parents' development. The more social support a mother has, research shows, the more responsive she is to the needs of her child.

Americans today so venerate the nuclear family that we often mistake it for nature's way. We cross the country for college, for jobs, or when a parent is ill. But extended family doesn't rate that commitment. What able-bodied parent or grandparent would pull up stakes just so three perfectly healthy generations can share daily life? What we've often forgotten is how ancient our need for kin outside the nuclear pod really is.

For modern hunter-gatherers and other pretechnological communities, help raising children meant the difference between life and death. The pillar of family structure was the equivalent of feisty Monica in her pink church hat and purple suit: a grandmother. Recent thinking about grandmothers coalesced in the 1980s, when University of Utah anthropologist Kristen Hawkes lived among Tanzania's Hadza hunter-gatherers. Carefully tallying the calories in each berry and edible leaf that tribe members brought home, Hawkes found that it was the grandmothers who hauled back the most calories.

Anthropologists like to study hunter-gatherers because their lifestyle remains similar to that of humans in the Pleistocene, when, it's believed, we developed most of our modern behavioral and psychological makeup. For 99 percent of the time we have existed, humans have been foragers. So it was after studying the hunter-gatherers that Hawkes developed a new theory about postmenopausal women in the twenty-first century, which she called the grandmother hypothesis. There's a good evolutionary reason, Hawkes theorized, why women live for so many years after their child-rearing function is past. These tough and energetic older women are still needed for the survival of the family's other children. Just as we evolved to depend on older women's help to keep families mentally and physically afloat, Hawkes suggests, older women are beautifully adapted to give it.

This Sunday night, while Sandra attends the christening, her mother and daughter have a date. They will bundle off to an aunt's house, make hot chocolate, and watch the *Wizards of Waverly Place*. You can't say Sandra will be out provisioning, exactly. But as she clacks down the stairs, she is plainly setting out for a sanity-saving, family-strengthening mission.

Her long, athletic legs are in stockings, and she's wearing a spectacular black cocktail dress. The ubiquitous flip-flops have vanished, replaced by stilettos with silver heels. Lisa, a connoisseur of princesses, looks stunned. "Mommy!" she shouts. Sandra smiles, knowing she's smashing.

Thanks to a grandmother, a woman who holds two jobs and spends nearly every unclaimed minute with her small girl is going dancing. The whole family, Jamaicans would say, will be stronger for it.

In seventh grade, I came across what I considered an important anthropological finding. "Did you know," I reported to my father, a psychiatrist, "that Japanese grandparents live with their children's family and have the final say in the household?" My dad, who grew up in a Jewish neighborhood in Baltimore and worked as an army doctor in Okinawa, knew from family gerontocracies. "Yes," he said. "And in my practice I've seen that it can be a very hard way for young people to live."

Thomas Wolfe to Philip Roth, Jack Kerouac to Bob Dylan, Patti Smith to the Ramones: for American artists, leaving home has been the defining experience of growing up. Conflict between parents and children seems part of the initiation, as biologically necessary as birds leaving the nest. We've even come to think of youthful rebellion as healthy. Yet widespread generational strife is fairly new. For most of American history, we were an agricultural society, and extended-family households were the norm. They had to be, for both children and farms to survive.

Then, in the nineteenth century, romantic marriage became the new core relationship in family life. The idea gained strength in the early twentieth century, as psychiatric theory began to portray the traditional family as a vat of psychological turmoil. This was certainly true of many immigrant families. Streaming in from conservative societies in Eastern and Southern Europe they careened into intergenerational battles as they adapted to U.S. life. But native-born Americans faced similar rifts.

From the 1920s to the 1960s, medical and mental health experts actively discouraged multigenerational living. "It was a moment in history when the differences between grandparents and parents were really intense," says Stephanie Coontz, director of the Council on Contemporary Families. "It was thought better to cut the 'silver cord,' as people called it, and introduce modern child-rearing practices." After World War II, subsidized suburban houses and affordable cars abounded. Returning GIs eagerly grabbed these opportunities. Far from their farms and tenements, their new, nuclear families transformed the culture. By the time I was pondering Japanese household practices in the 1970s, living with a grandparent or adult sibling in my neighborhood usually signaled some kind of trouble.

Yet the nuclear unit has always had weak spots. The cracks grew more evident in the late twentieth century, when an increasing number of women went to work, and the enormous cohort of Americans born after World War II started aging. The Greatest Generation "designed a social and fiscal system that has served their retirement years well," observed authors Sharon Graham Niederhaus and John L. Graham in a 2007 opinion piece. Their book, *Together Again,* makes a case for rethinking multigenerational living. "But their system breaks down with the onslaught of their kids' retirement. . . . We are just now starting to understand the substantial fiscal and psychological costs of separating the generations into so-called single family homes with the ideal of a mother, father and two kids."

In recent years, these costs have formed a national wrecking ball. Trapped in its crater, hundreds of thousands of Americans have been forced to reconsider family structures we abandoned a half century back. Curiously, in these new households, married couples and children may benefit most. In a society where couples often program their lives around a child's every mental and physical experience, having another adult in the house redirects them—toward each other. "We have this 'over-parenting idea' where parents can neglect their own relationship to pour all this time on the kids," says Coontz. "Multigenerational homes sometimes can relieve the pressure."

Especially in small families, kids, too, can benefit from more adults around. It dilutes their expectations that all needs be met by one or two exhausted, distracted, and fallible human beings. And despite an entire genre of comedy revolving around overbearing mothers-in-law, their presence can bring out the best in some couples. "Marriages, like all relationships, do far better when they have witnesses," write psychiatrists Jacqueline Olds and Richard S. Schwartz in their 2009 book, *The Lonely American*. "When any aspect of life is seen by others, it feels more real to the participants. The parts of life that are hidden start to feel a little split off . . . witnesses also provide a married couple with an audience to perform for as a married couple. People try to perform their best for an audience. Some of the performance lasts after the audience has gone home."

The American-style nuclear family works admirably as a fast, sleek vehicle for economic mobility. Children get a surge of emotional and economic resources, with no one else's needs slowing them down. Yet this superefficient machine is also delicate. Traditional breadwinning fathers often barely know the children for whom they spend most of their waking hours working. Depressed or alcoholic mothers can terribly damage children alone in their care. Today, with most American families relying on two full-time wage earners, the nuclear family structure looks more fragile than ever. Who cares for a sick child? And what happens if the parents' marriage dissolves?

There's also the matter of companionship. Americans may be more starved than we realize for engagement with people who know and love us. There's no point in false nostalgia: though we affiliate less in groups such as the Kiwanis, we socialize constantly online, with many of the same rewards. A BlackBerry, though, can't replace the blast of visual detail we get from face-to-face contact. We may even be hardwired to need that contact. In a provocative but unscientific project—he experimented on himself—a University of California psychologist recently proposed that viewing a life-size human face in early morning relieves some kinds of depression. If true, he said, it could recall a Stone Age need to know that the tribe is still there and we have not awakened, alone, in a world full of predators.

"You need to have a vision," Jamaican-born Altamont Morris said grandly one night from his armchair. Altamont was fifty-three years old and the indisputable lord of his manor. Sinewy and fit, with hair cropped like a Roman senator's, he presided over a big Union, New Jersey, house that easily fit him, wife Sonia, twenty-eight-year-old daughter Marie, twenty-three-year-old son Patrick, and six-month-old grandson Kyle.

Altamont's business, an auto shop with three employees, stood just a few miles away. Not bad for a man who dropped out of junior high to be a shade-tree mechanic. Forty years after moving to the United States, Altamont boasted all the attainments—the business, the wealth, the trophy house, the educated kids—for which middle-class Americans strive.

But the way Altamont achieved this, his vision of how to go about gaining those prizes, would make many of the same Americans flinch. Primarily this: until well into his thirties, Altamont lived with his parents.

Altamont grew up in Mandeville, Jamaica, the youngest son in a Seventh-Day Adventist family that worked furiously to stay solvent. Anytime he got a day off from school, he went to work with his father, roaming from house to house peddling tools and kitchenware. When he was fifteen, his father and two oldest brothers left to find work in the United States. And despite the Adventists' stress on education, Altamont left school to start an outdoor mechanic shop. A year later, his brothers sent him a ticket to New Jersey.

At once, Altamont enrolled in trade school to earn a proper mechanic's license. Two years later, barely out of his teens, he opened a repair shop with a friend, and a few years after that struck out on his own. Altamont's membership in the strong, supportive Adventist church, his teetotaling ways, and his natural entrepreneurship all sped his progress. But to get what he has now, he also took advantage of a less visible resource—one that may have made the crucial difference for a semi-educated kid with an oilcan. An ocean away from Jamaica, Altamont's siblings and father continued to live in a traditional, multigenerational Jamaican home.

For exactly one year, the Morris men rented. Altamont contributed next to nothing because he was in mechanic's school. No one complained, though. He was building economic power to chase down the family's two, quintessentially Jamaican, objectives: home ownership and higher education for their children. In 1970, the five men scraped together the money for a worn but affordable two-story, four-family house in Irvington, New Jersey, and sent for Altamont's mother. Working full-time now, Altamont could help with the mortgage; he'd also met and married Sonia, a canny, whippet-slender

Jamaican studying to be a medical technician at community college. By the time she got pregnant four years later, Altamont had squirreled away enough money for a modest house deposit. It was more than many Americans his age might have, if they'd followed the typical path of renting with roommates and then moving on to a solo apartment. For the expectant young couple, the next step was clear. They sold their share in the crowded house and bought a home—with Altamont's brother.

The brother and his wife Paula also had a baby, and, like Altamont and Sonia, soon had a second child too. In their new house, in a better neighborhood, the four adults and four children continued living together for more than a decade.

"Ten years?" I looked up from my notebook. "You mean, your daughter's whole childhood?"

"Ten years," Altamont smiled.

Yes, he was a homeowner. But to work from the age of fifteen, to leave your country for life—and still live packed under one roof with your parents or brother for forty years? Surely Altamont could have done better, I thought. Instead, the choices he made ensured that he and his family would not live on their own until his kids were in high school.

That, Altamont said, was the point.

Jamaicans are famous for certain obsessions: education, reggae music—and owning homes. Living with extended family helps them achieve the dream of home ownership while also building family bonds and saving money on child care. In a multigenerational household, "you're much more likely to have a higher ratio of adults to children," says Harvard sociologist Mary Waters. "That really has added benefits, because there are more people around to help with the kids, and there is higher-quality housing, because you have more earners per household. And you have a greater ability to extend your education because you're not alone."

And, curiously for many Americans, they find it a pleasure. In the blue-collar town of Irvington, where Altamont and his brother each paid about $400 for their mortgage, joint family life was fun, both generations told me. Altamont, Sonia, and their two kids took the upstairs, with its three small bedrooms, modest kitchen, and two bathrooms. The brother and his wife had the downstairs, which they shared with two daughters almost exactly the same age as their cousins. All the while, Altamont was tucking away part of his earnings for a house of his own.

"Oh, it was definitely worth it," he said. I noticed Sonia nod in agreement from the couch. Two decades before the crazed lending decisions and contorted mortgage schemes of the late 1990s, they also savored the knowledge they were not overextended. The house wasn't anything fancy. A stolid white clapboard, it had a small spit of grass on either side of its concrete front steps and a compact, sunny backyard. But as soon as the families moved in, Altamont's sister-in-law started planting. In went the tomatoes, basil, and a nutritious Jamaican green called callaloo. Later that year she added peach and apple trees—with fruit that now jostles the second floor windows in summer. But it was the neighborhood, more than the house, that influenced the family's decision to buy. Irvington offers relatively safe streets and far better schools than those Altamont's kids would have encountered if he'd had to pay by himself for housing in those early years.

Many West Indians, especially in the New York area, make the same calculation. The math is simple: the more wage-earning adults in the house, the higher their collective income. Though their language and visa status are the most potent factors, the efficiencies of longtime group living help Jamaicans reach a higher median household income, and a lower poverty rate, than most other immigrants. A multigenerational family of workers can also afford a better neighborhood than each member might individually. Since income distribution shapes the tax base, the family has also won access to better public schools, services, parks, police protection, and even political patronage.

Living together, in other words, Altamont and his brother were not only saving money for their children's futures. They were also crafting an environment that would strengthen their kids' ability to make the most of adulthood. It's still the household norm in most of the world, including well-to-do Western countries such as France, where living with several generations under one roof is considered mature and healthy.

In this country, it's common among first-generation immigrants of all backgrounds. In the New York area, Chinese Americans are actually the stay-at-home champs overall, with 49.2 percent of respondents in one study still with their parents from ages twenty-eight through thirty-two. Strikingly, though, many of these Chinese immigrants also put off marriage and childbearing during these years. The 27.6 percent of West Indians in the same age group who live at home stand out because they may be the immigrants whose goals most resemble those of native-born, middle-class Americans. Unlike typical Latin American migrants, who arrive here with radically less education, money, and mastery of English, most Jamaicans can soon graduate from subsistence status. And unlike first-generation Chinese Americans, Jamaicans don't seem as willing to defer the emotional satisfaction of partners or children. Jamaicans live with extended family because, as Altamont would say, they have a vision. But also, acting on an aspiration that is deeply American, a remarkable number of Jamaicans live with extended family . . . to be *happy*. In this culture, finding that possibility under the same roof as your parents has come to seem exotic indeed.

Americans' thirst to own property dates back to the conquest of the New World. But it became a civic virtue considerably later, when Herbert Hoover launched the first initiatives making home ownership more accessible. By the first decade of the twenty-first century, as we know, this policy ideal had puffed into a mass delusion that owning a home, regardless of ability to pay, was good for the individual and good for America. West Indians, like almost every other ethnicity, were snared in the subprime loan web that followed. The difference is that decades before subprime lending made it possible for nearly anyone, West Indians were already buying houses in impressive numbers.

Every migrant chases a vision that first flickered to life back at home. West Indians can sum up their ancestral obsession with one phrase: *I've got to get a piece of land.*

"The first thing your parents tell you, especially if you're a guy, is, 'Look for somewhere to cover your head before anything else,'" said a Trinidadian friend. "When a man starts looking for a woman, having affairs or whatever, and he decides to get married, they ask him, 'Where are you going to put her after you get married?' If you're a man in our culture, that's your responsibility." The sentiment is not unique. Russian, Chinese, Peruvian, and Bangladeshi peasants all yearn for land, because in societies without credit or reliable banks, dirt is still the best insurance that their families will eat. West Indians, however, continue to idealize home ownership in the United States—a culture where the most famous rich girl in children's fiction, Eloise, lives in a hotel.

Jamaica's unusual history helps explain why. Like the Africans in North America, the West Indies' black population was originally abducted from Africa and forced into slavery. Both populations endured centuries of horrendous brutality, stripped of homelands, rights, and physical autonomy. But the two slave economies differed in profound ways, including black land-ownership patterns.

From early on, even enslaved Caribbean Africans saw people of color who owned their land. Because blacks in the West Indies outnumbered whites by at least 95 percent, slave owners routinely made African slaves their concubines or even wives. Their mixed-race children, whom they educated abroad, returned to make up the island's professional class. In Jamaica, people of color were lawyers, craftsmen, and even local politicians as early as the eighteenth century. Even more important, Jamaica's emancipation, when it came, was genuine.

When slavery was outlawed in the United States, it was almost immediately replaced by Jim Crow and legalized discrimination. African Americans' economic mobility was nearly as restricted as it had been in slavery. In Jamaica, by contrast, ex-slaves could and did buy land where they wanted to. They could get decent land, at market prices, with the same legal protections available to whites. This very long tradition of ownership and access fueled Jamaican migrants' single-minded drive to own homes in the United States. They also knew they had a good shot at succeeding. West Indians are expert at adapting to new societies, having left the islands in great numbers ever since available land grew scarce in the late 1800s. To West Indians, the barriers to owning property were not institutional, or even psychological, but merely geographical, and they've been setting sail for their proverbial piece of land ever since.

Of the four Morris cousins, only Altamont's twenty-three-year-old daughter had ever lived on her own. It didn't last long. Soft-spoken but unabashed, Marie told me the story as her parents listened calmly. The previous year, she had gotten pregnant by the boyfriend she'd been seeing since she was fifteen. The pair decided to move into an apartment together, but he was in school, and Marie was simultaneously working and studying for a graduate degree. So Altamont encouraged her to come home. She did and, miraculously, her education missed not a beat. Having gotten her master's degree right before her baby was born, Marie was now an adjunct professor in graphic design at a community college. Her fiancé, as he was now termed, lounged in the gold-carpeted den at that moment, watching a basketball game with their baby son.

"When do you think you'll move into your own place again?" I asked.

"At least by thirty," Marie said. "I want to own my own place. And I want to have my own magazine."

Seven years from now—and only after owning a house and a business. My mental portrait of a chastened free spirit, forced to live with her disapproving parents, evaporated. For Marie, like her father before her, living together wasn't a stopgap. It was a game plan.

Suddenly the front door burst open. A lithe young woman in skin-tight leggings breezed in. It was Kareen, Altamont's niece. She too had just gotten her master's—also while living at home. She had come to show me her parents' place and how the second half of the big household had fared.

Eight years ago, after finally saving enough for a deposit, Altamont's brother had bought a stately house. Neither Kareen nor her younger sister, a college student, ever considered living elsewhere. Yet these were not Caribbean Emily Dickinsons, afraid to leave their parents' nest. Once, in elementary school, when they went through a phase of keeping little diaries with locks, their mother couldn't resist snooping. She nearly fell over laughing at the note she found scrawled on one page:

Okay Mommy, I know you're reading this. You think you know everything. Cut it out.

It was a most un-Jamaican tone to take with one's elders—and 100 percent U.S. smart mouth. So why, at the age of twenty-three, was Kareen still living in her childhood bedroom?

She did it for the same emotionally and economically layered reasons that her cousin still lived at Altamont's house—and that her own mother shared a house for fourteen years with in-laws. Most tangibly, it was a strategy to afford better education. By sharing the house in Irvington, Kareen's parents had sent their girls to one of the area's most prestigious Catholic schools. Now, living together cut the cost while they got their degrees.

The arrangement was also part of an understanding—almost a contract—that West Indian families have about education. When we got to the house, Kareen's mother instantly took my arm and led me straight to her kitchen. She was an English professor, with soft, slightly mussed hair and a droll smile. I could see instantly where her daughter's confidence came from. "Try this," Paula instructed, pouring me a sweet, cold concoction that looked like a milk shake. "It's carrot juice with condensed milk. West Indians love it." So did I. As I slurped it down, Paula outlined Jamaican school rules.

"Here's how it works," she said. "For as long as kids are in school, they get everything from us. Room, free meals, and school fees. As long as they want to study. The minute they stop school the free ride is over."

Obviously, not everyone can afford this. But as family units, many West Indians cooperate as much as humanly possible to help a child become economically stable. Unlike American parents, however, they don't see this as preparing the child to stand on her own. It's just one phase in a continuum. As parents grow older, and less able to earn, the team effort launched in childhood evolves. Children gradually slide into the role of caregivers.

"There's got to be something more to it," I said.

Paula had a big house, most of a PhD, and wouldn't need a caretaker for a good thirty years. And there had to be something more than tradition keeping a vivacious, Americanized woman like Kareen living with her mother and father. I had just seen a certificate in Gothic letters on the freezer, announcing perfect grades. She could easily have gotten a scholarship at a better school than the small college she chose because it was close to home.

"It's true," Kareen said. "I like it here. I love my mom. My sister's already asked her to move in with her when she gets married."

"It depends what I think of her husband," Paula said primly.

But she was evangelical, she admitted, about single young people living at home. Her reasoning reflected a classic West Indian blend of pragmatism and human insight.

"I tell my kids at the college, 'Come on,'" Paula said. "'Why pay your rent on someone else's property? Save your money and buy a condo, get that education. The only reason to move out is to have sex. It's cheaper to get a motel room. You're going to pay $800, $900 a month just to have sex? You're not going to be doing it every single night. Save your money.'"

Each time I met another extension of the Morris family, I had to ask the same thing: "How do adults live with parents or siblings without driving each other crazy?"

West Indian families, after all, are the same petri dishes of quirks as any other family. Especially at first, their lives here can be every bit as stressful as they were for newly arrived Jews, Italians, and Irish. Parents sometimes leave children back in the islands until they can afford to bring them here. And once reunited, West Indian families have to contend, for the first time, with being black. Every so often, some ill-informed commentator will point to Jamaican success as proof that U.S. racism doesn't exist. The opposite is true. Jamaican adults land here unscathed by racism and determined to ignore it while they pursue their goals. But their kids must craft a sense of self here. Often meeting the racism that U.S. blacks have faced for generations, some West Indian youths identify more with disaffected African American peers.

Considering all these obstacles, it's all the more remarkable how many Jamaican families manage to thrive. "How do people get along? Very well," said David Cort, a wiry, talkative Jamaican sociologist at the University of Massachusetts at Amherst. After years working on the East Coast, he spoke with an accent that was half Caribbean and half express-train Eastern Seaboard.

At the heart of West Indians' success living together, Cort said, is mutual understanding of goals. "A lot of it has to do with a framework of helping each other that is brought over from the home country," he said. "The children understand and the parents understand their shared obligation." No different, I thought, from the implied contract between any minors and their parents. The question is, What happens when the kids become adults, and they want to act on their own wishes?

"At the heart of this," Cort said, "is a disagreement between West Indian and American parents: when is the kid an adult?"

Americans typically think of our kids as adults at eighteen or twenty-one. But for Jamaicans like Sandra and Altamont, adulthood in many ways starts earlier, as soon as their children can grasp the family goal of improving their standard of living. By the time they're college age, kids are partners in a long-term strategy to pool expenses and get as much education as possible. What keeps them engaged? I asked Cort.

"This system works," he replied.

Seeing parents take several jobs and/or plunge into higher education in their thirties and forties, children learn to defer gratification themselves. Parents further shore up the family project by pointing out, with disdain, the frivolous ways of other Americans.

So much for the rest of us trying this system out. Actually, looking down on our fellow countrymen has been American meat and potatoes since colonial times. The Massachusetts Bay Puritans persecuted anyone who didn't share their notion of religious freedom, that is, being a Puritan. And in Appalachia, the early Scotch-Irish clung to clan structures that were centuries old. Families, too, define themselves in opposition to others, joining microcultures based on religion, food choices, parenting, schools, spanking, bilingualism, and sports teams.

Multigenerational families also require a certain formality. The closer the physical proximity of parents and adult children, a Jamaican family counselor explained, the stronger the boundaries need to be. "There's this understanding," another Jamaican told me, "that you let your adult kids do what they do, and you don't pry. And this is really weird, because you have this close level of interaction, all these adults living in the same house."

The more I talked to other West Indians, the more it sounded as if established roles between generations, instead of ratcheting tensions up, made it simpler to get along.

"Child, let me tell you something," my Trinidadian coworker said. "This is how I resolve things with older relatives. I have an aunt. She's the older one, I'm the younger one. If she wants to say something and I don't agree with it, I just turn a deaf ear."

My coworker is sixty-two.

"You mean, not communicating?" a college friend said when I repeated this to her. "The opposite of every value we've been brought up on?"

Yes. And no.

"We always say that white people make such a big deal out of little things," Kareen Morris mused as she drove me back from her parents' house. But as an adult, she explained, listening respectfully no longer meant you obeyed them. If a relative drives you crazy, just walk away.

You're going to be on the same team, in the same house, pushing for the same goals for a long while.

Parents and adult children don't always achieve perfect restraint, obviously. But even when they fight—if, for example, an adult daughter rolls in at dawn and her elderly mother objects—the dispute is less likely to end with a U-Haul. Everyone in the house is too clear on why they're together.

"Is there a certain lack of intimacy? Oh, yes," said sociologist Cort. "I've heard my dad say he loves me maybe three or four times in my entire life. But nothing will ever make me doubt it."

He saw the evidence. Parents give up so much in the quest for immigration, and children understand that. My friends and I worry about saying things right: telling our kids how much they're loved, praising with careful words to teach the value of trying. West Indian parents sometimes just show it: like Monica Brown working as a maid to buy her children a house, or David Cort's father quietly going without blood pressure pills to buy shoes for his growing sons.

Blind deference wasn't part of my upbringing. As a kid, I obeyed my mother and father because I authentically looked up to them. Not only did I adore them, they really did have skills and knowledge I didn't have. But I couldn't imagine, as an adult, living with the polite deference the West Indians described. Then it occurred to me I already did without thinking about it.

When my mother turned eighty a few years ago, something in me switched off (a bit late, I realize). I found myself trying harder to just let her be. There was something arbitrary about this: No one would call Marielena faltering, infirm, or even much mellowed. She has the same charisma and family influence she had forty years ago. Yet I figured the democracy was over. Something about the number eighty, in my mind, finally constituted a get-out-of-jail card. No reasonable person would expect a woman of this age to change the way she talked or ran her life, and she had earned the right not to try. For the first time it was unambiguous to me who would have to adapt—and holding my tongue some of the time grew somewhat easier.

The difference for many Jamaicans is that they assume their parents' inability to change from the beginning, and never, even as adults, revise that stance. Deference to elders, of course, props up traditional societies the world over. And as my father had seen in his practice, it can be a prison, making the old into tyrants, the young into servants, and, on a societal level, trapping everyone. Daring to defy gerontocracy, in my opinion, was one of the best gifts my parents made to their kids. If elders had their way in 1948, my parents' four-decade marriage would never have happened. A few years later, in Philadelphia, a friend's Irish American dad got kicked out of the house for dating a Korean girl. An Italian American friend's dad got punched for mentioning evolution.

As they try to find balance here, West Indians face real generational differences too. Yet the families I met often spoke of each other with a warmth I wasn't accustomed to.

"Americans," a West Indian woman told me, "think they should nurture a child and then when that child reaches a certain age they should be in their own life. Why? We look at it a different way. Turning eighteen doesn't mean you have to fall out of love with your parents."

Could a majority of my peers ever live with their parents, or even speak of them so sentimentally? I don't think so. We've been trained to prize our differences too much. But the generation that reached adulthood at the millennium may be very different. Even before the 2008 economic crash, multigenerational households were on the rise. From 12 percent in 1980, they increased steadily through 2008, when 16.1 percent of Americans lived in a multigeneration home. The spike reflected a tougher economy, yes, but also the family traditions of millions of immigrants and a greater number of unmarried people in their twenties, many of whom still lived at home.

Homebuilders had already noticed. "At building trade shows this year," the *New York Times* reported in 2006, "model homes for the first time specifically catered to multigenerational living. Bedroom suites are designed with private entrances and porches, halls are wider to accommodate wheelchairs, and light switches are lower so they can be reached by those in wheelchairs and by children. There are also bigger kitchens for social networking, as well as extra storage for belongings that now range from toys to Grandma's china."

Around the same time, a development company called Issa Homes built its first prototype of multigenerational homes in Celebration, Florida, designed to revive the best features of traditional American towns and based on the New Urbanism movement. Examining the same trend, the *Miami Herald* noted, "For others, a family compound—each family living in its own home but sharing a common yard—is the answer. 'It's like the saying, *juntos pero no revueltos* [together but not all mixed up],' one compound dweller said."

Immigrants, Hispanics most of all, have pushed the trend forward. Yet it may be retiring baby boomers who make multigenerational living outright common again. Boomers, and their exceptionally close adult children. In forty years, no one has seen the likes of this amiable generation born after 1982. They seem to defy the laws of what once seemed human nature: even as teenagers, these young Americans consistently, measurably, like their parents.

The trend was already underway around the time they were born. In 1983, three-quarters of American teens claimed they had "no serious problems" with their parents, compared with only 50 percent in 1974, according to the Mood of American Youth Survey. In 1996, the same study reported that 94 percent of teens felt "very happy" or "fairly happy" with their mothers (81 percent felt just as warmly about their fathers). The goodwill continued to rise in 2008, when 44 percent of students ages thirteen to nineteen named a family member as their role model, up from 42 percent in 2002.

They call their parents often; they seem to enjoy them. And parents yearn to be with their adult kids. Only 25 percent of parents, a homebuilding research group recently found, reported feeling happier after they leave. These are dumbfounding figures for Americans who came of age in the 1960s. They reflect normal life for many West Indians. Blessed with fewer differences than generations before them, baby boomers and their kids may end up reviving the once-common multigenerational home. If so, they stand to gain the same advantages that help West Indians achieve their own American visions.

6

How to Be a Good Neighbor:

Barrio Stoops, Sidewalks, and Shops

Little Village

I got to know Chicago's Little Village neighborhood the old-fashioned way: by stalking. It was early October, delicious walking weather, and the El had just dropped me at the portal of the biggest Latino community in the Midwest. I'd never before been to this area on Chicago's southwest hip, and was unsure where to head. Some streets, I'd read, were plagued by gangs. Then the turnstile behind me rolled, once, twice, three times.

A plump, middle-aged Latina with margarine-colored hair and a brisk expression marched out, clutching the hand of a boy who looked about ten and another who might have been seventeen. They lacked the spent, ill-tempered look I often wear myself, emerging from the train. All three, in fact, seemed to be in unusually chipper spirits. Both the younger boy in his cargo shorts and the teenager with his buzz cut looked content in their handholding phalanx. So I resolved to follow them home.

I was hoping the little family would lead me toward some answers in an epidemiological mystery. A magnet for Mexican immigrants, and one of the poorest and least educated communities in Chicago, Little

Village boasts surprisingly good markers of health and well-being. Of all these, perhaps the most enigmatic is Little Village's exceptionally low reported rate of asthma. According to an influential 2007 study in the *American Journal of Public Health*, foreign-born Latinos in South Lawndale, where Little Village is located, reported asthma diagnoses at less than one-third the average in either Chicago's white or black neighborhoods. Rich or poor.

And Little Village, overwhelmingly, is poor.

Even if it's controlled with inhalers, allergy shots, emergency room oxygen, and adrenaline, asthma cannot be cured. Something irritates the airways that deliver oxygen to our lungs, and they swell and narrow. Less air passes through. Chest muscles contract, and the airways respond by squeezing still smaller. With a tickle in her chest, or an itch in her throat, an asthmatic child starts to cough. In twenty minutes, the same child can be audibly, visibly suffocating to death. The sound is terrifying: a whistling, desperate wheeze. She may turn blue, lose consciousness.

We know it's triggered by allergies and by lung irritants such as diesel exhaust or cigarette smoke. It's aggravated by poor primary care: failure to visit a doctor early on can lead to an emergency room crisis that costs far more money to treat. Studies also strongly implicate psychological stress—a shorthand term for negative emotions that overwhelm our coping abilities.

Stress seems to correlate with asthma in many ways at once. Behaviorally, it's been linked to higher rates of smoking—a known asthma trigger. Physiologically, it alters the endocrine, immune, and autonomic nervous systems, all of which can inflame breathing passages. So it's not a big leap that the literature now shows strong links between asthma and low-income neighborhoods. In the United States, most of these areas are urban, with more mold and cockroaches, worse violence, and fewer medical services.

That's what makes enclaves such as Little Village so striking. In most obvious ways, the people who live here are at higher risk for bad health. And, according to what is currently known, they're particularly vulnerable to asthma. Something, or things, must be buffering Little Village's lungs.

Long before scientists ever tested the notion, Westerners have linked poverty with disease. Dumas, Zola, and Dickens electrified readers with their portraits of frail, overworked characters succumbing to tuberculosis and fevers. Throughout the twentieth century, research proved the intuition right. Poverty contributes to illness not just by weakening the body with malnutrition or more exposure to the elements, but through the side effects of lower income, social marginalization, bad housing, and worse medical care. Draw the poverty card in this country and you are overall more likely to get the whole, miserable hand. Higher infant mortality, more exposure to homicide, heart disease, cancer.

And you are far more likely to suffer from asthma.

Generally, that is. Asthma has dramatically risen among kids of all social classes in the United States and worldwide. Oddly, though, it is particularly fierce in developed countries, and in the inner cities of these countries. Based on data gathered in the 1990s, Chicago barrios including Little Village are the exception. In defiance of most public health formulas, kids skating on Little Village's congested sidewalks may have the healthiest lungs in Chicago.

We know a few of the reasons. A complicated, enigmatic disease, asthma is most likely a "gene by environment" interaction. In other words, it occurs when a mutation in the immune system, muscular system, lungs, or other system responds to an external trigger. So some aspect of Little Village's relative immunity is probably genetic. Mexicans, even in Mexico City, which has some of the dirtiest air in the world, have low asthma rates relative to Americans.

Another part of Little Village's asthma resistance—and again, no one knows how much—is surely migration selection, such a potent factor in immigrant health overall. Adults who make it here from Mexico tend to be constitutionally tough and mentally resilient. Mexican immigrants may also benefit from their past environment. According to what's called the hygiene hypothesis, children with more exposure to farm animals and other potential asthma-triggering allergens may be more resilient to asthma triggers later on in life. Yet none of these factors fully accounts for the disproportionately clear lungs found in enclaves such as Little Village. And whatever is behind its good health now has urgent implications for the rest of us.

Starting in the 1980s, asthma began spreading to epidemic dimensions. From 1980 to 1994, its prevalence in this country leaped upward by 75 percent. Today, it's America's number one chronic childhood illness, affecting nine million kids, and the single most common cause of prolonged absence from school, throwing already disadvantaged children hopelessly behind. Compounding the damage, it has skyrocketed highest among those least equipped to manage chronic disease: poor, inner-city dwellers, above all African Americans and Puerto Ricans. If we could somehow contain it tomorrow, asthma would still pose a public health crisis. Treating childhood asthma alone now costs more than $2 billion a year. But that's wishful thinking. Year by year, child by child, asthma in this country continues to rise.

It's a frightening, frustrating impasse, and in the last ten years a new medical movement has risen up in response. Melding epidemiology with a long-standing tool from social science, researchers are finding strong links between asthma and the psychological, behavioral, and physical world outside the door. They call it the neighborhood effect. The science is imperfect: the most striking findings so far are correlations, not causes. Do healthy people gravitate to certain neighborhoods? Or do certain neighborhoods promote health?

The metrics are still imprecise. How exactly do you measure stress? But the asthma/neighborhood link has proven so strong that in ten years it's gone from a medical curiosity to a regular topic of workshops, journals, and grant proposals. Far more than we'd realized, intangibles such as community may actually inform how well our lungs fend off irritants.

"I think the neighborhood effect is driving a substantial amount of asthma we're seeing. Substantial," says Harvard pulmonologist Rosalind Wright, director of the Asthma Center on Community, Environment, and Social Stress. The National Institutes of Health has funded several of Wright's studies on asthma and neighborhood violence.

The odd case of Little Village suggests a new twist to the existing literature. Some of the best tools Americans can marshal against asthma may literally be made of concrete. We can't sprout Mexican DNA or re-create a childhood on a Guerrero ranch. Nature determines our innate survival skills. But most of us can copy fairly easily the ways Little Villagers use ordinary stoops, shops, and sidewalks to re-create elements of a Mexican neighborhood. In the process we may buffer ourselves from a signature American disease.

From Little Village to La Villita

The purposeful mother knew her way around. Plus, she and her boys looked so amiable. Maybe, I reasoned, they'd talk to me when they reached their destination.

So I trotted behind them, pausing at lights to put space between us, sauntering across the street when I got too conspicuous.

I shouldn't have worried. The trio's pace and good humor didn't falter, and all three seemed strikingly unconcerned about threats from the street, including the inexpert spy loping behind them.

And Little Village was not exactly a seething cauldron of danger.

In a few blocks we reached Twenty-Sixth Street, a hectic commercial boulevard stretched under an arch reading Welcome to Little Village. Winsomely clumsy murals of children and community leaders coated the adjoining buildings. Beneath, as far as I could see, every inch of real estate was consumed by a small business. There were mom-and-pop grocery stores and an abundance of butcher shops (We May Be Small, but We're the Best!). Nearby were taquerias, auto shops, bakeries, and banks; block-long nightclubs and dusty *yerberias* peddling home remedies.

A few blocks later, the mother and boys turned onto a street where bungalows alternated with brick buildings, and abruptly the figures disappeared into a duplex. I decided to collect my thoughts in front of the block's crowning jewel: a white cottage with an actual picket fence and eight square feet of garden stuffed with sunflowers, squash, tomatoes, and swaying corn. It looked like a Thomas Kinkade painting.

At the beginning of the last century, little bungalows like this one housed thousands of working-class Poles and Czechs, then called Bohemians. Anton Cermak, a Czech who became mayor of Chicago by breaking through the Irish political machine, came from the area. So does game show host Pat Sajak. The immigrants' day jobs waited a few blocks away, on the assembly lines of mighty companies: International Harvester, Sears, Western Electric Company.

Starting in the 1950s, though, the neighborhood's employers began to relocate, and the upwardly mobile European workers headed to the suburbs. African Americans, migrating in huge numbers from the South, moved in, and for a few decades the new residents were sustained by the last manufacturing jobs.

But in large part because federal lenders refused to insure mortgages in racially mixed areas, the neighborhoods succumbed to real estate predators. Fraudulent house contracts, overcrowding, and decades of arson gutted once-solid neighborhoods. One of the most ravaged was

North Lawndale, a now desolate African American community just a few blocks from where I now stood.

Something different happened in Little Village. Because it always had far more homeowners than renters, the turnover here happened more gradually, less traumatically. In the end, one set of tenants completely replaced the previous one. Little Village filled up, becoming a destination for Chicago's Mexican Americans and torrents of migrants directly from Mexico. In fewer than twenty years, the neighborhood transformed, from a staid Slavic village to a jammed, impoverished, bustling barrio: the third-biggest Hispanic community in America. Its new occupants call it La Villita.

Today, more than 80 percent of Little Village residents are Mexican American or Mexicans, some of whom trudged through mountain and desert to cross over illegally. They're construction workers, janitors, maids, bus boys. Never the poorest of the poor in Mexico (you need a few thousand dollars to pay a coyote), they are also not the poorest by Chicago standards. Most have jobs. But they do, by many measures, teeter just above the city's bottom economic rung. In 2006, for instance, incomes in Little Village were lower than those in 84 percent of Chicago's other neighborhoods. Or, to use another common socioeconomic measure, Little Village has fewer high school graduates than 99 percent of the city's other neighborhoods. Most people here speak English as a second language, if at all.

So it's easy to guess some of its features. Two coal-burning plants churn out toxins nearby. The hideous Cook County Jail shadows the main thoroughfare, sending forth a stream of exhausted-looking women ending visiting hours. Local schoolkids have only one or two dingy parks to visit, though the city has promised to build on the campus of the defunct Celotex plant. Unsurprisingly, for many Little Village residents the American Dream consists of getting out as fast as possible, ideally to a modern, roomy suburb like Cicero on the West Side.

They may not realize what they're leaving behind.

Sharing the Streets

I took a last peep at the Cottage of Light and zagged to the opposite curb. On the Little Village street where I'd trailed the small family, four men were positioning milk crates. A half dozen kids on skates caromed around them. Two of the men had tucked liter beer bottles near their feet; another pulled a Modelo from a cooler after shooing away the little girl perched there.

"Ah, Chicago," he said.

It was four in the afternoon on a weekday; these men were drinking in public, unabashedly, apparently, while supervising their own children. Behind them sagged a three-story apartment building, its concrete yard enclosed by a fence. Yet the mood felt benign. The little girls flitted close to their dads, aiming empty water pistols and cracking up into giggles. Then a fifth man, muscled and mustachioed, emerged from the building and headed for the party's lone boy. He was a clean-cut child, about eight, with fawn-colored skin and glossy black bangs. But the man looked unfriendly.

"I mean it," he was saying as I edged closer. "You need to go inside. Go now."

The boy hesitated, weighing the options.

"I'm counting to three," the muscled man growled. He bristled three fingers. "Do you want me to go to your mother?"

The little boy sprinted.

"What was that about?" I asked the group, all of whom had been watching raptly.

"He came with a plastic gun, and he was pointing it at our eyes," a wiry girl piped up. "He lives across the street. That's my stepfather." Her name was Maritza, she said, and she was thirteen. And after only the briefest introduction, in which I satisfactorily established I did not work for the government, the adults pleasantly offered their names too, or at least parts of their names, and slid me a crate.

"Grandpa Manny! Grandpa Manny!" Maritza leaned on her skates to bellow. Whizzing by on a mountain bike, a slightly menacing-looking boy with a shaved head and white undershirt waved. "That's his nickname," Maritza said. "He's a friend of my older brother's. I think he thinks he looks like a grandpa."

I personally thought he looked like a gang member. But in crowded, interconnected Little Village, the lines between child, adult, kin, neighbor, and compatriot smudge more easily than they might in a more compartmentalized neighborhood. It was perfectly likely, in fact, that bald-headed Manny was indeed a *gangero*. For more than a decade, residents here have bitterly complained about gangs and their trash and graffiti. Some also probably enable them. In low-income neighborhoods, the same social ties that can do so much for physical health also keep gangs robust. Gangbangers keep their home turf secure, and neighbors hesitate to turn in their own nephews, godchildren, or ex–altar boys. In Little Village, gangs seemed to respect a rough decorum, concentrating in a known handful of streets and reserving their mayhem for night.

"When it gets dark," Maritza said gloomily, "my mother says we have to come in because of the gangbangers."

Daylight, though, belongs to upstanding citizens. When Maritza's mother emerged from the apartment building, the girls on skates swarmed her, begging to walk to Twenty-Sixth Street for ice cream. She shook her head, hovered for a minute to hear the men's conversation, then headed back inside. Emboldened by all the activity, I unfolded a notebook page on which I'd jotted questions that other researchers had asked in this area.

"How often do you and your neighbors get together, outside or inside someone's house?" I asked the skaters.

"Two or three times a month," Maritza guessed. "Holidays."

"Do your parents and the neighbors do each other personal favors—like shopping if someone is sick or taking care of each other's kids?"

"Yes," a younger girl called. "Just a few days ago, the neighbor upstairs told us not to step on the grass after they just put it down."

"Then the neighbor told my mom," Maritza added. "And then my mom said not to step on it so it could grow." We both reflexively looked down, where Maritza's skates were mutilating the few remaining green shoots. The neighbor upstairs was very friendly, Maritza went on. She had a huge van, and all summer long, along with her own five kids, she'd drive Maritza and her four sisters and brothers to the lake. That *was* friendly, I thought, and definitely a relic of a past era. Not only would I never take on that responsibility, I don't think I'd let someone else take it on for me.

I glanced at my last question, half-thinking it wasn't worth asking a thirteen-year-old girl.

"Do you think if there were a fight outside, the people in this neighborhood would get involved?"

The entire entourage nodded fiercely.

"It happened just the other day. Right in front of this building," Maritza said. "The gangbangers beat up a guy, I don't know why. They broke his hand and then he went to the hospital." A man stepped into the fight to save him, she said. She pointed to where he lived, on the ground floor of her building. And she skated off to get him. It may seem inconsequential, but Maritza's dash to summon her neighbor said much about Little Village's health. It hinted at the neighborhood's social cohesion, an ephemeral-sounding trait that for a poor neighborhood can be the health equivalent of a stack of gold bars.

The Asthma Hunters

Kathleen Cagney, director of the University of Chicago's Population Research Center, grew up around asthma.

"My father had it, so I thought it was interesting from that standpoint," she told me after I first visited Little Village. But Cagney didn't consider asthma a subject of study until fairly late in her training.

Cagney has straight dark hair and a blunt speaking style that doesn't brook whimsy. She likes to stick to the data. But in her research she is passionate. "I've always been concerned," she said, "with inequalities." Earning her degrees—master's in public policy at Chicago, doctorate in public health at Johns Hopkins—and working in Harlem cancer clinics, Cagney saw firsthand how Americans' outcomes for certain diseases differ according to socioeconomic circumstance. That's why she turned her attention to asthma. Because it was so unfair.

While many Americans with asthma are, like Cagney's father, white adults, and even more are white kids, asthma differs from other diseases that have a powerful genetic component. In the past decade, an avalanche of studies have suggested that your chances of suffering from the disease are significantly predicted simply by where you live. Its prevalence and ethnic breakdown are similar in big U.S. cities, affecting about one in five blacks and Puerto Ricans, and about one in ten Mexicans and Caucasians.

But Chicago's asthma outcomes are far, far worse than those in any other U.S. city. Compared with the national average, an inner-city Chicago resident is twice as likely to need hospitalization during an asthma attack. And, stunningly, an asthma sufferer in Chicago is twice as likely to die from the illness. For African Americans in Chicago, the asthma death rate is simply astronomical: five times the national average. "Why? What's going on in Chicago?" asked Maureen Damitz, senior programs director for the Respiratory Health Association of Metropolitan Chicago. Nobody knows.

Chicago may also be the city to offer asthma researchers a breakthrough. Parsed into neighborhoods, divided by race, the city's ethnic communities have for the past fifty years been studied minutely by social scientists, who have developed a data trove unrivaled anywhere in the world. What it reveals about health in places such as Little Vil-

lage, could help beat asthma nationwide. The mother of all these studies was a multi-phase, interdisciplinary project launched in the 1990s
that probed how families, schools, and neighborhoods shaped the
well-being of Chicago residents. Some of the techniques were uncon-
ventional. Creeping through 196 neighborhoods in customized SUVs,
researchers scribbled notes on what they saw while video cameras
whirred behind them. They also quizzed residents in detail about their
social habits. How often, they asked, do you:

1. have parties or get-togethers where other people in the
   neighborhood are invited?
2. visit in each other's homes or on the street?
3. ask each other's advice about personal things such as
   child-rearing or job openings?
4. do favors for each other?

The researchers then graded each neighborhood for, among
other things, "social interaction." But what did this have to do with
asthma? A lot for Kathleen Cagney and her colleague Chris Browning,
researchers at the crossroads of social science and public health policy.
In 2005, they led a team that overlaid the neighborhood data with
three years of findings from an enormous study of asthma rates in nine
thousand Chicago-area residents. The researchers then controlled for
age, gender, race/ethnicity, home ownership, insurance, income, regular source of health care, smoking habits, and whether a physician had
diagnosed the respondent with a weight problem. What they found
defied the classic equation that poverty equals illness.

The first numbers looked familiar enough. In Chicago's white population, just under 19 percent had been diagnosed with asthma-type ail-
ments, compared with 22.2 percent of African Americans and slightly
under 15 percent of U.S.-born Latinos. (About three-quarters of Chicago's Latinos are of Mexican descent.) Latinos who were born abroad

showed a sharp asthma-resistant advantage. But Cagney's next finding was startling. In the city's main Mexican enclaves—Little Village is one of two—the reported asthma diagnoses were a mere 5 percent.

Now, it's likely this figure was artificially low. Immigrants visit doctors less often, and so receive fewer diagnoses of respiratory disease, for example. But the numbers still fell below asthma levels for Mexican immigrants overall. Even stranger, they fell far below asthma levels for Mexican immigrants who lived *outside* the barrios.

Of all the groups Cagney studied, in fact, foreign-born Latinos in nonimmigrant neighborhoods were slammed by asthma the hardest. Away from Chicago's Latino ethnic enclaves, a full 22 percent of foreign-born Latinos wheezed and gasped. This was something that neither selection nor genes could explain. Whatever it was, the immigrant advantage did not reside simply in being Mexican or even in being foreign born. To enjoy the asthma protection found in Little Village, it seemed, a Latino in Chicago needed some ingredient found in Little Village itself.

Cagney hypothesized that this enclave effect worked in two ways. First, ethnic homogeneity might "increase information exchange through a common language. Shared culture or lifestyle behaviors might also be at play." It made sense. Imagine being a rural, non-English-speaking Mexican, still dazed by your journey and ignorant about the U.S. medical system. You'd be a lot healthier if you could ask someone for a lift to the clinic. And in an enclave, peer pressure still enforces old-country values. A new arrival from Guerrero, settling on her steps for a smoke, might freeze mid-puff if a passerby glared at her disapprovingly.

But Cagney discovered a second link between asthma resistance and a Little Village zip code. And this one didn't require being Mexican. Considering its poverty, Little Village scored surprisingly high in social interaction. That social interaction "significantly increased the protective effect of foreign-born status," the researchers wrote.

"Causation is always hard to claim," Cagney told me later. But, she said, "these findings suggest that the level of social connectedness affects asthma levels—and can be a buffer to asthma."

It sounded so cozy.

But it begged several questions. What kind of socializing was this that could have such an effect? The key factor, Cagney and other asthma specialists say, is likely *where* that socializing takes place: outside, on sidewalks and stoops, and in local stores. When it comes to managing asthma, as a Chicago pulmonologist put it, "outside is definitely better."

Sidewalks

"Do you feel your neighbors have your back?" That's called collective efficacy, Kate Cagney told me. It shows a social norm—the idea that I do something helpful, not because I expect a return from you but because that's what is right. "It's picking up a letter from the sidewalk and putting it in the mailbox," Cagney said. "It's stepping in if there's a fight near your house."

"Do your neighbors come by your house?" That's social interaction, Cagney went on. "Little Village has both of these features, and it has more of both than even some more affluent Chicago communities. There are ways in which money can't buy everything."

In fact, money can pare away social interaction and the good that comes with it. While a well-to-do family can hire a babysitter with no emotional strings attached to the deal, neighbors in a poor but relatively high-trust community—like Little Village—have to depend on each other for most of their child-minding. Swapping this favor helps knit the social bonds that have such a complicated, protective effect on their health.

Even more influential than their child-care practices, though, is the way Little Village residents get around. Because many here can't afford cars, they have to walk. Vexed by graffiti, pestered by litter, Little Villagers nevertheless perambulate their sidewalks day and night. Most would probably prefer their own wheels, but from a pulmonologist's viewpoint, the place is nirvana.

True, by walking around you inhale outdoor pollutants—but it's a much less intense blast than the invisible fog of insect droppings, chemicals, and mold found in apartments and houses. And though they'd rather do it in a more pleasant way than slogging to the bus stop for their night shifts, Little Village residents burn calories more consistently than most people with gym memberships. And obesity is linked closely with asthma.

The walkers' army is also fending off crime. A city sidewalk, as Jane Jacobs declared in her 1961 book, *The Death and Life of Great American Cities,* "must have users on it fairly continuously, both to add to the numbers of eyes on the street and to induce the people in buildings along the street to watch the sidewalks in sufficient number." Jacobs' observations seemed radical in a decade when public housing and sealed-in office complexes seemed the best tools to vanquish crime and urban malaise.

In recent years, though, she's become the muse of the New Urbanism movement, a trend toward reclaiming traditional community features such as the front porch, the walking path, the town square. Whether all New Urbanism principles—and there are a lot of them now, not all of which Jacobs endorsed—reduce crime is still in the lab stage. But she was onto something about eyes on the street—though they seem to work only in city neighborhoods where people are visible on more than half the block fronts. Any less than that—for example, the barren streets of North Lawndale—and walkers actually become targets.

But in places like Little Village, where most streets whir with activity until nighttime, the street army forms a deterrent. In fact, Little Village—like immigrant neighborhoods in other major cities—boasts one of the lowest violent crime rates in Chicago. Between 1995 and 2002, Harvard sociologist Robert Sampson found, Mexican Americans in Chicago committed fewer violent crimes than either their white or African American counterparts. In Little Village specifically, burglary levels in 2006 ranked in the city's bottom 20 percent. For at least a decade, its crime rates have trailed those citywide overall by almost two-thirds.

You don't need to romanticize Little Village life—God knows its residents don't—to see the paradox here. In this neighborhood where residents live in fear of deportation, crowd into shoddily partitioned buildings, and mostly speak Spanish, a little girl like Maritza is nevertheless safer from violent crime than most other kids in Chicago. Like asthma resistance, Little Village's low crime rate—relative to its income level—has many sources, says Sampson, who has studied the area extensively.

He ticked some of them off. Again, the selection effect ranks high up there. "These are people who are migrating to this country, leaving their homes," he said. "If you're motivated to do that, that's connected to certain characteristics that would be protective against crime." This is also a population that doesn't want undue attention, and probably underreports crime. On the other hand, Sampson has pointed out, it's pretty difficult to hide homicides. And finally, the torrent of new arrivals from Latin America, with their demand for accessible shopping, continually flush Little Village's sidewalks with human activity and commerce.

With its casual, free-floating outdoor life, Little Village revives an old truth. You don't have to be best friends with your neighbors to see them, talk to them, and benefit—deeply—from knowing them. In fact, Los Angeles urban planner James Rojas told me, some barrio dwellers characteristically create those bonds by building . . . fences. I knew exactly the kind he was talking about. I'd spent the afternoon by the fence at Maritza's building, a new-looking iron cage around a front "yard" the size of a carport. A much comelier example stood across the street, where the owner of the exquisitely landscaped Cottage of Light had installed a tiny picket fence around the corn and squash.

In East Los Angeles, Rojas said, fences are the most distinctive Mexican adaptation of the 1950s Anglo neighborhood. And with fences, he theorized, comes sociability. Marking out an extra parcel of home, fences encourage barrio dwellers to personalize their front yards with fountains and adornments. Walking becomes more entertaining, as passersby peer into the yards for socially sanctioned snooping.

"With a fence you can be in front of your house and not be exposed," Rojas explained. "Without a fence you feel very vulnerable. So the fence becomes a way for socialization. People talk over a fence. It makes the front yard both a quasi-public and private space, rather than, say, an American suburb where you have a big front lawn and the front door becomes the point of interaction. There you either have a formal visit or no visit at all."

Yet picket fences, or for that matter, front lawns, aren't really traditional in the towns and villages many Mexican immigrants left behind. High concrete walls, yes, for those with the money. But for most others, leisure time outside the house largely means a stroll on a plaza.

Find a bench at dusk in a Mexican town to this day, and you can still see the full pageant of plaza culture unfurl. Preening teenagers clump on the bandstand or promenade in circles as they have in such towns for hundreds of years. Grandmothers stake out the benches. And in the big open spaces—up on the bandstand, or under the trees near the ice cream seller—toddlers careen joyously, parents eyeing them from a relaxed distance.

"The plaza does about a million things at once," a writer friend who lived in Mexico put it. "Everyone is getting out, and getting to know each other. It shows kids how to behave, and the ones who don't are shunned. No one wants their kids to hang out with the *marijuanero.* You are constantly being watched. You can't get away with anything."

Relaxing in a fenced-in front yard, planner Rojas thinks, re-creates this experience for many immigrants. But socializing this way is also a throwback to a very American tradition: the boundaried relationship. We once cherished it for sound reasons. Good fences make good neighbors, the old wisdom went, echoed in our nostalgic tropes of white picket fences, housewives gossiping over the hedge, TV dads jawing over a fence in the backyard. Cars rocketing us from home to the workplace blurred that social middle ground. The fencelessness of electronic media has almost erased it.

On social networking sites, which are often described as virtual neighborhoods, people broadcast details (the divorce, the childbirth, the medical procedure) to enormous groups of acquaintances with no gradation in closeness. (Facebook is starting to offer such gradations, however.) Conversely, on the streets where we live, our craving for privacy often propels us inside as quickly as possible.

There's relief in that distance—life is too clamorous without having to befriend strangers just because they bought real estate on the same block. I know I feel that way. Applauding its goals in theory, each year I dread milling around on National Night Out, making conversation by the foldout table with an unknown person who lives three streets away.

Using sidewalks for transportation, for exercise, for idle snooping, seems to me a more organic way to know your neighbors. It may work even better if you can follow the sidewalk to a store.

Shops

A few summers before visiting Little Village, I went to a barbecue in the kind of neighborhood thirteen-year-old Maritza might dream of. Katy, Texas, is an airy, reasonably priced subdivision about thirty minutes' drive out of Houston. Its wide lawns are resplendent thanks to the humid air and diligently applied chemicals. Packs of kids Maritza's age bike past, roaming far from parents' anxious eyes. Car traffic here is scarce, and unknown pedestrians more so. Furthermore, parents know that if their offspring want to congregate at a mall or any other public spot, they'll have to enlist an adult to drive them.

"Welcome to *The Truman Show*," said my friend Carlos, a newspaper editor, opening the door. He and his wife had bought a GPS when they moved in, finding houses and lawns so alike they got lost. But their kids, natives of Mexico City, relished Katy's offerings: the excellent public schools, the lush soccer fields, the incredible amount of house you could get for your dollar. It was the kids, in fact, who'd voted to move to the suburbs.

Even so, Camila, a swanlike thirteen-year-old, did have one complaint. I'd pried it out by accident, with the question I was asking most of my foreign-born acquaintances that year.

What habit do you think people from your country should hang on to when they move here?

Camila answered promptly, "Little shops you can walk to."

I could see the thirteen-year-old's logic. Who wants to beg a lift to buy gum? But Camila's complaint, it turned out, made sense from a public health perspective too. Simplistic as it may seem, the welter of shops just blocks from Maritza's house were probably the neighborhood's single most tangible buffer against asthma. In Mexico, where most people live in the bursting-at-the-seams capital or in villages, the human foot—augmented by buses and take-your-life-in-your-hands collective taxis—remains the most common vehicle.

The Mexicans who come to Little Village bring with them, of course, their poverty, and for a while, at least, their poverty-based transportation habits. But, as Camila suggested, they also bring a certain aesthetic delight in local shopping. It's the same pleasure that once made American Main Streets the place to peer at and to judge your neighbors. Today, its heartbeat amplified by new arrivals, Twenty-Sixth Street is effectively Chicago's Main Street, churning out more economic activity than any other thoroughfare in the city except North Michigan Avenue.

The commercial cacophony would wake a zombie. Even if you're just buying a pound of beef, you can stroll in and out of a dozen different butcher shops, favoring the one whose proprietor makes you laugh or saves you soup bones. When I asked Kate Cagney about the one practice that non-immigrants might borrow from Little Village to fight asthma, she answered as swiftly as Camila had two years before.

"I would have the same response as the young woman from Mexico," Cagney said. "The commercial piece is just really important." Street-level neighborhood stores, she explained, work as a kind of community multivitamin. If there's someplace nearby to shop, people in a neighborhood will walk more, both to buy and for the stimulation of seeing what's for sale and who else is shopping. Heading out to the store, a Little Village resident ups her lung function, immunities, and possibly the safety of all the neighbors out shopping too.

The health benefits keep refracting, sometimes in unexpected forms. In July 1995, Little Village's barbershops and *carnicerías* proved protective against a health threat very different from asthma: a heat wave that killed as many as 739 Chicagoans. For over a week, shocked emergency teams piled body after body into meat-cooling trucks. The elderly, the alone, minorities, and the poor died in hugely disproportionate numbers. Yet many of those who perished, rescue workers saw, could have survived if they had left their roasting apartments. Once again, Little Village seemed to be surrounded by an invisible force field.

In Little Village, the heat wave killed just three people. But in the shattered neighborhood next door, North Lawndale, nineteen people died. Translated into the grim math of statistics, Little Village had a death toll of a little less than four per hundred thousand. The toll in North Lawndale was fully forty per hundred thousand—or a death rate ten times as great. In his devastating book *Heat Wave*, a study of the social and institutional failures that helped cause these deaths, sociologist Eric Klinenberg noted that the two neighborhoods shared "similar microclimates and almost identical numbers and proportions of seniors living alone and living in poverty."

Browning and Cagney led one of the early research teams that dissected the tragically distinct outcomes. Similar as the two neighborhoods were economically, they discovered, their physical environments—their ecology—were polar opposites. North Lawndale was physically abandoned, its buildings burned or crumbling, almost devoid of commerce. Little Village, blessed with such a different history, bustled around ebullient Twenty-Sixth Street.

So when the heat descended, an elderly woman in Little Village knew there were street-level shops that she could safely walk to, with air-conditioning. Once inside, she could then benefit from social cohesion. With one glimpse of her pallid face, a neighbor could call an ambulance. The shops' effect was so direct, so vital, that it probably even saved lives of the neighborhood's elderly Czechs and Poles, still grieving for the lost landscape where they had raised families.

Stoops

"I came to this country because of curiosity, desire. Or error," Andrés Juarez, the owner of Maritza's apartment building, declared jovially. Maritza didn't have to ask twice when she skated to his ground-floor window and invited him out. He'd been watching us the whole time. "I have a very interesting story," Andrés said. "Sit down and I'll tell you."

He didn't invite me in, though. Instead, he ushered me through the high wrought-iron fence that enclosed the asphalted square in front of the building. A white delivery cart affixed to a mountain bike leaned on one wall. Offering me a low folding chair, the kind you'd take to a fireworks display, Andrés settled on the stoop beside me.

Trim and youthful, with an indulgently groomed mustache, Andrés was fifty-nine years old. Born in a small village in the state of Guerrero, he took a bus to Mexico City as a young man, when, as he put it delicately, "possibilities dried up." Starting as a janitor, Andrés taught himself to use a computer and became a manager at a clothing factory, designing knockoff patterns. He married, became a Jehovah's Witness, had kids. Then, a decade ago, Andrés and his wife decided to try their luck in the United States. They weren't starving. They were simply struggling, without any way to progress. So they left.

In Chicago, Andrés and his wife set to work, making dolls out of straw, cleaning offices, and packing shipping crates. Then a semi-miracle occurred. A fellow Jehovah's Witness asked Andrés to buy a small apartment building from her at an unheard-of bargain, and other church friends helped with the deposit. Now a landlord, Andrés kept his box-packing gig, and added a second job wheeling through the neighborhood selling icy Acapulco-style shrimp cocktails. In a good week the *mariscos* brought in $700, and between the four adult family members' many jobs and a full roster of tenants, the building was starting to pay for itself.

Andrés looked toward the sidewalk. A slender girl in skintight capris, a small child in a pink school uniform, and a brawny young man leaned on the fence. "Don Andrés," the teenager called. He hopped up, conferred with her for a moment, then disappeared into the building. When he returned, he was carrying three Styrofoam cups of shrimp cocktail.

"Delicious!" the young woman said. "We came to buy one for our daughter but ended up getting three."

"Sorry, Papi!" the little girl chimed as they walked off.

But Andrés didn't get to resume his story. A disheveled boy with a nest of overgrown black hair wheeled up on a bike. "Don Andrés," he murmured in a strange, wheedling voice. "How much are the *cocteles*?"

"Five dollars," Andrés said evenly. "And you owe me two dollars from last time, remember?"

"I don't have any money," the boy said. I noticed that he, like the girls on skates, carried a plastic gun. While they had been playing with silly orange toys, though, his looked real. The strange boy lingered, rolling a pellet cartridge between his fingers.

"That's a disturbing kid," I muttered.

"He is in a situation where his family makes him something he doesn't want to be," Andrés replied. "Maybe tomorrow he'll be on a corner selling drugs."

When the boy finally pedaled away, Andrés told me how he knew his family. They were among those who had seen the fight.

It had happened only a few months earlier, a sultry midnight in August. For some reason—no one seemed to know why—a lone member of a rival gang arrived on their street. Andrés awoke to the sound of shrieking. Peeping through his front curtains, he saw half a dozen local gang members at his front fence, hammering the outsider with fists and beer bottles. "I ran outside," Andrés said, "I opened my gate, and I grabbed him. But they followed me through the gate. They trapped me against the bicycle"—he motioned with his chin to the shrimp cocktail cart—"and kept beating us both. So I grabbed him again. I embraced him, like this." He clutched his upper arms with both hands. "I pulled him into my house and I slammed the door."

The police pulled up within minutes, and the attackers scattered. Though he didn't know—still doesn't know—the bloodied victim, Andrés may have saved his life.

I asked Andrés why he did it, and why, in general, there was so much social interaction on Little Village sidewalks. He shrugged. "This is how we do it in Mexico," he said. Digging through a satchel, I found my copy of Kathleen Cagney's asthma study and paraphrased a few lines. Andrés listened politely. But you could tell he was wondering why anyone bothered to write this stuff down. It reminded me of the afternoon I'd spent at Restaurant La Flor in Ohio, asking about the cuarentena. Everyone knew the rules, and considered the benefits so plain that studying them seemed redundant.

Obligingly, Andrés reflected on my question a bit further. He'd never thought much about asthma, but the link between street life and better health made perfect sense to him. Maybe that was what cured the preemie twins on his top floor. They'd moved to the neighborhood three months earlier with breathing problems and now no longer needed inhalers.

Andrés was a bold guy, daring enough to leave Mexico, brave enough to wade into a Chicago street fight. But a lot of his behaviors—monitoring the street from his window, pedaling the shrimp cart, lounging on the front stoop—were also throwbacks to life in Mexico. Here in Little Village, economics and pleasure have kept those old-country habits alive. Those habits, in turn, may make Little Village more healthy.

The Neighborhood Effect

The street darkened. The milk crate men chatted on, but their daughters had hurried home, ceding their play space to gangs. The last vendor, rolling a canister of tamales as if she were walking a schnauzer, had passed an hour earlier.

"Is it safe to walk back to the El?" I asked. Definitely, Andrés said, but added, Don't wait too long. Little Village was safe, for a poor neighborhood, just as it was social—relative to its disadvantages. But this was still a barrio, with gangs, overcrowded apartments, and low-paid manual laborers worried each day about their rent. Romanticizing it would be stupid—and incorrect.

Yet the rhythm really did differ from that in typical U.S. neighborhoods, and after an afternoon hobnobbing with Andrés's tenants, I imagined my breathing was slower, my mind refreshed. Fifty years ago, many American neighborhoods, and not only poor ones, looked similar. Affluence, commuting, and air-conditioning all helped undermine those community habits. But it doesn't take great sacrifice to regain some of them. All over the country, in neighborhoods of all ethnicities and income levels, residents connect as well as they do in Little Village.

In Chicago, multiethnic, ultra-educated Hyde Park shows an even higher interaction level than Latino, low-income Little Village. Curiously, neither Hyde Park's population nor its built environment are products of any deep tradition. Designed for wealthy merchants in the 1850s, the orderly neighborhood drew in scholars, administrators, and social scientists after the nearby University of Chicago was founded in the 1920s. In the 1950s, like so many city neighborhoods, Hyde Park fell apart. Prosperous residents fled, and the city's poorest took their place in the decayed housing. Only in the 1960s, after a controversial urban renewal project destroyed many of those buildings and drove out most low-income inhabitants, did Hyde Park become what it is now: a racially diverse, high-income community with the social interaction of a . . . Mexican village.

On the surface it looks nothing like Little Village. "The shopping is nonexistent," said longtime resident Laurie Bederow, a social worker.

"No one sits on the stoops, or hangs out the windows like they did when I was growing up in the Bronx, and women used to prop their elbows on pillows to watch the kids."

Hyde Park, though, has its proxies. Bederow's apartment lies spitting distance from Lake Michigan, a sort of aquatic town plaza where families, dog walkers, and joggers can get their exercise and people-watch at the same time. The University of Chicago, and its adjacent theological schools, constitute Hyde Park's nerve center, both as workplace and ever-changing bazaar of concerts, lectures, and workshops. Egged on by all those social scientists and seminarians, Hyde Park is, famously, activist: Bederow and her neighbors see each other constantly in a circuit of social justice activities, interfaith seminars, and meet-the-candidate coffees (all this social cohesion was particularly healthy for Bederow's former neighbor, the then–state senator Barack Obama).

All this examination of social connectedness, and the unseen ways it feeds our well-being, shed light on why I'd stayed so long in my own Houston neighborhood.

When Mike and I moved back from Central America in 1995, we were quickly smitten by Montrose, a shabby bohemian neighborhood five minutes from downtown. Though gay homeowners were beginning to beautify it, the neighborhood was dodgy, a haven for renters, transients, halfway houses, artists, bar employees, and journalists. It was a riotous, diverting place to live. Shortly after we moved in, the police knocked on the door to ask if we had seen a naked man with a blue turban running past. My friend Julie once rolled back her carpet to find a giant pentagram scorched in the floor under the Barca-lounger.

I truly fell in love with the neighborhood, though, when the bachelors moved in across the street. Every night around nine, the three sloppy single guys would assemble on their collapsing front porch and play poker. They drank, they gambled, they cackled over their private jokes. But they were also partaking in the area's communal night, along with revelers ambling to the Ripcord nightclub and the wordless, nocturnal Urban Animals, an in-line skating tribe.

As the child of a porchless Maryland suburb, I was fascinated by the way the card players lived outdoors and indoors at once. So when we bought our house from our landlady, the first thing we did was build a porchlike front patio.

The card-playing bachelors moved on; their replacements, Bill and Kirste, have proved even better. After rebuilding the porch, they now, more or less, live out there. Deep into the evening, I love to see the aura of their laptops, hear their civilized murmurs. "Why don't you move someplace bigger?" visitors to our not-that-small, 1,400-square-foot house sometimes ask. The short answer is, this is what we can afford. The longer answer is that it's a modest house with a spacious addition—our street.

Neighborhood connections, in other words, can be cobbled from all kinds of materials. What makes Little Village so unusual is its suggestion that urban poverty need not be a sentence for social dysfunction. We can't all own lakeside property near a university. But most Americans do have a sidewalk, or front stoop, or porch, over which we can make some decisions. The few who don't tend to be those who most need it. Among these are the residents of North Lawndale, now too dangerous for people to linger outdoors. After seventy years of arson and isolation, it's hard to see how the remaining neighbors could rebuild the area on their own.

"I don't know if there is a human on the planet who doesn't wish North Lawndale could have the same community attributes" as Little Village, one Chicago epidemiologist told me angrily. "We know the importance of the neighborhood effect. So why is there no intervention?"

It was 7:00 p.m. Clutching a cup of Acapulco shrimp cocktail, I thanked Andrés and left him watching the night. In just a few years,

I knew, this street might look wholly different. Little Village was gentrifying, and while this would ease out the gangs and litter, it was sure to disperse many who now live here. I wondered how that would change the habits of those who stayed behind, perhaps even Andrés. Some of Little Village's healthiest behaviors, it seemed, stemmed from nothing more than an old-fashioned attitude toward public space. I hoped Andrés would prosper, but keep his barrio habits alive. As the train slid off, leaving Little Village behind, I hoped, too, that I would remember to nurture those habits once I reached home.

7

How to Eat:

Vietnamese Monthly Rice

The Crash

After nine hours in a cubicle, lunch spent researching science camp for her kids, and forty ugly minutes on the freeway, Lana Khuong opened her front door and knew the truth.

She did not feel like cooking dinner.

This was a woman who had lived through the Vietnam War. She'd waited years under the Communists for a visa and built a new life as a Houston legal secretary. She did not lack fortitude. But, opening the door to her house where her hungry husband, sons, and two-year-old granddaughter waited, she felt her energy funnel away. She had pitched into the time of day when organizing even a simple meal can seem insurmountable. But the alternative—family members scattered throughout the house with snacks or sandwiches—seemed even worse.

Most parents have heard dire warnings of just what befalls families that don't sit down for evening meals. Their children earn worse grades, get lower test scores, dabble more often with drugs. They're prey to more asthma attacks and eating disorders. They are less resilient, for God's sake, to catastrophes such as 9/11. But those are just correlations. For first-generation Vietnamese such as Lana, scientifically proving the value of family dinner is pointless. Eating with others, no matter how late in the day, is psychologically, even spiritually, essential.

Not that it's easy. The Vietnamese template for dinner is also considerably more involved than the American one. Always, for instance, the meal must include a clear soup and steamed rice. There should be crisp vegetables, savory protein, tart pickles or salad. And rather than one hunk of protein per diner, meat or fish must be hand-chopped to bite-size chunks. No wonder Lana didn't feel up to the task.

I often felt that way myself, even when I hungered to slide down at a table with food waiting, warm and fragrant. After work I craved the chance to sit down and stitch the day's events together with people I love. But at six thirty or seven I didn't want to be the one cooking. As a result, too often when I finally pulled something together it was seven thirty, when the apex of a three-year-old's social skills is asking if she can leave the table and sleep. The difference, on evenings like this, was that Lana had a solution.

Fast Food

Monthly Rice Delivered Here, the signs promise from the window of Quan Di Tu, one of dozens of Vietnamese restaurants in southwest Houston. Inside the little shop, two hours before dinnertime, thirty-two-year-old Trang Nguyen is stirring a deep pot bubbling with fish broth. Dipping out precise ladlefuls, she decants the soup into plastic cups, each with a scrawled name on the lid. Those names are all that Trang and her business partner, Betty Nguyen, need for their next step. At 5:00 p.m., one of the women will disappear from their pocket-size restaurant, poising a cardboard box laden with Styrofoam containers across her solar plexus. For the next hour, she'll knock on the doors of ranch houses, lean over gates toward coolers, or open up apartments with her ring of keys to drop off the dinners the two women have just cooked.

This is home-style Vietnamese food. It has less oil, less salt, and more assertively redolent fish sauce than you'd find at a restaurant. It's cooked differently too. Braised and simmered rather than flash-fried, which looks more impressive but dries out faster, it will still be savory later that night, as leftovers for anyone who arrives home late. And it's much cheaper than takeout, because the ingredients are humbler, and because subscribers accept whatever menu Trang has chosen for them that day.

Thus, when Lana arrives home from work at six, the day's freshly cooked dinner is waiting by the front door. There's a nest of vermicelli, flecked with coriander and dried shrimp. The main course is simmered catfish, as comforting to Vietnamese as meatloaf is to Americans. Today's soup, dipped from the stovetop just a half hour before, is a clear broth flecked with shreds of chard and scented with star anise. Lana has even ordered dessert, a jiggly vanilla pudding dotted with green jelly cubes. All Lana has to do is set the table—making dinner happen is still up to Vietnamese women—and her husband, sons, and granddaughter can troop in for a hot family meal.

Com thang, or monthly rice, is the American version of a generations-old tradition in Vietnam. There, where women traditionally didn't work outside the home, com thang probably evolved with family cooks who prepared meals in their own homes and delivered. The custom branched out into a cottage industry, feeding scholars and soldiers who were far from home but still determined to eat as they would with their families. As more Vietnamese women entered the workplace, the custom not only changed but thrived. When Vietnamese refugees came to this country beginning in the mid-1970s, they brought it with them.

"Com thang comes down to taste and economics," Tran Van Hien, a University of Houston-Clear Lake computer instructor, told me. He has used the service himself, and his sisters, all doctors and all working mothers, use it now. "There's no point," he added, "after a long day of school or work and fighting traffic, to going home and cooking." Com thang is the Vietnamese answer to the six o'clock crash. In its traditional version, monthly rice is just-cooked, homemade food delivered to your house each day at dinnertime. It is dinner made from scratch, from ingredients bought that day in the market. And it's cheaper than a meal at McDonald's.

The Rules

In both the United States and Vietnam, com thang hinges on two core Vietnamese values: the importance of tremblingly fresh ingredients and the need to eat with other people. To serve these demands, com thang cooks in Vietnam have devised a varied repertoire of services. Most common is daily home delivery, like Lana gets in Houston. Clients decide whether to renew month by month. Alternatively, they may also stop by the cook's house or restaurant each afternoon and pick dinner up. A young man in the military, or a university student, might place a standing order for a full year.

Imported to the United States, com thang diversified further. In Orange County, California, stunning real estate prices have spawned an old-fashioned boardinghouse boom among Vietnamese American young adults. Their rental rooms often come without kitchens. Craving the food of their childhood, they sign up with the area's on- or off-the-books com thang cooks. The luckiest ones get meal deliveries from their own mothers. Three decades after the first refugees landed in Orange County, their children have enrolled by the thousands in area colleges. Mothers commonly cook a week's worth of comfort food—soups, catfish, pickled vegetables—and dispatch it in coolers on $5 buses.

Vietnamese Americans living farther from home have revived

another version of monthly rice. When The Pham, a photography editor now in his thirties, went to graduate school in Missouri, he couldn't find a Vietnamese restaurant. Armed with a name from his parents, Pham located one of St. Louis' handful of Vietnamese home-makers and hired her to cook his dinners—which he ate at her family table.

"I was paying as much for the family setting as for the fresh meals," Pham said. Back in Vietnam, shrewd homemakers care-fully screen the applicants for such meals, picking the ones whose work ethic and intelligence look most promising. Such a fellow adds ambience, naturally. But he might also marry one of the household's daughters. What better way for everyone in the family to vet him first? The suitor is nicely positioned too, able to assess his potential wife's personality, her parents' temperaments, and, it goes without saying, her cooking.

"That happens here in Orange County all the time," Anh Do, the vice president of *Nguoi Viet* newspaper, told me, laughing. Do's paper features an entire classified column of com thang providers and also hires them to deliver subsidized lunches to its staff.

Still, the whole idea of Vietnamese subscription meals—finding a contact, tracking down someone's home business—seemed, when I first heard of it, out of reach. If I'd thought carefully, I might have had doubts about the food too. My first sip of *pho*, Vietnam's fabled long-simmered noodle soup, was one of the experiences that made me want to stay in Houston when I moved here in 1996. But the pho joints I visited were tiny specialty businesses, and the only other Viet-namese dishes I knew were, well, restauranty. Tasty enough. But heart-seizingly salty, bright with cooking oil, and, especially when they were nothing more than a stir-fried handful of greens, way too marked up to buy with regularity.

So I didn't think much about com thang until almost a decade after a friend mentioned it. A lot had changed. Mike and I now had a couple of three-year-olds, I commuted to an office, and every night I faced the wilting challenge of trying to sit down to family dinner as I had loved doing as I grew up.

Settled now in Houston, I also had lots of Vietnamese friends. One, luckily, was Lana, a working mother who herself was on the hunt for monthly rice.

The Quest

"In fact, I'm looking for someone new," Lana told me the next time I saw her. It was always good to have Lana at work on your case. Compact, a faithful gym devotee, Lana is deliciously blunt and always, as I knew from watching her raise her sons, finds a solution.

Lana's com thang provider had retired a few months earlier at the age of thirty. Not, mind you, because she'd made her fortune. Com thang is not that kind of business, with its small clientele and vermicelli-slim profits. The cook, or rather her family, had succumbed to burnout, a common ending in this line of work.

Maybe, Lana and I agreed, an ad on Radio Saigon would net a good selection. "Searching for excellent com thang provider, individual working from home, southwest area," Lana wrote in Vietnamese. "Delivery preferred," she added at my request. A few days later she called me, chagrined. "I've been getting calls all day," she said, "but Vietnamese don't listen carefully! Every single caller has been *looking* for a com thang deliverer."

Had com thang somehow disappeared? No: it was alive and thriving. Only its logistics have changed, explained Ann Le, author of *The Little Saigon Cookbook*. Com thang had gone legit. "In the past few years in Los Angeles, there's been such a crackdown on health codes," she said. "You're not supposed to be cooking from home, of course. The result is that fewer cooks dare to run com thang operations from their kitchens." Houston, she theorized, might be feeling the reverberations.

But there was a second, more cheerful reason for the radio silence. Fewer com thang cooks have to deliver. In the past, ambitious newcomers barely factored their own countless hours of labor as a business expense. What choice did they have? In Vietnam, com thang providers were often former servants or widows scrambling to support their families. During their first years in the United States, most Vietnamese worked with the same desperation. By now, though, many have advanced spectacularly. Some are rich, even famous. The children of those refugee "nail technicians" and clerks are now buying the convenience store chains and nail salons where their mothers used to toil. They're doctors and lawyers and chemical engineers. They're also branching out into more creative endeavors: luxury shoes, like designer Taryn Rose, and even space travel, like astronaut Eugene Trinh. Fewer of them, in other words, need to labor in hot kitchens, sautéeing, steaming, and schlepping for fifty other families. And their kids and husbands no longer have to deliver for $1 to keep in business.

You can even find a variation of com thang in the deli case at big Vietnamese markets. The price is the same, $2 or $3 a dish. But some, Lana for one, wrinkle noses at this variation. The food may not be fresh, and is certainly prepared by more than one person. Real com thang is cooked by someone you see week after week, someone you can look in the eye to tell her you like her grandmother's soup. For that, you need to hunt down the minuscule com thang joints in storefronts and strip malls, the ones with three tables and a Magic Marker sign that says, in the world's least accurate translation, Fast Food.

Auntie Four's

How different, really, is com thang from takeout? Like many Houstonians, I am a Vietnamese food fan, every few weeks slurping a $5 bowl of pork-flavored pho. I sprinkle it, as I've been taught, with basil, cilantro, sprouts, and jalapeños. But according to my friend Dai Huynh, a *Houston Chronicle* food writer and trained cook, Vietnamese home-style cuisine differs from this entirely, in preparation, ingredients, and seasoning. To show me, she picked me up one day at lunchtime and drove me to a new com thang place she'd found. This wasn't a conventional restaurant, Dai cautioned. It was more of a way station for people to pick up their monthly rice. But it had three bite-size tables where we could eat while Dai schooled me on com thang essentials.

Auntie Four's Food to Go didn't bother with details like waiters or table settings. The little shop was designed for customers to grab and go. Right now, around 1:00 p.m., it was quiet. Most office workers had already come by on their lunch breaks or would start filing in around 5:00 p.m. Peering through the glass shield at the steam table, Dai whispered, "This is the real thing. You can't get what they have here in a restaurant. It's not showy or expensive enough. But we"— she meant anyone who'd grown up in a Vietnamese home—"can't live without these flavors."

She pondered our order. At the back of the steam table stood five white platters, each heaped with just-fried or just-roasted whole fish. There were mackerel, sardines, tilapia, and others I didn't recognize, each topped with frizzled fried onions or shredded herbs. On the heat, in a deep metal tub, chunks of beef and preserved eggs floated in a brown sauce. Another vat held pale chicken broth with bitter melon rings and pork nuggets. Other tubs held tofu in copper-sheened gravy and potbellied tomatoes stuffed with minced beef. A volcano of fried anchovies towered on a plate.

Altogether, there were three soups, and about ten other dishes to choose from. Except for the larger fish, each dish cost $2.

"Vietnamese food is all about texture and contrast," Dai said as we sat down to wait for the dishes she'd chosen. "Every meal, including com thang, has to include dishes that are salty, sour, crunchy, and soupy. And rice, of course. So"—a plate of vinegary bean sprouts with dark green shreds arrived, which Dai plucked with her chopsticks— "the sour part of the meal is this mix of fresh sprouts and pickled spinach. I adore this spinach. My mom used to make it and preserve it in a big jar on our counter." I pinched up a taste. The sprouts tasted familiar and refreshing, while the greens were fermented and musky. Together their effect was tonic. I helped myself to more.

"Now, this way of serving food: this is family-style," Dai said.

I wasn't sure what she meant. Doesn't every family eat family-style?

"At restaurants, or even in your house, Americans take their servings complete from the plate," Dai said. "You take the breast of chicken, or your steak, and you try not to touch the other food while you're doing it. But here"—she paused, prying a strip of catfish from a caramel-colored fillet—"you break off from the whole. Then you keep going back to get more. It's okay to double dip, and you are touching other people's food every time you get your own. It means a lot to us, eating this way. It is intimate. An exchange of energy.

"Watch out for bones," she added as I hacked off a wedge of catfish. The meaty flesh bristled with translucent splinters. "This is a dish that kids eat?" I asked.

"All the time. You just learn to be careful. If you get a little bone in your throat, eat some rice. That's what they told us when we were kids."

I tried a bite of the firm, light-colored flesh. It had been braised in fish sauce and syrupy, caramelized sugar, a combination Dai said was typical of southern Vietnam. The flavors were creaturely and delicate at the same time. The texture rolled, like good chocolate. I hadn't realized catfish had fat, but peering into the serving bowl, I saw a broad ring of it surrounding the meat. "You're supposed to eat that," Dai said. Good. I took more.

Dai grinned, expectations confirmed. "We don't get tired of this food," she said. "This is what our mothers made for us growing up. And after a while without it, even as an adult, you start to crave it."

The Table

Dai was improvising with her theory of energy transmission via catfish. But I was struck at how many first- and second-generation Vietnamese had the same notion. Communal meals, they said, are not just a pleasure. They are necessary for mental balance. Eating alone can actually foment psychological problems, Tran, the computer science teacher, told me. I'd never thought of family meals in quite those terms. But dinner in my own home, growing up, is without question the most distinct, consistent memory of my childhood. I can see it as if it were a play: each person in the same seat every night, candelabra always lit, the rubber Marimekko place mats for each child—lion for Adam, monkey for Jason, fish for Luisa, and for me a red hen.

Years later, when I was around thirty, my mother, in a spate of preemptive organizing, asked each of us to name the possessions we wanted after her demise. There was rash talk of printouts and stickers. In the end each person named one thing he or she really liked. For me it was the waxed, taffy-colored dinner table with the broad, upholstered chairs that we had occupied in formation for twenty years. I remember slumping with laughter at that table over my brothers' jokes. I stormed away from it to house arrests in my room. Uneasily, I tried to ignore the empty seat when my sixteen-year-old sister briefly ran off to Florida. I sat mortifyingly mute for an entire meal when my beloved sixth-grade teacher Mr. Carman joined us for dinner.

Even for the 1970s, when fewer women worked outside the home than today, those Kolker dinners were unusually elaborate. In the decades since, such meals have gotten ever harder to create. According to one influential study, Americans reported a 33 percent drop in family dinners between 1981 and 1997, in part because children's free time had dropped by almost twelve hours a week.

Yet we really are programmed to eat with others. And home-based family meals, a relentless cascade of studies show, are perhaps the signature habit of functional families. The quantity of mealtime that a family shares is the strongest predictor of low rates of behavioral problems and high academic scores—stronger, oddly, than the number of hours spent in school itself. The big question, of course, is whether family meals improve family functioning, or if families pull off nightly dinners because they are functional. For all the stacks of data pronouncing that dinner is magic, all we know is that it simply correlates to outcomes we want.

But the number of those correlations is striking. In *The Surprising Power of Family Meals,* writer Miriam Weinstein details a multitude of positive influences linked to communal meals. As she suggests in her subtitle, eating together can make us "smarter, stronger, healthier, and happier." She's not the only one to find such connections. Some are logical. Diet counselors, for example, say regular family dinners help patients learn what a moderate helping looks like. Families can supersize portions at home, but it's easier to make good decisions if a McDonald's marketing campaign isn't shaping the choices. Talking while you eat also slows a meal's pace, which in turn reduces consumption. Vietnamese cooking exemplifies this principle. You can't just wolf it down, because you're occupied prying, pinching, lifting, or ladling. This is probably rooted in necessity, not some ancient insight about weight loss. With fewer big trees for fuel, many Asian cultures chop ingredients for speedier cooking.

The weight control effect of family dinner may be self-evident, I thought, but the emotional part not necessarily. What about families that doggedly meet for dinner every night, only to repeat the same nasty fights? What about dinners that combust because someone is drinking? I was lucky to really enjoy my brothers and sister and parents and look forward to seeing them at the end of each day. But I remember with special clarity the pall on meals when we fought. Surely some families would be happier if they didn't keep climbing back in the ring.

But here the findings are counterintuitive. Even for kids growing up in volatile households, dependable family dinners create a continuity. They show how to keep a commitment, crucial for kids at risk of impulse-control problems such as addiction, research suggests. Eating together also seems to build survival skills for ordinary families. In a study of thirty-two families, a team of Emory University psychologists tried to gauge the long-term links between family meals and emotional resilience. The research was well under way when the 9/11 attacks shook parents and children around the country. When the researchers completed the next phase of their work, they found higher levels of emotional resilience in the children who'd been eating dinner regularly with their families.

The explanation was not what you might guess—that those kids had calmer, more organized parents, for instance. Instead, the resilient kids enjoyed a strong inner "locus of control," the sense of having some power over what happened to them. People with an external locus of control believe their lives are buffeted by luck or by others more powerful than they are. But people with an internal locus of control believe, to an important degree, that they can shape their own lives.

While families talk in all kinds of situations, they tend to share the most information at mealtime. And the kids who ate regularly with their families, the Emory researchers found, knew measurably more about their relatives, from the pioneers to the wastrels. That family knowledge correlated strongly with internal locus of control— and with the kids' resilience. Hearing stories at mealtimes, the lead researcher wrote, built "perspective-taking, critical thinking, theory building and relationship roles within the family."

All these links reflect correlation, not cause. We really don't know why regular family meals are so closely linked to good health. What's appealing about dinner, though, is how neatly it attaches our psychic needs with the unmistakable demands of our bodies. At the end of the workday, we know we want to get home. We want to eat. And we want to tell someone what happened that day.

We'd feel even better, many Vietnamese think, if we could satisfy those requirements with wholesome food that's cooked, if not with love, at least with care.

After reading one too many reports on the consequences of neglecting dinner, I resolved to step up my own patchy efforts. Causation or not, why not elbow my way into the statistical winner's circle? The problem was that I got home from work at six thirty or six forty-five, and Mike, the better and more efficient cook, got back even later. It then took at least forty minutes to cook dinner and set the table, a process I admittedly slowed by observing my grandmother Lydia's ritual of transferring all condiments from unsightly jars to saucers. Just as ritualistically, at 7:15 p.m., Anna and Elena would start to fall apart.

Often enough, maybe three nights out of five, I managed to pull something off. But two nights out of seven, it was 8:00 p.m when we finally got to the table and I would laboriously begin my stories about relatives and their life-altering personality traits. Elena would drape herself in an upside-down U on her chair and Anna would find it more comfortable to digest standing up. Mike would find it a teachable moment for what Texans call "home training" while I frantically flipped through my latest journal article clearly stating that for maximum effect, family dinner must be positive and relaxed. In general things got loud.

I know now some of this was because I was new at coordinating meals for four people. But it also reflected the limits many parents, no matter how adept, face when women work and home fires must be lit anew at six each evening. My mother, the author of those leisurely, laughing dinners I remember so well, hated putting them together on a deadline each night. It's part of the reason I was so slow to learn cooking myself.

Working women find that deadline even more draining, a researcher named Reed Larson concluded in 2001. Intrigued by how families used their time, Larson looked at fifty-five two-parent working and middle-class families in suburban Chicago with at least one child between fifth and eighth grades. He even rigged up a way to measure these parents' emotional state throughout the day. Using what he called the Experience Sampling Method, he fitted out research subjects with pagers or alarm clocks for one week. When Larson signaled them at random moments, the subjects reported what they were doing and feeling.

Averaging their answers, Larson found that women with full-time jobs outside the home reported more happiness in their daily lives than stay-at-home mothers. Single mothers were the exception, reporting most happiness at the moment they returned home. But for most of the working women, those with partners and children, shortly after opening the front door, "their average emotional state fell substantially."

Larson labeled this the six o'clock crash.

But what did it mean? That working mothers didn't want to see their own kids? No. What plagued them was the specter of cooking dinner. When the inquisitive Larson paged his subjects at 6:00 p.m., he found mothers were arriving home to the general expectation that they would make supper. "It was not uncommon," Larson noted, "that our ESM signals during this period found a wife working in the kitchen and her husband relaxing in front of the TV."

Fifty-five families is a small sample, and I think more men experience the six o'clock crash than Larson's research conveyed. But the crash itself—that part, I knew, was authentic. Lana, an experienced cook whose children were all nearly adults, knew it too. That's why com thang was invented, Lana said in one of our frequent phone calls.

"Under pressure," Lana said, "I just cannot cook well. I need time and concentration. After work I'm just too tired. It's too much. And I still have to take care of my baby granddaughter. Com thang is a lot of convenience."

Then she said, "I found someone for you."

The Triumph of Tiffin

Teetering on an appliance box poised on a three-legged stool, I poked a spatula at a kitchenware shelf in Viet Hoa Market. The vast store had a full aisle devoted to dried mushrooms in gift boxes, and another department with nothing but household shrines. But there was no one to help me reach the humble object of my desire. I was trying to reach a stainless-steel stack of canisters known as a tiffin box. In fact, I wanted eight of them. I needed these tiffin boxes before dinnertime the next night.

The tiffin box, called a *portaviandas* in Latin America, where it's also used, is an engineering triumph. Four shiny cylindrical serving bowls snap, one on top of the next, into a metal frame with handles on top. The containers are sealed with a latch that swings over the very top. Made of tin or aluminum, they look like sturdy Towers of Pisa without the lean.

Traditionally used to transport home-cooked meals to the workplace, they're still in heavy rotation in Latin America, India—by the millions—Thailand, and Vietnam. The word, though, is British: it means "light meal." The modern, metal version of the boxes was supposedly popularized by colonial British in India who insisted on bringing their own food to the office. That was before, it goes without saying, chicken tikka masala became Britain's most popular dish.

For generations, tiffin boxes also transported monthly rice. But when I visited the restaurant that Lana told me about, I discovered it had abandoned them entirely. Dismayed at the idea of sending an armada of Styrofoam boxes to sea every week, I asked the owner, Trang Nguyen, if I could do com thang the old-fashioned way.

Sure, she answered, amused. She directed me to Viet Hoa, where she bought her own kitchen supplies. At about $16, the price of a tiffin box was very reasonable. For my purposes, though, the bill was going to be higher. Because I lived forty-five minutes away from Trang and her partner Betty's neighborhood, they couldn't afford to cross town to drop off one meal with the usual $1 surcharge. Four customers, though, would work. So I signed up for four com thang meals to be delivered to my house at 7:00 p.m. every Friday. Trang and Betty asked for my food preferences (lots of fish, little pork). Now all they needed were four starter tiffins to fill and deliver, and four clean empties to collect when they did the drop-off.

Price for a meal that feeds four: $7.

"Seven? Like this?" I wrote the number on a bit of newspaper. "With delivery? For a four-course dinner?"

"That's right," Trang said. She was a small, burly woman with a weathered face, and the fact that she'd learned English in Texas gave her speech a pioneer twang. "We've only been in business six months," she explained. "Delivering food, and keeping the price competitive with everyone else, helps us get new customers."

She ushered me to the kitchen to meet Betty.

It was a tidy and maniacally organized little space, smaller than the kitchen in an average ranch house. Every single cooking object was neatly stacked or wedged in one square island of shelves. Almost no food was in sight. The day's meal had been cooked by 11:00 a.m. and was already spooned into the ten-compartment steam table out in front. The only edible in the room was a large, cooked lump of brisket in a Chinese-style bowl.

As a closed-circuit TV of the shop flickered over her head, Trang sliced the meat with a cleaver. She'd been cooking in restaurants like this since she was nine. Trang's family and Betty's family had owned a restaurant in Saigon together. Now they were both in their early thirties: Trang came here as a refugee twenty years ago, while Betty arrived only in 2005. In the United States, Trang first worked at American and Vietnamese restaurants as a waitress. "In my time off, when the other waitresses went home, I went to help in the kitchen, just to learn," she said.

A few years after arriving here, Trang divorced. Waitressing, nail salon jobs, and six years of moonlighting as a com thang cook from her apartment kept food on the table for her kids. Then Betty arrived, and within months, married Trang's older brother, who worked at a toothbrush factory. The two women got along and, they found out, had complementary talents.

"Betty is good at appetizers and soups," Trang explained. "I specialize in chicken with lemongrass, salted ribs, vermicelli and noodles with beef in spicy sauce." She made her way to the stove, where she slid the beef slices into a big pot and turned her attention to a wok the size of an umbrella. Turning up the flame, she tipped a cup of garlic, onion, and lemongrass into some already-shimmering oil.

The year before, Trang said, she noticed an ad announcing a com thang business up for sale and decided to buy it.

"I don't want to work for other people. I don't want to worry about losing my job," she said.

Inviting her new sister-in-law to be a partner, she took out loans from family and friends and they founded their com thang shop. Now the two women worked fourteen hours a day. Betty got in at 6:00 a.m., Trang a couple of hours later. They cooked together until 11:00, when they took turns darting out to deliver as many as forty lunches a day. This worked because, except for me, all their clients lived within a few minutes drive.

Trang's dream was to buy a real, sit-down restaurant, one that would cater to non-Vietnamese as well as Vietnamese. This place, though, cost much less than an actual restaurant: just the two of them, with no waiters to pay, and no silverware or glasses to buy.

Neither Trang's kids nor Betty's new husband could stand the place. "Our family members say this is too much work," Trang said, fishing lemongrass slivers from the wok. But they didn't understand the independence it represented to them, the just-within-reach step up from waitressing. Owning your own business is the most important thing, Trang said.

"Yeah, yeah, yeah!" she trilled, doing a dance step in her high-heeled flip-flops.

Delivered

After eight hours staring into a screen, an hour editing, and twenty minutes reading proofs, I called it a day at work and drove home. When I opened the door, the girls were mountaineering over Mike's exhausted form, which was prone on the floor. But gleaming on the stove stood four shiny tiffin boxes, each packed with a full family meal cooked by someone I liked. Garlic and shrimp filled the air.

Trang's brother had stopped by just a few minutes earlier to deliver the meal, Mike told me. Now the six o'clock crash, the dread at the end of the day, had been supplanted by . . . Christmas.

"I want to see, I want to see," Anna yelped, clambering forcefully over Mike's skull. I wanted to see too. Gathered around the table, we took turns unlatching the tidy cylinders and peeking inside. My neighbors Bill and Kirste knocked on the door as we looked. They had signed up for one of the weekly tiffins in my subscription, and I'd invited two other neighbors to take home the remaining pair. Somehow, though, the suspense of unpacking one savory dish after another, and the gradual unfolding of a meal that none of us had lifted a finger to create, turned a takeout plan into a party. Spreading the $28 banquet across the table, we opened the door for the rest of the neighbors and sat down for a feast.

My grandmother Lydia would have approved. Unpacked, the tiffin boxes made a neat line of bowls, each embossed with sunbursts, leaves, and flowers. In the middle, I'd plopped a glass of lacquered chopsticks. The first bowl contained chicken broth, practically clear, with Asian greens swaying under the surface. When I sipped it, the soup was so light that it seemed more like tea than a food. That's intentional. Vietnamese frown on consuming cold drinks, which they say shock the body and congeal fat inside the gut. Instead, at mealtime you're supposed to sip a light broth like this between morsels.

With four different tiffin boxes holding eight different entrees, the morsels were varied. I'd been surprised the first day I'd dropped the boxes off, when Trang asked me what foods I liked. I'd thought I had no choice. But it's part of the com thang cook's business, I learned, to prepare enough options that clients don't get bored or forced into eating something they dislike. "Ask him what's good," Trang had said as I considered the unfamiliar dishes. She nodded at a very lean young black man eating at one of the tables. He waved me over.

"Try the catfish, and the beef with lemongrass," he suggested. "That's what I'm having. I come here every day. I'm a dancer. I teach at a studio just a few blocks from here—ballroom, tap, kids, hip-hop. I can't afford to eat a lunch that makes me sluggish. So I come here and for the price of a meal at McDonald's I get a different lunch each day."

Plenty of com thang subscribers do let Trang and Betty decide for them. They know the food will be good. For me, the sense of surprise made the meal even more tasty. It was a throwback to being a child.

Much of the fun of restaurants is the chance to be a pasha, determining every detail of what you eat. But at least as seductive, I found, is the comfort of being parented: the sensation that someone knows what you like and will make it for you. All you need to do is show up and be fed. On the table that first night were two fish dishes, because Trang already knew from my lunchtime visits that I loved seafood. One tin held chunks of pungent grilled sardine; the other, Trang's version of that swoony caramelized catfish. I peered like a birdwatcher as Kirste, a sparse eater, tasted the catfish. I saw her empty chopsticks pause in the air. Her eyebrows rose.

"This is good," she said as the fish sauce, the soy sauce, and the melted sugar all registered. "This," she said a second later, the alchemy deepening, "is amazing."

Mike, meanwhile, sampled the grilled sardine with a martyred look. "I'm from Amarillo," he told the group. "I don't trust fish." But he soldiered on, this time to the barbecued pork nubbins, each with a tiny rectangular cap of fat. Mike's tragic look vanished. Even to the most American palate, these savory Chiclet-shaped morsels were irresistible. The ribs' tiny size tempered their decadence. Vietnamese typically salt meat and chicken heavily, to a point that makes the same food impossible to eat in supersized portions. It's a strategy that heightens a protein's bang per buck. Rather than gobble meat in costly slabs, you learn to savor one bit at a time, balancing the saltiness with soup and white rice before going back to the next bite.

As I picked, slurped, and surveyed the table for my next serving, my neighbors tried to figure out the economics. You could see, on examination, how a smart homemaker could make a profit here.

One of the yummiest entrees, buttercup-yellow eggs scrambled with bitter melon, must have cost Trang merely pennies. Not only was it satisfying enough for a main course, but a Vietnamese diner would have appreciated the melon's medicinal qualities. Not everyone could have cooked it, as Trang did, just so: the eggs soft but not runny, meaty but not tough. That is where the art came in.

Trang's most onerous expense at that time was likely not food but gas. Still, we reckoned that the $1 surcharge for each tiffin box added up to twice what Trang's husband needed for a round-trip to my house. Added to that, I was so incredulous at the low price of the meal that I tacked on a $1 bonus per box. Since tipping isn't ordinarily part of com thang protocol, Trang was actually earning more delivering to us than she would in her own neighborhood.

But our tabletop calculus neglected two crucial elements: the sliver-thin profit margins all this hard work produces, and the hours of planning and labor needed to keep the business afloat. It's these ingredients that prompt most com thang operators to quit just about the time they get their footing. They are constantly replaced by entrepreneurs willing to snap up the tiny kitchens and storefront shops they leave behind.

A few days later, it happened: I craved more of Trang's cooking. As Dai predicted, the caramel catfish was excellent the next day. So were the sautéed greens, the eggs, and the surplus white rice. No pork ribs remained. I took absurd, thrifty pleasure working through the various tiffin boxes in the refrigerator until every last scrap was consumed. But I was also savoring the memory of that impromptu dinner. It had been, I reflected, a feast interesting and pretty enough to serve to six guests, yet cheaper than a meal for two in a restaurant.

Mike was less enthusiastic. We have such different taste that it's taken years, and a reliance on his excellent cooking, to come up with a family cuisine we both like. Convinced he would contract a fatal vitamin deficiency without pasta, he felt neutral about the merits of monthly rice. But that, Lana told me, is a liability at her house too.

"My sons don't like com thang," she said after I reported on the first delivery. "And I guarantee you will get sick of someone's else's cooking after a while. But the point is, I use it on and off. I stop for a while, I get my energy back, and I cook again. Then when I need a break I sign back up." Nor, Lana warned, does monthly rice totally smooth the obstacle course of assembling her teenagers, husband, and toddler granddaughter for a meal. "We still fight over setting the table and cleaning up," she said. "The kids still come home at different times, and they don't honor my trying to sit down together." But at least organizing a meal is more a personal challenge, and less a physics equation.

In this challenge, the com thang cook and the consumer are allies. Unlike many extremely cheap services, com thang isn't, at its heart, exploitative. It's a confluence of interests between an ambitious small business owner and working parents who may be only a few steps ahead economically. The people who use com thang know fluidity is part of the system. Cooks, meanwhile, know it's a grueling job, but with luck, one that pushes them to a goal: independence, a better restaurant job, or maybe a less labor-intensive small business. I wondered, in fact, why of all the immigrant entrepreneurs in this country, only Vietnamese have developed this particular mix of services.

Indians, it's true, use a service akin to monthly rice, in locations from London to Silicon Valley to Mumbai. It's traditionally delivered in tiffin boxes, and based on Indians' similar pickiness about food provenance and flavor. The great difference is that these hand-delivered meals are almost always lunches. Though wholesome and cheap and homemade, they do nothing to ease the pressure on working women. To the contrary, the mother is usually cooking the food back at home, outsourcing the delivery so she can focus on fixing dinner.

Other variations on the monthly rice formula—cheap, fresh food cooked by someone you know—may well exist in this country on a small scale. When I last talked to cookbook writer Ann Le, she was hot on the trail of a rumored Honduran dinner delivery business in Brooklyn. Though I'd seen the signs a thousand times, I was oblivious to com thang's existence until a Vietnamese friend tipped me off. I would now know to hunt for Fast Food signs in Los Angeles, San Francisco, northern Virginia, Washington, D.C., and Philadelphia, all Vietnamese hubs.

Maybe, though, it is time for other frugal and talented cooks to broaden the niche. Though food historians don't seem to document anything like com thang in U.S. culture, I would wager numerous stones remain unturned. In any case, Americans excel at spotting good ideas from elsewhere and fixing jet engines onto them. An aspiring chef wanting to show off her creativity, an artisan working with a community farm alliance, or a pair of single mothers renting an old Domino's: if any of these could make meals that were cheap and fresh and real, I'd consider subscribing. As it was, at least one of my crash hours between 6:00 p.m. and 7:00 p.m. had been transformed. With monthly rice, for the most modest sum imaginable, Friday night dinner was now a ritual I craved all week long.

8

How to Collect:

The American Money Club

M Y FRIENDS WATCHED silently as I closed the living room curtains. It was February 2007, and after six weeks of recruiting,
I'd finally assembled enough takers for my own Vietnamese savings
club. A hui. Though based on the half-dozen huis I'd visited or heard
described, this one was undergirded with some very American con-
ventions meant to reassure the nervous pioneers.

Detailed explanations. Codified rules of conduct. *Many* e-mails.

To a few members who, reasonably enough, worried about someone absconding, I quietly promised to cover their losses if something
bad happened. For the rest, I'd composed a letter—well, a memo-
randum of understanding—outlining how, exactly, the thing would
work. Two hundred dollars a month. No checks or IOUs. Show up
in person (to forge bonds of personalized trust where none really
existed). And, I promised, the whole operation would last only one
hour, from 8:00 p.m. sharp to 9:00 p.m., every second Wednesday
of the month. Unless, of course, you were having fun and wanted to
stay longer.

Even so, as I turned from the window, my guests' expectant faces
unnerved me. This clearly wasn't a party. Otherwise all these boozy,
animated writers and artists wouldn't be sitting docilely in a circle like

Cub Scouts. So what are we doing? they seemed to ask mutely. Technically, of course, we were collecting accounts payable and disbursing them according to a predetermined rotation. But abruptly I was seized by dread. Of all the risks I'd tried to anticipate, I hadn't considered boredom: that I might have inadvertently trapped a dozen lively and extremely busy people into the equivalent of waiting in line at Home Depot.

It began to dawn on me how many other potential calamities I had failed to imagine: Someone going insane, forgetting or just denying his debt. A freak hurricane tearing off the front of the house just as we took out our cash. A maniac bursting in to grab the money from the winner's hands. In an act of God, I wondered, would I still have to compensate everyone? Gazing around the living room, I realized I would. Even if my guests didn't demand it, I couldn't afford, literally, even the faintest residue of unease among this many friends.

It was scary even to contemplate. We weren't Vietnamese, but we were closely connected, most of us mingling, if not every day at the newspaper then in a kaleidoscope of parties, small-business endeavors, and neighborhood encounters. And here I was, mixing money and friendship. No good, I'd always believed before, could come of that.

About half of the people I originally invited, and who turned me down, certainly agreed. My friend Lucinda, a lawyer pretty much game for any new social endeavor, sounded so anxiety-fraught about the experiment that, even though she was willing to try it, I told her not to. It would make her miserable, wondering for a full year if the hui, and maybe our friendship, would go up in the same sulfurous fumes as the failed investment club she and her husband had just fled. Mostly, though, people just couldn't see the profit in it—especially when I explained that there *was* no profit, financially speaking. *I don't see the economic advantage over the rate of interest derived from traditional financial instruments,* one acquaintance e-mailed. Another crafted a spreadsheet comparing a hui's (nonexistent) earnings to those of a 401(k) gaining 10 percent in the same time period. It was as if we were talking on crossed phone lines, and it was easy to see why the communication might falter.

In the last quarter century, Americans have been presented with countless new tools for investing our money. It was hard to convey that a money club wasn't a financial tool at all—any more than a clay jar under the goat pen. In our FDIC-protected economy, even a bank account makes better financial sense.

A hui was instead a behavioral tool, one that, obviously, not everyone needed as much as I did. But corralling social relationships into the same space as your financial life is in any case close to taboo for Americans, and rightly so most of the time. Few are the friendships–turned–business partnerships that survive to retirement. Investment clubs, probably the most accepted way to mix friends and finances within the middle class, require an even higher grade of financial trust than huis—too high, in fact, for me. Part of the security in a hui, to my mind, was its modesty. The profit—such as it was—would be psychic.

I definitely needed the psychic help. With a decent salary in an inexpensive city, I didn't have any debt besides a mortgage. True, child care and taxes devoured most of my wages, but I was diligent about that 401(k), in a good year socking away 12 percent. What I hated, though, was all the money I managed to waste.

"I want," I told the group in my living room, "to stop spending my money on $10 boxes of salad and $4 tea bags." They laughed, more at me than with me. Apparently not everyone felt quite as victimized by the snack industry. In fact, as we piped up our motives in a 12-steppish litany, I was struck by the variety of reasons drawing us to this one, rather rigidly structured, Asian ritual.

The Mexicans—and there were five altogether, including my mom, Marielena—barely thought twice about joining. When I'd first broached the subject with each, they were the only ones who hadn't plied me with questions, including, What is the point?

"Oh, that's a tanda," said my interpreter friend Elena Vega, who grew up in Mexico City. "We had them in my apartment building. You'd use them to buy a TV or a blender." She could use the cash for visits to her mother, she told the group. But the truth is Elena Vega relished any cozy, wine-drinking gathering, evidenced by her role in charity auctions, a cabal of bocci enthusiasts, and a *rosca de reyes* cake party every Christmas.

My movie producer friend Yissel, also born and bred in Mexico City, instantly signed on as well. "I want a new laptop," she told the circle. Always prepared, she unfolded a computer printout with a Chinese character on it. "I looked up *hui,*" she said, passing the handout around. "One of the definitions is secret society."

Jack, a tall, debonair ad man, was a third-generation Mexican whose ancestors had been San Antonio ranchers. He knew all about tandas too. "Yeah, I'll do it," he'd said casually as soon as I asked. To the group at my house he said simply, "It's nice to have help saving. And a glass of wine is always welcome." He planned to feed his IRA.

I looked curiously at the next player: my mother. True to her word, Marielena had moved here from Washington, D.C., six months after the girls were born. She and I now flowed in and out of each other's social activities much as we had when I lived at home thirty years before. But I wasn't quite sure, myself, what the hui meant to her. Of all of us, she needed it least. For the twenty years she'd been on her own, she'd lived comfortably and extremely sensibly on money my late dad had left her. She'd seen it earned faithfully over a forty-year marriage, and treated it with love and respect. Most likely, of course, she joined the hui just to be with me.

Or not. "I joined," Marielena declared, in her NPR diction, "because I have always wanted to be in a club."

My neighbor Kirste, a sylphlike graphic designer, spoke next. She wanted to save for taxes, she told the circle. "Seems like everyone I know who's self-employed is in the same boat," she said. "It also seems a good opportunity to force myself to save money. Kind of like having a workout partner."

Her husband, Bill, owner of a high-end media installation business, admitted he joined mainly to humor me.

Next came Sarah, also a neighbor and a year into a reporting job at the *Chronicle.* "I'm in my twenties," Sarah said, "and it's just really hard to save. I don't know how to do it."

I wasn't sure that the last couple, my friends Bob and Hanan, felt like explaining their reasons at all. They were last in the circle, and they were also going to be the first to receive the payout.

"We need a lump sum to pay off a bill fast," Hanan had said after I outlined the rules in the *Chronicle* ladies' room. "If I join, can I collect first?" Absolutely, I told her. It was my hui, so I could make decisions like that, traditionally speaking. But I also was thrilled. This was a real, urgent need for no-interest cash—the reason why money clubs developed in the first place. Typically, in fact, it's the leader, or *chui-hui,* who needs that lump sum, which is why she forms the club. Because I am personally motivated by treats, surprises, and showy desserts, I wanted my payoff last. Nothing would make me happier than actually seeing the hui fix a problem. Though I didn't ask exactly what the bill was, I could guess. Hanan and Bob, old-school reporters who never lost their passion for journalism as an instrument of social justice, had endured years of medical bills after an out-of-control car almost killed Bob. The financial and emotional pressure, as long as I'd known them, had been merciless. I'd never known any family who lived with such prolonged stress, or, despite it, worked and laughed with such valor.

"You don't have to say your plan for the money," I hastily announced, as clumps of $200 began streaming Bob's way. But no one was listening. Something odd and sublime was occurring. Whatever Bob and Hanan's particular need was, I could see before my eyes the growing power of a jolly reprieve. Jolly, because it wasn't a gift of richer to poorer, or a loan compromisingly granted, or indeed a loan from one person to another at all. It was a fully entitled, no-strings attached, cash advance delivered as cheerfully as a birthday gift. It formed a blanket that threatened to fall from Bob's knees. The cash totaled $2,200.

"We don't mind saying what it's for," Hanan called from across the room. She waved her glass of wine in a toast.

"IRS," Bob said. Staring down at the unruly mass of twenties and fifties and hundreds, he was glowing.

Who wouldn't be? We could see a millstone, the kind of expense that haunts without any compensatory good memories, just . . . going away. And not because it was fobbed off, but because someone's planning and good reputation made it possible. It was a rare sight. Power, relief, bounty, good wishes: all manifest right in front of us, in a heap so big that Bob had to scoop it up with two hands.

Three months later, shortly before the hui was to start, Mike wandered past our bedroom and saw me hunched on the floor, poking a blue bottle with a wire hanger.

"What on earth are you doing?" he said.

"It's my money bottle. I'm getting my cash for the hui," I answered, clacking the wire. It was a bit like that boardwalk game where a metal claw dips in a box to grab a fresh $20, but always collapses at the moment of contact. My money, however, could not be called fresh. Over the past three months, I'd begun taking a delicate relish in collecting stray bills—the two singles in change after a Whole Foods run, a folded dollar found on the dashboard. Twirled into cigarillos, each went in the bottle. Getting them in there took thought. For the first time in years I was paying deliberate attention to small scraps of money, denominations of one or five I once dismissed as too small to keep careful track of.

I was an American Express girl, in any case. For close to two decades now I'd used the charge card as often as I could, even for glancing sums that provoked open hostility from cashiers and taxi drivers. I liked the paper trail of my spending. And I liked paying in full, collecting frequent-flier points like Green Stamps. When it came to money, I craved streamlining. Paycheck into bank account, payments to vendors electronically whisked out. By 2007 I'd become the kind of parent whose children had never spied her using currency. Money, the girls believed, was a small card with which you got stuff. There was always one of it, and it was indestructible.

So the money bottle proved an unexpected lifestyle enhancement. I began finding it easy to change my minor but squandersome daily ways. The $10 to replace a forgotten lunch: no longer frittered. I envisioned those dollars going instead to the bottle, accounting for one-twentieth of my month's tally to my friends. I was damned if I was going to waste it on a salad. Almost immediately, I began thinking ahead in ways I never had before: hoarding bags of fish and peas in the freezer at work, finding a tiffin box in which to spoon leftovers each morning.

Because I intended to squeeze savings from better habits, rather than divert money from other savings, I tried not to pay the hui from my salary. Instead the bottle slowly filled with single bills fished from my pockets and book bags. I began to fancy my savings as old-fashioned butter and egg money, and myself as a resourceful, leathery farm wife like Elizabeth Taylor's mother in *National Velvet*. Unhealthily, possibly, I positioned the money bottle high on the bookshelf in front of my bed where I could lay eyes on it first thing on awaking. The sight, I found, was uplifting.

At this moment, however, shortly before my guests were due, the bottle sat on the floor right in front of me. I could not pull one dollar from its murky depths. With thirty minutes to go, I seemed mainly to be twisting and spindling the contents.

"Give me that," Mike said, grabbing the hanger. He had stoutly refused to join the hui, which violated most tenets of his practical and generally catastrophic worldview. "Look," he said. "I'm a photographer. We can't fake it like you reporters if something goes wrong. I need to anticipate everything that can possibly fall apart."

But he couldn't stand to watch me manhandle cash or misuse even a primitive tool. Fifteen minutes later, $200 in small bills lay smoothed and lovingly stacked next to the bottle.

"That was kind of fun," Mike said. "It really has that smell of money. You know, sweat, people's pockets, their underwear."

I knew what he meant. Although my transactions now were as sanitized as if I were Queen of England, the rescued bills instantly reminded me of when we'd worked together in Haiti. There the bills known as gourdes seemed to have the texture and warmth of human flesh. Too precious to be risked in anything grabbable like a purse, most money traveled the country jealously tucked inside pants and brassieres. When you touched it, you could almost feel the charge of the countless, minute, urgent transactions it had fueled. Now, clasping my slowly accrued American dollars, I imagined I again felt a charge. It was almost as if I were holding something alive, a small creature. This was my projection, of course, but it wasn't mine only.

An hour later, gathered around my dinner table, it was time for me to collect and count up the money. By now, our nervousness had melted off. Our links actually resembled the ones that keep ethnic money clubs stable. Members of the same small media tribe, even those of us who didn't know each other knew people in common or wanted to talk about the same events. Flushed with this new sense of comfort, I set to counting. After three months, we'd settled into a sensible system in which I, as the leader, collected, counted, and wrote down everyone's contributions. Then I passed them along hand to hand to the month's recipient. And for the third time in three months, performing this perfectly sensible task, I became completely addled.

"This money's from Jack," I began. "All right. Twenty, forty, sixty, eighty." Wait—had I counted two twenties stuck together as one? Best to make sure. Start again. Unaccountably, my hands were shaking, and they had been last month as well. "Two, four, six, eight, ten, twelve." I stopped again.

Had I counted the twelfth bill or was it coming up next?

The others at the table ate cheese and crackers and jeered. "Watch out! I saw her put twenty bucks down her shirt!"

But I really was flustered. The more I tried to thumb through each person's cash in an orderly fashion, the more jittery, the less methodical I seemed to get. I managed to count up Jack's $200, but stalled again on Yissel and Carlos, who had passed down a combined brick of $400, and yet again on my mom, who sent along a bank envelope. "My $200 is in there, and there's also $200 for you, for paying my dog sitter," she said as it made its way toward me. I had to go through it twice.

Finally, two times in a row, I demonstrably counted $2,200—the correct sum for our pool, which included nine people at $200 each and one at $400. But I'd taken forever. People were fidgeting with boredom and I felt, obscurely, less than confident about my handiwork even now that it seemed to be right.

"Make sure you count it," I said wearily as I handed the bundle to Elena Vega, the week's collector. Everyone clapped. It really was fun to see all that dough in the hands of its new owner. You half-expected someone to set a paper crown on her head.

I snapped a picture with my iPhone. A wine bottle began a pilgrimage along the same route the money had traveled. "What're you going to do with it, Elena?" someone called.

"Acapulco," she said. "Acapulco and taxes."

But the next morning, at the respectful hour of 10:00 a.m., Elena called. "Ay, Claudia, that was so much fun," she said. She hesitated. "But listen, could I ask you something? Just between us—please don't bother mentioning it to the others. But could you look around and see if there's $200 from the hui anywhere? I realized when I got home it was missing."

Oh no! I remembered my pitiful stop-and-start accounting all too well. "You didn't count it?"

"No—I was too embarrassed," she said. "I know! It's just that it felt so rude having to confirm that my friends had paid me."

How could I fault her? Much as I thought money didn't intimidate me, I'd utterly lost my head trying to count it that night. Large sums of cash, it seemed, really did possess energy, stimulating and bedeviling those unused to handling it. Now I thought back to the previous week, Kirste's turn. As rattled as I was, trying to count straight, I hadn't paid much attention to Kirste's own troubles that night. One, two, three times she had counted before she could finally confirm she had the right sum. After hanging up with Elena, I circled the house. Immediately, I found her $200 on the coffee table where I'd set it, thinking it was my mother's repayment to me. Elena laughed when I called and told her. But I was horrified.

The next month, I asked Bill, who has a staff, hires contractors, and buys expensive equipment, to count on my behalf. He did it unimpeachably. Elena and I joked about the mishap, but we also picked it apart seriously. Loath to even say it aloud, we wondered if, in spite of running our own businesses much of our adult lives, some undetected force of female socialization had thrown us into a tailspin when handling large piles of money. Kirste, who'd been self-employed for ten years, later confessed she'd asked herself the same thing. It didn't sound quite right, but there was no doubt that some conflict about all that cash had snakebit my ability to count beyond twenty. And money conflicts, as my father used to say, are rarely just about money.

In my own case, I decided, the issue was not gender. It was unfamiliarity. I needed to relearn that even small bits of money had power. The hui was forcing me to confront this. *Cash slows you down,* I wrote in a note to myself a few months later. *It's a reminder—in front of witnesses—of how you manage your money. You touch it. It's real.*

Handling my friends' cash, it occurred to me, was like chatting while preparing dinner with an enormous cleaver, or peeking over a lethally rocky gorge. I'd never attack someone with the cleaver, of course, and I wouldn't hurl myself off the cliff. But I could, and the results would be cataclysmic. It seemed a bit Freud for Freshmen to deduce that deep down inside I wanted to run away with everyone's money. But I do think I feared, really feared, harming people I loved—or having them doubt me—by making an error. Usually our shortcomings are well known to those who are close to us, and they can step, judiciously, out of the way. People joined the hui because they trusted me. But who had ever gotten a chance to assess my dollar-counting skills? In a money club, some of the most common flaws—forgetfulness about dates, a tendency to spend your last dollar—become potentially dangerous weapons. Maybe that's what made my hands shake.

On a visit to Astro Dry Clean, I told Dan about our various travails counting the money. She smiled gently. In traditional Vietnamese huis, she said, it's always women who manage the cash. Husbands hand their pay to their wives, who carefully portion out an allowance for them and steward the rest. Men, it's believed, just don't have the knack.

I had learned to harvest the money bottle the night before the hui. For my humble goal—controlling stupid impulse buying—the money club had worked amazingly quickly and well. When the guests came now, the table was set just so, with two sets of each snack at each end to allow everyone to graze as they pleased. Each month, the previous month's winner would supply a few bottles of wine; Yissel, a virtuoso cook who'd once prepared an all-white mole for Gabriel García Márquez, reliably supplemented my frumpy Costco vegetable trays. At the end of the table, waiting for Bill, was a little Indian notebook with a blue Baby Krishna on the cover.

In the past few months, I'd discovered, counting the $2,200 had completely lost its anxious charge. But though I could now matter-of-factly riffle the cash like a teller, I preferred having Bill take the ceremonial role. People were always imposing such duties on Bill. His calm, silverback-gorilla authority strengthened the hui's pleasing routine. It had become like church for the unspiritual, with ritual, amusement, and gentle fiscal discipline as the earthly rewards.

This month, I was enjoying an additional reward for my efforts. At the cost of exactly $2,200, I now sported a set of space-age iBraces®. The brand-new German orthodontia customized painful but undetectable hardware to the insides of my teeth via computer.

"Guess what. I yoothed my hui money for brathes," I announced as the group settled around me.

The response was universal.

Um, why?

Well, mainly because now I could. At forty-four, I told myself, I was showing signs of wear and tear. Shouldn't I shore up the infrastructure before true decline set in? And after contributing my share to the hui, I had a $2,200 payoff the next month. Money amassed by virtuous scrimping, it was not, technically, classifiable as robbing the girls' college fund. Symmetrical choppers, I told myself, were an investment in keeping up appearances.

*   *   *

In January 2009, the end of the money club was drawing near. I began to ask the players for their thoughts.

I knew I wanted to continue. I'd figured, though, I'd gotten more out of it than others. The low-stress festivity—I was still serving up those Costco vegetable platters—softened the pinch of saving $200 extra each month. I liked, too, this distinctive species of peer pressure. I wasn't striving to overtake anyone, just working to maintain a standard I'd decided in advance was in my own interests. And the money paid to maintain my friends' respect in the end came right back. I'd even found the hui multitasking for me. I'd started traveling for research and was spending weeks at a time on my own, rather than around a conference table with hyper-articulate coworkers arguing about current events. I hungered for the hui's social contact.

The time away from work was also unpaid. Even living frugally, zero income is zero. For six months, I'd expected, I wouldn't be able to save. Yet, thanks to the preexisting obligation to my friends, I had to set money aside.

Though I hadn't planned it, and though it meant scrounging the dregs of the money bottle, or getting partial loans from Mike, the money club's mechanism had taken care of me. Whether we were successfully self-employed (like Bill), comfortably retired (like my mother), or occupying an odd limbo of temporary unemployment (me, on leave), $200 looked and felt the same in all of our hands. Pulling it together, even if I was scrambling for it now, was a comfortingly respectable feeling.

By now, several original members had left town. Yissel and Carlos had moved to Mexico City. Elena Vega and her husband had gone to the Reuters bureau in Cuba. Sarah, the young reporter, had used her hui money to move to Iowa City, where she was beginning grad school. Leveraging peer support to finance her education, Sarah may have been the closest of all of us to using a hui for its traditional economic purpose.

"New tasks are supposed to be good for your brain," she said. "I think that's socially true too. I liked the shared financial risk. My dad was really doubtful about it—why not just put it in the bank? But I think it's like some people who are incredible athletes and can't understand how hard it is for other people to get off the couch. It really helped me to save, and also transition to living on a grad school salary."

From Havana, Elena Vega e-mailed with her usual good cheer. "I have to say I am very organized about money, have something put away, no credit card debt," she wrote. "So for me, the hui didn't really help in any particular way. In fact, I found myself jealous of the people who came later. After I got my money, it was hard to keep paying that $200 with nothing to look forward to. But I liked making the new friends."

The rest of us decided to start a second year. A doctor friend joined, relishing the *National Velvet,* butter-and-egg aspect. She planned to surprise her husband with a Prius down payment. A financial reporter from the *Chronicle* wanted in. So did James, my cherished former boss on the editorial page, who'd retired during one of the paper's increasingly frequent paroxysms of downsizing.

My prize catch, however, was Mike.

"What finally changed your mind?" I asked.

"You made me," he said.

There was some truth in this. But it's not as if all my other suggestions carried that kind of weight. Eventually, Mike conceded that, like most of the other self-employed players, he wanted to put aside money for taxes. Perhaps another detail pressed the scales too. A year ago, the hui's general risk and loss of interest or investment earnings seemed to defy economic good sense. Now the state of our 401(k)s challenged that logic. People were starting to leave their monthly retirement statements unopened. My paper, the biggest in Texas, had carved its company match to almost nothing. Even more jarringly, the paper had shed dozens of staffers, well-established ones, twice in the past year.

We chattered about the upheaval at our next meeting, opening purses and wallets as we talked. Gradually, I noticed everyone looking at Mike. Opening his black photographer's bag, he was methodically fishing out bricks of money and stacking them on the table. His entire share, in new one-dollar bills.

One night in March, I leaned on the patio doors to let in the warm air. I wanted to see my friends. Earlier that week, every hui member who worked at the *Chronicle*—including me—had been laid off.

Chicaaaaa! Yissel e-mailed when the news lightninged to our friends in Mexico City. She offered any help she could give. But there was nothing to do. An American industry was collapsing and the fissures had merely opened later in Houston than elsewhere.

Still, it was hard to believe. The *Chronicle*—the rich, slow-moving giant of Texas? We'd all known layoffs were looming, but few of us really guessed the extent. No buyouts this time. A full one-third of the writing staff: gone. And this time, the third round in eighteen months, many targets were prominent staffers, people who'd maybe flattered themselves they were immune. Dai, the food writer who'd won more national awards than anyone else at the paper. Maria, who analyzed and reported on finance in two languages. Hanan, who'd been writing about women's issues for twenty-five years. Gone, too, were nearly all the editors I'd ever worked for, including the foreign editors who had sent Mike and me to Haiti, Cuba, India, and Japan. Almost all my friends, in one day, dispersed. The brash, talky tribe we belonged to had expelled us. I remember my hands and feet went cold that afternoon, and recalled reading somewhere that our body temperatures plunge when we are excluded from groups.

A few nights after the layoffs, friends threw a party for Hanan. The hosts were cheekily calling it her debut, and they'd laid out a Cajun feast in one of the most poetic gardens I'd ever seen. Old oaks reached above us, and a little Mexican fountain splashed in a corner. It was so proper and deserved, I remember thinking, toasting Hanan in this beautiful place. Yet we all looked awful—almost ghoulish. Everyone was in shock, of course. Later, a few months after the layoffs, people actually began looking great: younger, skinnier, rested. "The *Chronicle* face-lift," a coworker called it. But the party, or whatever we called it that night, felt bleak. It was a farewell to a creative life, attended by dozens of people who'd just lost their own.

I saw several of the same faces the next week at the hui. Yet to my imagination, they looked different. Solid. Those who hadn't been with the *Chronicle* looked good to me too. I felt soothed just seeing them. Maybe the difference was that here, every one of us was exactly the person we'd been a month ago: simultaneously lenders and debtors, each person a crucial contributor whose absence would cause a crisis.

Even the hui's drawn-out schedule now seemed to reflect the decency of a different era. You showed up, you did your part, and (barring a sociopath robbing everyone blind) you would be rewarded. A simple enough formula, except that for almost 10 percent of American workers that year, one that no longer balanced out. A year ago, the money club, with its odd interpretations of words like "investment" and "winner," had seemed tantalizingly foreign. Now it represented something utterly conventional: the promise that you could play by the rules and not be betrayed.

We sat at the table in our familiar spots. Bill and Kirste, fully at home at our place (Kirste cast the deciding vote on our paint), settled in by the wall. Near the head of the table, but not at it, sat my former boss James. As always, I plopped down across from him. For the first time it hit me why I liked this spot. James and I had sat across from

each other, at just such a long table, every morning for four years during editorial meetings. With eight other staffers, most of them now
gone as well, we'd parse the day's papers and decide how to pontifi-
cate. (It really was a fun job.) Though it hadn't occurred to me before,
the money club re-created that experience—the faces, the routine, the
lively opining. I felt fortified tonight by the sense of normalcy, and my
friends' expectation of normalcy from me.

It was Bill's turn to collect. After a year and a half of gathering
cash by the fistful, I could have coolly done the accounting myself.
But there was something pleasing in the ritual of passing our money
down to the silverback. With his nickel-colored hair and unflappable,
small-town banker's manner, Bill embodied the hui's comforting pre-
dictability. With each month that passed successfully, each member
had built an invisible line of credit. We all trusted each other so reflexively by now that, coming in, we just concentrated on the wine and
the party. It was, as my mom had described it that first day, a club.
But unlike most clubs, your true right to be there kicked in only after
you'd proved yourself, month after month, by coming through for
your friends.

Bill peered at the green fan in his hand. "Hey, I think you're short
five bucks," he whispered to me.

"No, really? I counted it out," I said, vexed.

"Yup, missing five."

I dashed upstairs, praying that the spilled guts of the money bottle would add up to five ones. I actually didn't have any other cash
than that. There was money in the bank, in funds and certificates and
inaccessible accounts carefully tended for the future. But after three
months of unpaid leave, cash flow was thin. I felt nervous enough
about it that I'd made sure two weeks back that the money bottle contained all the money for my share.

Four ones and four quarters, in my earring dish. I hurtled down
again, smiling sheepishly.

"Sorry," I told the room.

Bill smiled and recounted. I had my back to him, extracting a wine cork in the kitchen, when he called, "Oops. You're still short."

"No!"

"Missing five."

I whirled around, mortified.

What was wrong with me? I'd long ago overcome my nerves about handling cash. Thoughts forking like lightning, I mentally scanned for household nooks that might yield $5 more. An IOU, after all, was not an option.

Then I reexamined the faces around the table. Bill and Kirste were giggling into their wineglasses. Mike, his arm draped on my mother's shoulder, was laughing openly. So was she. They were pulling my leg, of course. Because it was still easy to pull.

More than a year into the hui, I could now resist the mindless spending that once had plagued me. I could lick a thumb and count $2,200 with the best. But cash, to me, would always have a life to it, an electric charge that no card or automatic deposit could ever possess. Touching, counting, passing money hand to hand, all seemed to link me physically to the choices I'd made to collect it—and to the other hands it had touched before mine.

Anchoring

O N A RAINY night in Atlanta, at an unremarkable airport hotel, a jaw-dropping cavalcade of men and women are sailing into a ballroom. Burly African men, resplendent in skullcaps and lavish brocade tunics; towering women in mermaid gowns and metallic headdresses looming two and three feet high. All are immigrants from the Nigerian village of Agulu, and all belong to the Institute for Agulu Development, whose members gather from around the United States once a year to feast, dance, and reminisce for three days.

This year they have come with a mission—one no other Nigerian Americans have yet attempted. They want to revive a beloved custom that has helped fuel their extraordinary triumphs in the United States, but that they have neglected to pass on to their children.

The Agulu natives are Igbo, an ethnic group famous for their entrepreneurship and their dislike of central government. The Igbo are also known for assigning every one of their members to an involuntary association called an ogbo (pronounced, imperfectly, as "oar-BUH"). No one signs up; everyone born in the same year is in, automatically. Were you born in 1958? Welcome to the 1958 age grade. Born in 1972? You're in the 1972 group. In some villages, the age grades may span three or five years; in others, they're defined by momentous events, such as the Biafran war, or the year the electricity came. But regardless of the way your ogbo is designed, it will shape both your opportunities and your responsibilities for the rest of your life.

The Agulu doctors, academics, and architects dancing at the Atlanta hotel tonight still participate ardently in their ogbos. Many first came here decades ago, as students in the 1970s and 1980s, when Nigeria was flush with oil money but lacked higher education to match. Equipped with fluent, British-inflected English, most of these well-heeled young men and women thought they were here temporarily—until a military regime upended the government and their safety back home.

Agulu's exiles leaned heavily on each other in those days, especially on their age mates. Miles and years away from the village, their old ogbo network still bound them wherever they were, like a lifelong fraternity. But perpetuating the exact tradition in this country seemed hopeless. Numbers, mostly, were the problem: there were rarely more than a couple of Nigerians of the same age in any one city. In the American fashion, the immigrants had to rush to earn a living. No one lived in a community that in any way approximated Agulu.

But a few years ago, Sampson Oli, a professor of criminal justice in Florida, felt a sweep of regret. Though he kept in close touch with his age mates, and diligently took part in their projects, he knew his children would never grow up with the same kind of bond. It wasn't just the missing social network that made him sad. He wanted his children to feel the obligations an ogbo built, the sense of duty that lasts a lifetime.

Almost from the moment he can walk, each child in an ogbo is expected to contribute to the community. It's extreme Montessori from the start. At age ten, in addition to romping with other children, you're expected to sweep the *ilo*, or central meeting space. As a teenager, you are meant to build and patch huts for the needy. As a young man you guard the village, providing at once a cheap police force and an institution that keeps you and your peers out of mischief.

But the true genius of an ogbo unfurls in maturity. Fueled by a brilliant mix of team spirit and competitiveness, ogbos keep their members deeply engaged in community service for life. Wherever they are in the world, age mates expect to keep in touch with one another in order to improve life in the village. They pave streets. They hire doctors. In a country where government routinely fails to provide, ogbos may be the most dynamic force in development.

"There is something important about being responsible for your community from an early age," Oli told me wistfully as institute members filed into the hotel ballroom. Now he and his friends, he said, were determined to adapt the ancestral system for their American kids.

After a year spent traveling from Los Angeles to Nashville to Painesville, I came to understand that the immigrant customs I most admired all resembled the ogbo. They were not valuable merely because they were traditional. All cultures come up with some good traditions and some miserable ones. But the ones that remained relevant filled a gap. They met a desire or a need that the inhabitants of the world's richest country still share with those in the poorest. They worked because they channeled universal impulses, changing them like wind or water into energy.

The fundamental insight of the cuarentena, for example, is that rest, companionship, and transition time are as critical to new mothers in the United States as to women on the remotest mountain in Mexico. In some ways, they are more critical here, because we have so few rituals attending those needs. Instead, we've developed a communal expectation that the weeks after a baby's arrival must be an ordeal. I remember walking through my neighborhood one summer day when a woman I knew staggered out of her house dazed and disheveled, as if she'd just left a plane wreck. Smart and entrepreneurial, she had just a few years earlier opened an art gallery near my house.

When I heard she'd had a baby, I assumed she was bustling happily inside her bungalow, absorbed with whatever mysterious activities new mothers did.

But that's not how she described it. "This is rough," she said. "No one tells you what it's like. I'm alone all day in there. Now I see why Mayans raise their babies communally." As much as any Chiapas villager, she could have used a cuarentena's mix of care, companionship and a smattering of peer pressure to make sure she really rested.

American women, let alone American men, don't hear much about the first weeks of motherhood. In an embarrassing display of my own ignorance, it never occurred to me that day to ask if I could come in and help. I thought it would be intrusive. Now, though, I'm evangelical. If I know someone who is expecting a baby or planning to adopt—adoptive parents run the risk of postpartum depression and anxiety too—I ask who will be helping out. Physically and emotionally, I'm now persuaded, those first forty days should be sacred. If you mother the mother, then she, the baby, and the whole family will be healthier.

But even though pretty much every traditional society in the world is familiar with this idea, I stumbled across it only by accident. Other mothers, fathers, and babies would have an easier time if doctors, policy makers, and employers treated the cuarentena weeks with the seriousness they deserve.

Assisted marriage is another old custom that reflects surprisingly current emotional insight. I have to say I resisted the idea at first, averse as I am to any notion of checklists or coercion in love. But in the months I worked on this book, I was startled at how immediately my American-born friends of all generations grasped the idea—and loved it. They were right. Most of us eventually long for a life companion. Why hide it? Why leave it only to chance?

In our society, we have accepted a trade-off: young people enjoy education and adventure in exchange for late marriage. But after thirty, the search for a life partner can be punishing. Romantics though we are (and as I write this, fifty-two-year-old soap star Lorenzo Lamas has giddily announced his fifth engagement, to a twenty-three-year-old), Americans also respect efficiency. Plucking from two traditions, young South Asians here have shucked off the oppressiveness of arranged marriages—but still see the value of getting help. In talking to them, I gained some serious respect for what it takes to supply this help.

Screening suitable boys or girls is not for the dilettante! Yet there's also no reason it must be a job only for DNA-sharing relatives. So many Americans feel closer to their friends than their biological families. Openness to assisted marriage, I think, would encourage more of us to be honest about our emotional goals—and to choose people we trust to send over good candidates. It's the loving eye, not the biological link, that makes these searches work for so many South Asians. That, and a carefully tended little black book. I plan to keep one myself—maybe I'll get another chance as a screener in twenty-five years.

Efficiency and effectiveness are easy sells in this society. But many of the practices I admired most traded on a less-appreciated quality: what Spanish speakers call *calor humano*, or human warmth. When I first found Betty and Trang's monthly rice business, I marveled at its practicality. I couldn't believe it was possible to get fresh meals, so cheap, delivered to my house. It took me even longer to understand the full value of what they purveyed. "You know the people who cook for you. And they want you to like what they make," a friend pointed out. "You're not buying from a teenager who's spitting in your hamburger in the back room." I savored the dinners Betty and Trang made because they were tasty, because they showed up at my door, and because I liked the women who cooked them.

Then, as Lana predicted, I took a break for a while. When I abruptly found myself with more time and less cash, I tapered off on the com thang. A few months later, when I went back, Betty and Trang were gone. They'd sold the business to another family. The catfish was still as mouthwatering, but they didn't deliver, the couple's daughter informed me, translating for her parents. Now I pop by when I can, gathering Friday dinner or impromptu lunch with the one com thang aspect that has become permanent: my metal tiffin boxes. I had, at last count, a dozen, and that doesn't include the ones given away as gifts. I use them to stash leftovers, haul cupcakes to school, and pack picnics, never tiring of their pert design and perfect sustainability.

If I lived closer to a Vietnamese enclave and could get delivery, I'd still subscribe. And in any of the other cities where Vietnamese congregate, I'd make sure to scout the closest "Fast Food" shop. But I also know that if an enterprising American cook in my neighborhood could supply her own down-home, freshly made meals for four, I'd happily pay double the $7 I'd paid Betty and Trang. It would still be cheaper than pizza. And most importantly, it would be real food, cooked by someone who cared.

Caring, of course, takes numerous forms. In 2011, Yale law professor Amy Chua detonated a national tizzy with her tale of browbeating her daughters into musical virtuosity. I couldn't see the point. In China and Korea, I knew, the whatever-means-necessary approach also includes beatings. "With something more creative than a belt, though—maybe involving kneeling," a Chinese American friend opined. But this extreme pedagogy reflects a foreign educational landscape, where a decent college education is desperately hard to reach, and economic progress absolutely depends on it.

The result may be straight A's or prodigious feats at Carnegie Hall. It might also include burnout, stunted innovation and leadership skills, and high suicide rates. Middle-class Americans can demand better. For all the flaws in our school system, it aims to educate the

most economically varied array of kids on earth, and that demo-
cratic spirit has enriched many old-fashioned techniques. When
Jews emigrated to the United States, their rigorous Hebrew afterschools helped give the same, seemingly mysterious edge that Asian
afterschools do today. The immigrant kids got more hours of study
time, a serious peer group with whom to learn, and the mental agility
that comes of knowing two languages. It was America, however, that
induced these Jewish families to offer afterschooling for the first time
to their girls.

Today, Korean hagwons also deploy traditional tools we know
really work: adult engagement, peer support, more hours on task. And
they offer all this enrichment preemptively, not after the students are
floundering. At the same time, the hagwons are evolving as well. The
best are placing less emphasis on the rote learning that's still common
in Asia and more emphasis on critical thinking. All this afterschooling
isn't free, of course. But it still costs far less than private school—especially in the early years, when all you really need is a slightly older
student tutor, or perhaps a talented Indian mentor on Skype.

There's a deeper social benefit to it too. Low-income public schools
improve with a certain percentage of middle-class kids in the student
body. The kids thrive on the peer effect, and the school culture overall basks in the attention of engaged, affluent parents. Even teaching
improves, because better teachers are drawn to schools they sense are
more prosperous.

Before I began working on this book, the whole idea of preemptive
tutoring was foreign to me. But it's a good example of an immigrant
tradition that speeds its users toward American goals by allowing
adjustments en route. Blatantly copying my Asian and South Asian
friends when I signed the girls up with Tess, I had no intention of
forcing them to afterschool five days a week, or employing the yelling cure if they fell short of academic perfection. All I wanted was
for them to learn to sit still and feel entitled to be mathematicians.

Will their weekly talks with Kerala catapult them to calculus? I have no idea. They're six. But I am grateful for the personal attention I see them receive. And I'm inspired to know there's more in my power than I'd guessed to get the most from public school.

There are other lessons to learn from Little Village, where some of the healthiest communal habits barely register as traditions. Apartments are cramped; parks are scarce. Zooming down the sidewalk on skates, passing the twilight on the front stoop, or strolling to shops doesn't seem "traditional" to immigrants: they're just living life as they once knew it in Mexico. Together, though, these habits create an alchemy that Americans with a lot more choices want too. Something about street life in this barrio actually creates a safer, healthier environment than Little Village's threadbare economic status would ever suggest. And it costs nothing to emulate.

As soon as I got home from Chicago, I eyed my house differently. The front step—there was no stoop—I realized, was better real estate than the entire back patio. Now I make it a point to loiter there. As the milk-crate men demonstrated, this is a pleasure. Taking the air outside your door is the least labor-intensive form of community building in existence. Yet people see you, and it bonds you. "I've watched your girls grow up, you know," a neighbor recently surprised me by saying. She lived in the townhouse across the street, but I didn't even know she spent much time in town. "I saw their first steps in your front yard. I heard their first words in Spanish."

My reaction surprised me too. "Tell me everything you remember!" I said. While no one wants to live their entire lives in the front yard, it feeds us, emotionally, to be witnessed.

From lung function to street safety, it also feeds physical health. "Outside is better than inside," the asthma specialists say. So do the obesity doctors. And unless your neighborhood is already too dangerous, law enforcers agree too. The neighborhood effect in places like Little Village seems so pronounced, in fact, that while individuals should factor it into their housing and lifestyle calculations, governments have a stake in encouraging it. Incentivizing sidewalk-building, zoning for small stores, and houses with porches or street-friendly space in front costs little, but can pay off handsomely in public health and safety costs.

After visiting Little Village, I also started thinking more about what I call middling relationships. Like shoppers whose selection of apples is a fraction of the array our grandparents enjoyed, I tended to pick my relationships from just a few bins. There were emotional intimates, relatives, work friends, and professional relationships.

Biodiversity, though, is good for us. Nineteenth-century Americans regularly dined on pigeon, lamb, turtle, goat, deer, duck, and buffalo as well as beef, chicken, and fish. Colombians in the Andes savor nutrients from a variety of potatoes vast as the shampoo selection at Wal-Mart. After watching the array of social bonds that immigrants cultivate, I'd say many of us lack diversity in our relationships. What do you call a sister-in-law who brings you breakfast for forty days? The sibling with whom you share a mortgage, but not your personal life? The neighbor you confidently lend $200 a month, but never see for so much as coffee? Really, I thought, these were all varietals of friendship. The immigrants I met understood their uses—they had to, in order to survive.

The Jamaicans I stayed with were connoisseurs in this domain. They cultivated family relationships in ways I'd never considered. One of the strongest memories from my teens is of standing with my parents near our house in Maryland, and my mother saying, "How nice it would be if you kids came back and lived here when you're adults." I recall it because it seemed unthinkable—depraved, even. Until recently.

Our house was sold long ago, after my father died. It was a roomy old house, in a good school district. It would have been easy to expand. Although I don't share a roof with my mother today, she does live down the street. Thirty years ago, I could never have guessed how much fun it would be.

"That old idea of yours made sense," I recently told her.

"You're misremembering," she said mildly. "That was your father's dream, not mine." My dad—a psychiatrist who devoted his career to freeing patients of the burdensome past. From the same work he must have known there's nothing healthier than being near the people who help us thrive. Nature doesn't mandate that we fall out of love with our relatives. Common sense, Jamaicans would say, dictates that sometimes we'll be happier *with* them. I'm not truly sure if I would be. But I wish I hadn't absorbed the twentieth-century notion that living with parents was a script for, well, *Psycho*.

Less wedded to the nuclear family, immigrants and the children of baby boomers enjoy far more options. College without debt? Decent house payments? The extraordinary advantage of doting grandparents? Recently my daughters declared their intent to live together when they grow up and place Mike's and my room in the middle of the house. I told them it was an excellent plan.

In the end, though, it was the money club that most transformed my definition of normal. The clubs are not a substitute for banks: I still faithfully revere professionals, contracts, and regulated institutions. I'd venture to say most migrants learn to love them too. There's nothing like losing your savings to a marauding militia, or seeing your business bled dry by gangsters, to make you appreciate the FDIC. It's also hard to live in Houston, the city that spawned Enron, and pile all your financial eggs in one basket. I wouldn't invest more in a hui than I was already wasting on blunders like $10 salads.

But the money club did prove a magnificent saving machine. Oddly, the behavior-modification part was most impressive when I was flush. Prosperity is like a fast current of water, rushing you along and sweeping small expenditures from your mind before you can really examine them. The touch and talk of cash made those transactions real again. When the torrent dried up, being mindful was easier. Each expense stood like a boulder on a dead creek bed. The hui, a particularly large rock, loomed in my vision weeks in advance.

"I'm surprised no one backed out after the layoffs," an investment banker friend said. "They must have really enjoyed it."

"We *couldn't* back out," I said. I could hear my voice rise just considering it. "We all owed each other. It was nonnegotiable."

The hui's power lies in that mix of financial and emotional bonds. Once, when I first began writing about refugees, I proposed a story about a money club to a women's magazine. The top editor didn't just hate it. She declared the idea dangerous. Indeed it was—which is why anyone who starts a hui, and who is responsible for its outcome, ponders hard whom to invite. Choose well, though, and the successfully shared risk transforms into shared self-respect and a special social bond. "We're keeping on, aren't we?" a neighbor asked me anxiously recently as the last month approached. "I'm addicted."

The practices in this book are like intricate irrigation systems, each calibrated over centuries for a specific climate and crop. That they've adapted so well to the United States suggests they channel some universal impulses.

The power of social parties is one of the strongest. Introverts or extroverts, humans evolved to need approval from the rest of the pack. Probably thanks to the Puritans, Americans mainly think of parties as an indulgence: letting our hair down, shedding the responsible workaday self. But for the traditional societies that send migrants here, parties can be incredibly effective at enforcing good behavior.

Over-imbibing aside, social gatherings bring out the best in us. We clean up a bit, arrive when expected, and do what we can to amuse. When people exercise their party manners, they're less prone to whine or shirk. That's why Americans used to routinely hold parties for daunting projects like quilting or barn raising. And that's how a Vietnamese money club works now. The endorphins from hobnobbing with friends soothe the pinch of handing over your money.

I'm using "party" in a loose sense. For many struggling immigrants, a party consists of little more than a pot of beans in someone's kitchen—and the mysterious electricity of face-to-face contact. Chopsticks clicking over a shared platter of catfish have the same spark.

Americans, with our super-programmed daily schedules, often postpone having anyone over until we have the time and money, and maybe the new addition, to do something really nice. But we underestimate our need for time with the pack. According to research in the newly trendy field of happiness, "the short answer to the question of what makes people happy is this: other people," writes Tina Rosenberg in *Join the Club: How Peer Pressure Can Transform the World*. Joining a group that meets once a month, she notes, boosts happiness as much as doubling your income.

The smartest immigrant practices also capitalize on the urge to invest. It's an odd word, I know, to use in the context of 37 million people who mostly come here from poor countries. But precisely because they lack financial capital, they tend to be wizards with social capital—the relationships that accomplish many of the same things as money. As with any investment, there are risks. Ask anyone who's fled a neighbor-on-neighbor riot or civil war.

But in general, social capital is so powerful that immigrants typically lavish great energy on building it with their neighbors, parents, churches, and families. Latinos, whose incomes are lower than those of most Americans, nevertheless invest heavily in time with extended family and other social networks. Though native-born Americans used to do this as well, today one-fifth of us regularly visit friends and neighbors and three-quarters don't know our next-door neighbors at all.

The more that goes into relationships, naturally, the greater the payoff. Spend forty days cooking chicken soup for a mother, and she might do the same for thing for you. It's only in recent decades, though, that researchers have really measured the tangible benefits of such investments. They're considerable. In a 2002 study of 137 couples, for example, mothers with highly satisfying friendships suffered lower rates of postpartum depression.

And although many of them spring from the world's most traditional places, the practices I saw all granted some kind of *permission*.

You're not imagining it: babies are tiring. Rest.

It's normal to want a life partner. Ask for help.

No human can manage a freshly cooked, perfectly balanced, four-course meal after work every night. Get a subscription.

How alluring these offers must sound in poor countries, where the roar of the collective often drowns out one person's needs. But we Americans, who are so bent on self-reliance, can get pretty starved for permission ourselves. Asking for help usually trails after some kind of failure. Maybe we would feel less depleted if, like immigrants, we instead turned to friends, neighbors, and family in pursuit of success.

A few days after finishing my research, I treated myself to a morning at the girls' school. My mother was already there. Through some dark art I could never have mustered, Mike had goaded her into leaving the house each morning at seven thirty and tutoring for three hours a day. A cult of personality quickly boiled up in the six-and-under set. When I got to the cafeteria, kindergarteners were hurling themselves at my mother's legs as she tried to pour herself coffee. She was chatting with the lunchroom custodian, a Salvadoran woman who had a soft spot for her too.

"Just look at your mother!" the lunch lady cried when she saw me. "So strong! She's just like my mother who lives with me. These old people are indestructible! They're made of iron!" Leaning on her broom, she added, "You know why? We take care of ourselves. Forty days in bed, that's what we do. We don't mess around when we have babies. No going out to the mall."

Then she raised a finger. "Mark my words. The generations that come after are different. They're weaker. They won't live as long."

Someone give this woman tenure, I thought. Not only had she just summed up decades of research on the immigrant paradox, she'd articulated the theme of a recent Brown University symposium: "Is Becoming American a Developmental Risk?" The good habits many immigrants bring with them, in other words, are not rocket science. They're based on common sense, the outcomes intuitive. But even though these traditions promote values we Americans treasure—entrepreneurship, maternal health, social bonds—they tend to fall away after a generation or two of exposure to U.S. life. Their positive effects fall away too.

The Brown symposium suggested that this now plays out in schools. Children who are immigrants themselves, and the young children of immigrants, show more academic engagement and higher aspirations than their second- or third-generation American peers. According to one study of national databases, foreign-born students who come to this country at an early age show better health and avoidance of such risky behaviors as drinking, drug use, and teen sex. Factor in all the obstacles many families face—lower incomes, isolation, poor language skills—and the kids' relative success really does seem paradoxical. Except for two things: They come from cultures where survival was their own responsibility. And, as immigrants, their families have already shown the gift for spotting the main chance and grabbing it.

These traits have always characterized immigrants. First-generation Americans have been more likely to be self-employed than their native-born counterparts, at least since 1880. And they're defined by their work ethic. As political scientist Francis Fukuyama points out, "[Who are] the true bearers of Anglo-Protestant values . . . who in today's world works hard? Certainly not contemporary Europeans with their six-week vacations. The real Protestants are those Korean grocery store owners, or Indian entrepreneurs, or Taiwanese engineers or Russian cab drivers working two or three jobs in America's free and relatively unregulated labor market."

So it should be no surprise that 95 percent of U.S. immigrants are employed. Growing up in a different country equips people with alternative ways to solve problems—one reason why the foreign-born score higher on creativity tests. Nor should anyone be surprised that immigrants are almost a third more likely to launch their own businesses. Google, eBay, and Intel were launched with immigrant cofounders, and more than 25 percent of patent applications in recent years have flowed from immigrant imaginations. Between 1995 and 2005, one out of every four U.S. tech and engineering start-ups had foreign-born CEOs or chiefs of technology.

Yet not all is well with the second and third generations. Signs of a health and behavioral slide have surfaced among the children and grandchildren of numerous immigrants—the very offspring whom immigration should help most. In research on both Hispanic and Asian students, for example, the foreign-born Asian students outperformed their second- and third-generation peers academically, and the foreign-born Latinos accelerated faster, at least in the elementary years.

What's going wrong? Perplexingly, researchers suspect it's the influence of U.S. culture. In their groundbreaking book *Legacies,* sociologists Alejandro Portes and Rubén Rumbaut surveyed thousands of adolescents in immigrant families. They found that the more years they lived here, the more urgently the youngsters wanted to break with their parents, speak only English, and emulate longtime Americans. Even language is a double-edged sword. English, so essential to join U.S. culture, is closely associated with Latinos staying in school and enjoying higher earning prospects. We know it's indispensable for fully taking part as a citizen. At the same time, English proficiency is a marker for other, pernicious behaviors like smoking and eating fast food—the habits of longtime Americans.

"It's a bit of a twist," the director of the National Longitudinal Study of Adolescent Health told the *New York Times*. "Linguistic isolation is a positive thing because it slows assimilation . . . [and assimilation can mean] adopting unhealthy behavior and risk factors from which they are protected by their own culture."

A paradox indeed. To fully participate in the culture they sought out, first-generation immigrants need to keep living like . . . immigrants. Being an immigrant is not, after all, any one nationality. It's having a backstory in a land that forced resourcefulness, joined with an individual drive to better the future.

It's what being American was, just a few decades back.

I admit I was thinking strictly about my own needs when I began asking people, "What's the smartest habit people from your country bring here?" But as I explored the traditions in this book, I was struck by the delicacy of their insights into human motives and what the body and psyche really need to be well. All for little or no cost. Now I think the kids and grandchildren of immigrants should be encouraged to pose the same question to their own parents. And while it's not our custom to dwell on the past, maybe native-born Americans should start asking too.

It was near midnight at the airport hotel, and the Agulu Institute was in glorious swing. I felt as if I had crashed a celebration on Mount Olympus. Hundreds of men and women danced with grave majesty. The men's robes phosphorescent in the dim light. Swaying over the crowd, enormous headdresses made every woman seven feet tall.

For most of us, parties bring out our best selves. The Agulu gathering revealed what many Ibgo consider their *true* selves.

"Igbos as a people are very, very independent," explained Dr. Oli, the Florida professor. We were pushing through the crowd toward a long table piled with fiery tilapia and corn fritters. "When you look at the part of Nigeria where Igbos live, you find that it's the least fertile. And then other tribes in Nigeria had kings, organized governments. Igbos did not have anything like that. But we survived."

They did more than survive. Entrepreneurial and migratory for centuries, the Igbo are also among Nigeria's highest achievers. They represent the majority of the highly educated Nigerians in the United States. Their success, at least in their view, springs in large part from their social structure.

Instead of answering to kings, Igbo defer to their elders—an aristocracy that, in theory, anyone is entitled one day to join. Ogbos provide an important counterweight, occupying and empowering the young. Poor or prosperous, every member of an ogbo sits on the floor at their gatherings and has one vote. Starting in grade school, each performs public service assigned by the elders. Ogbos stay cohesive because of the closeness the members share as adolescents—and because of their rivalry with all other age grades.

Like Americans, Igbos tend to be sociable, public-spirited, and intensely competitive. But only the Igbo have age grades, which achieve a trifecta of diversion, lifetime social support, and the channeling of individual aggression into helping others. The structure is so compelling that even while many members now live abroad, their ogbos at home continue to thrive. You can get a glimpse of how this all works in an endearing photo book called *Ogbo: Sharing Life in an African Village.* In one shot, a line of giggling ten-year-olds is sweeping the village plaza. One boy is tall, nicely fed, with sturdy new blue jeans. A few spaces down the line, holding the exact same type of broom, a shabby little fellow laughs his head off dressed in nothing more than a shirt and red underpants.

As they get older, the members' jobs grow increasingly demanding. Elders will assign them to clear a stream, build huts for widows, and, for the young men, protect the village. But the spirit is festive, not grudging. "No one's going to come after you if you move to the city and break off," one woman explained. "You do it because it's fun. You want to be part of it. Doing the assignments, you're singing together, all your friends are there. You know what it feels like? Almost like having an identical twin. As soon as someone has a problem, you have another family—someone to share your problems."

Once members begin working, they start paying modest dues. When an age mate shows up in a new city, members put him up and try to land him a job. If he stumbles financially, some ogbos even give a one-time pick-me-up of several hundred dollars. But what really bonds them is perpetual, simmering competition.

"There's always another age grade you're competing with," Oli said. "Which one has a better name? Which has more respect? No one wants to be the ogbo that let the village down." Oli would know. Though he has lived in the United States for decades, and chairs the criminal justice department at Bethune-Cookman University, he counts an ogbo achievement in the 1960s as one of his life's greatest triumphs. "We saw the village needed electricity and the government was not prepared to supply it," he said. "So we raised money, bought a transformer, and dug the ground for placing the poles." He smiled. "They still call us the age grade that brought electricity."

How can you create an ogbo, however, if you've never even seen the village you want to improve? This is the conundrum that Oli's friends and some of their American-born children wanted to unsnarl. About a dozen have come to the hotel this weekend to meet each other, a step that in Nigeria would be for toddlers. Yet the young people were determined to stay in touch.

"Our parents are always sending money home, always building stuff," one young woman, now in medical school, said. "We would like to do that service component too. It's part of us."

I couldn't at first see how this would work without years of face-to-face comradeship or attachment to place. But age grades have proved to be very flexible. Nigerians in the United States today organize their cohorts around a larger age range, or the year they arrived here, or even just shared roots in the village. Most radical of all, a system that was strictly gender separated at home has gone coed. "This is the United States," Oli said, laughing. "You can't go and have a club excluding women."

I wondered if the ogbo system should now be turned toward the United States. This, after all, is where the second generation lives. The unique mix of team spirit and competition both strike chords in this country. Americans like the idea of volunteering, but we're on our own figuring out how, and we loathe the idea of being coerced. There's even a certain silence around volunteering, since it can be annoying to hear others carry on about their saintly deeds. Shrewdly, ogbo culture ignores the saintliness angle. Service, it's implied, is just what you're expected to do as a human. Team spirit and competition make it exciting.

A national service movement could take advantage of these insights, rewarding and recognizing age groups that contribute the most. Perhaps the idea would work best in a limited geographical setting, like a school district: the third graders would know they're expected to write to local veterans, sixth graders would expect to visit animal shelters, and eleventh graders would expect to ladle soup at a shelter. Some U.S. groups already use cohort pressure in limited ways: KIPP charter schools, for example, require students to include their projected graduation year whenever they sign their names. Using cohorts and competition to spark national service could produce lasting rewards for U.S. children. Helping other people—like joining any sort of club—is one of the most reliable paths to individual happiness.

Outside the packed ballroom, a tapping sound rose. It coalesced into drumming, joined with high voices, and suddenly a team of singing boys and girls in orange sarongs dashed into the room. The adults sprang to their feet.

"I used to sing this when I was young," cried a woman standing near me in the crush. When the song ended, dollar bills filled the air around the children like moths. More villagers pressed in from the hall, magnetized by the music and the brilliant, swirling robes.

Thirty years after establishing themselves here, the children of Agulu were determined to remember their origins. If they could find a way to translate their ogbos, I thought, other Americans would willingly remember along with them.

NOTES

Embarking

4 *The term first appeared as the:* K. S. Markides and J. Coreil, "The Health of Hispanics in the Southwestern United States: An Epidemiologic Paradox," *Public Health Reports* 101 (1986): 253–65.

4 *Later studies showed Latinos:* K. Eschbach, J. P. Simpson, Y. F. Kuo, and J. S. Goodwin, "Mortality of Foreign-Born and U.S.-Born Hispanic Adults at Younger Ages: A Reexamination of Recent Patterns," *American Journal of Public Health* 97 (July 2007): 1297–1304.

5 *In 2010, the Centers for Disease:* U.S. Department of Health and Human Services, "United States Life Tables by Hispanic Origin," *Vital and Health Statistics*, series 2, no. 152 (October 2010): 11.

5 *They give birth to healthier:* Margie Shields and Richard E. Berman, "Children of Immigrant Families: Analysis and Recommendations," *The Future of Children: Children of Immigrant Families* 14, no. 2 (Summer 2004).

5 *Asian, Latino, and Caribbean:* "Disentangling Mental Health Disparities," a series of six papers, *American Journal of Public Health* 97 (January 2007): 52–98.

5 *What can explain this?* For a useful overview on this issue, see Kyriakos S. Markides and Kerstin Gerst, "Immigration, Aging, and Health in the United States" in R. Setterson and J. Angel, eds., *Handbook of the Sociology of Aging* (New York: Springer, 2011).

5 *Selection, we know, is the biggest:* The impact of elderly, ill Mexicans returning home before dying, known as "salmon bias," may somewhat distort their U.S. longevity statistics. But this appears to be a minor influence and does not account for other health phenomena such as birth weight. See C. M. Turra and I. T. Elo, "The Impact of Salmon Bias on the Hispanic Mortality Advantage. New Evidence from Social Security Data," *Population Research and Policy Review* 27 (October 2008): 515–30, and A. F. Albraido-Lanza, B. P. Dohrenwend, D. S. Ng-Mak, and J. B. Turner, "The Latino Mortality Paradox: A

Test of the Salmon Bias and Health Migrant Hypotheses," *American Journal of Public Health* 89 (October 1999): 1534–48.

5 *Especially among Mexicans, the paradox:* Juliet Chung, "Healthier Than You Might Expect," *Los Angeles Times*, August 28, 2006, and Paul Simon (physician with Los Angeles County Public Health Department), correspondence with author, March 2011.

6 *Behavior, many researchers think:* Nevertheless, the paradox remains—a paradox. "There is no definitive, scientific proof for immigrant selection bias or behavioral effects, only speculation," says health scientist Elizabeth Arias, an expert in immigrant mortality at the Centers for Disease Control. "They appear to be the most logical explanations for the advantage, but there is no conclusive evidence yet. Both things are very difficult to measure scientifically with statistically representative data. But there is considerable anecdotal evidence and perhaps even some small scale non-representative studies." Correspondence with author, March 2011.

6 *Immigrants smoke and drink less:* Shields and Berman, "Children of Immigrant Families."

7 *Many headed to Washington:* Cecilia Menjivar, "El Salvador," in Mary C. Waters and Reed Ueda with Helen B. Marrow, eds., *The New Americans: A Guide to Immigration Since 1965* (Cambridge, MA: Harvard University Press, 2007), 413, 416.

8 *And uniquely, perhaps, among America's:* Stephen L. Klineberg, *Public Perceptions in Remarkable Times: Tracking Change Through 24 Years of Houston Surveys* (Houston: Center on Race, Religion, and Urban Life, Rice University, 2005), 20–21. Klineberg points out that Houston has more Hispanics than San Francisco, more Asians than Miami, and more African Americans than Los Angeles.

8 *As a majority-minority city, though:* Klineberg, *Public Perceptions in Remarkable Times*, 22.

10 *In 1776, 70 percent of white settlers*: Stephen L. Klineberg (professor, Department of Sociology, Rice University), correspondence with author, December 2011.

10 *From 1820 through 1925:* International Sociological Association and the International Economic Association, *The Positive Contribution by Immigrants* (Paris: UNESCO, 1933), 19.

10 *A wave came from:* Stephan Thernstrom, ed., Ann Orlov, managing ed., and Oscar Handlin, consulting ed., *Harvard Encyclopedia of American Ethnic Groups* (Cambridge, MA: Belknap Press of Harvard University Press, 1980), 363, 409, 528, 750, 971–72.

10 *The 1924 National Origins Quota Act:* Klineberg, *Public Perceptions in Remarkable Times*, 20.

11 *By 1960, in a country:* Mary Beth Norton, Carol Sheriff, David W. Blight, David M. Katzman, Howard P. Chudacoff, and Fredrik Logevall, *A People and a Nation: A History of the United States*. Vol. 2: *Since 1865* (Boston: Wadsworth, 2010), 779.

11 *The number of newcomers who:* Klineberg, *Public Perceptions in Remarkable Times*, 20.

11 *Today, more than 37 million:* Erin Andrew, Susan Golonka, Martin Simon, and Mary Jo Waits, "Rising to the Immigrant Integration Challenge: What States Are Doing—And Can Do," National Governors Association Center for Best Practices, Issue Brief, November 4, 2009, 3, 5, and Norton, Sheriff, Blight, Katzman, Chudacoff, and Logevall, *A People and a Nation: A History of the United States*, 779.

11 *It was a radical change from the:* Princeton University sociologist Douglas Massey in testimony before the Senate Judiciary Committee, 2005, quoted in Ashley Pettus, "Uneasy Neighbors: A Brief History of Mexican-U.S. Migration," *Harvard Magazine*, May–June 2007.

12 *Now, according to 2006 census estimates:* Leslie Casimir, "Bachelor's and Beyond," *Houston Chronicle*, May 20, 2008, A1.

12 *Driven by the fall of Saigon:* Rubén G. Rumbaut, "Vietnam," in Waters, Ueda, and Marrow, *The New Americans*, 658.

13 *The Mexicans deemed his knockoff:* Patricia T. O'Conner and Stewart Kellerman, *Origins of the Specious: Myths and Misconceptions of the English Language* (New York: Random House, 2009), 106.

13 *It was the Germans who pioneered:* Thomas Sowell, *Migrations and Cultures: A World View* (New York: Basic Books, 1996), 54, 78.

13 *Italian Americans, meanwhile:* Sowell, *Migrations and Cultures*, 160–61.

13 *Italian cuisine, the social reformers:* Simone Cinotto, "'Now That's Italian!': Representations of Italian Food in American Popular Magazines, 1950–2000," Italian Academy for Advanced Studies in America. www.docstoc.com /docs/19685266/"Now-Thats-Italian!"-Representa.

13 *Roam any street in the South:* John Michael Vlach, "The Shotgun House: An African Architectural Legacy," in Dell Upton and John Michael Vlach, eds., *Common Places: Readings in American Vernacular Architecture* (Athens, GA: University of Georgia Press, 1986), 58–78.

14 *Soul food, bagels, salsa:* Culinary historian Jessica B. Harris argues that Southern hospitality itself is an import: "Indeed, hospitality was and remains an especial virtue in some countries of western Africa, where it is a religious as well as a civic and a personal duty to take in and feed the traveler and the stranger. It's called *teranga* in Senegal among the Wolof and *diarama* among Mandinka. These notions of hospitality and propriety crossed the ocean with the enslaved Africans as well." Jessica B. Harris, *High on the Hog: A Culinary Journey from Africa to America* (New York: Bloomsbury, 2011), 108.

14 *Their backwoods "familiarity":* David Hackett Fischer, *Albion's Seed: Four British Folkways in America* (New York: Oxford University Press, 1991), 754.

14 *Ethnic hostility, in other words:* Fischer, *Albion's Seed*.

1 How to Save

20 *Among Asians, money clubs:* Shirley Ardener and Sandra Burman, eds., *Money Go Rounds: The Importance of Rotating Savings and Credit Associaions for Women* (Oxford, U.K.: Berg, 1995), 204.

21 *Eleven years later, another survey:* Joel Garreau, "For Koreans, 'Keh' Is Key to Success," *Washington Post*, November 3, 1991, B1.

21 *Fifty miles away, on the Gulf of Mexico:* Christine Gorman, "Do-It-Yourself Financing," *Time*, July 25, 1988.

28 *This, after all, is how more than:* David U. Himmelstein, Deborah Thorne, Elizabeth Warren, and Steffie Woolhandler, "Medical Bankruptcy in the United States, 2007: Results of a National Study," *American Journal of Medicine* 122, no. 8 (August 2009): 741–6.

29 *Some victims had been:* Ivan Light and Edna Bonacich, *Immigrant Entrepreneurs: Koreans in Los Angeles, 1965–1982* (Berkeley: University of California Press, 1991), 252.

33 *"I've been wanting one of those":* John Leland, "Debtors Search for Discipline Through Blogs," *New York Times*, February 18, 2007.

33 *His instincts proved right:* Thomas Sowell, *Migrations and Cultures: A World View* (New York: Basic Books, 1996), 166.

2 How to Mother a Mother

40 *Except for in North America:* Though practiced in Germany, France, Spain, and elsewhere in Europe, rituals such as the cuarentena didn't take hold in colonial America, maybe because most immigrant women arrived without extended families to help them—or the wealth to hire surrogates. Robbie Davis Floyd (medical anthropologist, University of Texas at Austin), interview with author, December 2010. See also Carol P. MacCormack, "Biological, Cultural and Social Meanings of Fertility and Birth," in Carol P. MacCormack, ed., *Ethnography of Fertility and Birth* (London: Academic Press, 1982).

41 *To the Babylonians, forty days:* C. Butler, *Number Symbolism* (London: Routledge & Kegan Paul, 1970). In "The Myth of 40," an unpublished paper, Michael Moore of Shaanan Teacher's College in Haifa, Israel, argues that the mystique of the number 40 continues in contemporary life.

41 *Ancient peoples knew they could:* Brian Bayles (medical anthropologist and assistant professor, Department of Family & Community Medicine, University of Texas Health Sciences Center at San Antonio), interview with author, March 2010.

42 *But they also had little to say:* Postpartum symptoms, which can include feelings of worthlessness, anxiety, and emotional distance from their newborns, can affect not only women but their bonding with their children. Katja Gaschler, "Postpartum Depression Epidemic Affects More Than Just Mom," *Scientific American*, March 20, 2008.

43 *The few ethnographers looking:* Laurence Kruckman (cultural anthropologist in the Department of Anthropology, Indiana University of Pennsylvania), interview with author, April 2007. Also see Laurence Kruckman, "Rituals as Prevention: The Case of Post-partum Depression," in Ruth-Inge Heinze, ed., *The Nature and Function of Rituals: Fire from Heaven* (Westport, CT: Bergin & Garvey, 2000), 213–228.

47 *Through their first hour:* Robert A. Hummer, Daniel A. Powers, Starling G. Pullum, Ginger L. Gossman, and W. Parker Frisbie, "Paradox Found (Again): Infant Mortality Among the Mexican-Origin Population in the United States," *Demography* 44, no. 3 (August 2007): 441–457.

48 *A study based on 568 low-income:* Kim Harley and Brenda Eskenazi, "Time in

the United States, Social Support and Health Behaviors During Pregnancy Among Women of Mexican Descent," *Social Science & Medicine* 62, no. 12 (June 2006): 3048–3061.

48 *By bolstering a mother emotionally:* In her 2008 book *The Jungle Effect* (New York: HarperCollins), physician Daphne Miller methodically analyzes traditional cuisines in cultures with some of the world's lowest rates of depression, diabetes, and other chronic illnesses. Once they were brought to the industrialized United States, Miller suggests, those cuisines often mutated into actively unhealthy diets because they left out or replaced key traditional herbs, condiments, and spices that often had true medical benefits.

48 *In a rhapsodic essay, gardening:* Joan Huyser-Honig, "Purslane," National Gardening Association. www.garden.org/subchannels/edibles/herbs/?q=show&id=175.

50 *That role reversal takes place:* Kathleen Niska, Mariah Snyder, and Betty Lia-Hoagberg, "Family Ritual Facilitates Adaptation to Parenthood," *Public Health Nursing* 15, no. 5 (October 1998): 334–335.

50 *Allowing the mother:* In Chiapas, the housework ban takes the form of a taboo. Merely touch a broom, a woman is told, and air will enter your bones, dark spirits will swarm to your house, and your womb will fail to heal. Medically speaking, all this resting shouldn't be necessary: women getting over an ordinary delivery should get moving again as soon as possible.

But one of Anarosa's neighbors in Akron set me straight about the reason for such stringent rules in rural Mexico. The forty days after childbirth, she told me, were the only time during her life in Mexico when she did not have to walk miles to the river for cooking water and carry it back to the house on her head. She didn't have to grind the day's corn, then pat and fry it into two dozen tortillas. And for the first time in married life, she was exempt from roaming the hills for firewood, dragging it home on her back, and chopping it into kindling. For a Mexican woman whose routine resembles those of our nineteenth-century pioneers, the cuarentena enforces a respite from a daily life so punishing that after giving birth it could kill her—jeopardizing all those who depend on her.

51 *And yet in the United States:* U.S. doulas—who more typically support the childbirth process—have begun to offer services addressing the lack of postpartum support many women feel. See, for example, http://www.birthsource.com/scripts/article.asp?articleid=240.

53 *According to one study, even mothers:* Vicky Lovell, Elizabeth O'Neill, and Skylar Olsen. "Maternity Leave in the United States: Paid Parental Leave Is Still Not Standard, Even Among the Best U.S. Employers," Institute for Women's Policy Research, August 2007. www.iwpr.org/publications/pubs/maternity-leave-in-the-united-states-paid-parental-leave-is-still-not-standard-even-among-the-best-u.s.-employers.

53 *Dana Raphael, a pioneering breast-feeding:* Dana Raphael, *The Tender Gift: Breast Feeding* (New York: Schocken Books, 1976), 24.

3 How to Court

63 *No statistics chart the number:* Madhulika Khandelwal (director of the Asian/American Center and associate professor in the Urban Studies Department,

Queens College, City University of New York, and author of *Becoming American, Being Indian: An Immigrant Community in New York*), interview with the author, September 2008. Also see Neil MacFarquhar, "It's Muslim Boy Meets Muslim Girl, Yes, But Please Don't Call It Dating," *New York Times*, September 19, 2006.

66 *It just reinforced her belief:* And even assisted marriage is quickly evolving, magazine editor Hakki notes. "Things are changing rather quickly here in the Western world," she told me. "People are more easygoing and social media is playing a large part in how people are interacting. For example, I just heard of someone who met his fiancée through Facebook. They're both Indian, both lived in Saudi Arabia when they were kids and the girl knew the boy's older brother. The boy currently lives in Canada and the girl lives in India. They started communicating on Facebook, the parents got involved, everyone said yes and now the wedding is set for this autumn in India." Correspondence with the author, March 2011.

66 *In the developing world, complications:* Save the Children, *State of the World's Mothers 2004: Children Having Children*, May 2004, 4.

66 *And "no dowry requested" signals:* Juliette Terzieff, "Pakistan's Fiery Shame: Women Die in Stove Deaths," *Women's eNews*, October 27, 2002. www.womens enews.org/story/domestic-violence/021027/pakistans-fiery-shame-women -die-stove-deaths.

69 *In Puritan New England, young:* David Hackett Fischer, *Albion's Seed: Four British Folkways in America* (New York: Oxford University Press, 1991), 80.

69 *Then, in the prosperous midcentury:* Martin King Whyte, "Choosing Mates—The American Way," *Society*, March–April 1992, 75.

69 *Free to "shop" for our partners:* Stephanie Coontz, *Marriage, a History: From Obedience to Intimacy, or How Love Conquered Marriage* (New York: Viking, 2005), 263.

70 *According to Whyte:* Whyte, "Choosing Mates—The American Way," *Society*, 76. Some later studies have shown that cohabiting couples can expect a higher rate of divorce, but many scholars call that data controversial, since it may reflect couples who were more ambivalent about marriage to start with. Also see Coontz, *Marriage, a History*, 297.

71 *A few research teams have:* Jane Myers, Jayamala Madathil, and Lynne R. Tingle, "Marriage Satisfaction and Wellness in India and the United States: A Preliminary Comparison of Arranged Marriages and Marriages of Choice," *Journal of Counseling and Development* 83 (Spring 2005): 183–190.

71 *At about the five-year mark:* U. Gupta and P. Singh, "Exploratory Study of Love and Liking and Type of Marriages," *Indian Journal of Applied Psychology* 19 (1982): 92–97.

73 *"We wonder what's wrong with us":* Anita Jain, *Marrying Anita: A Quest for Love in the New India* (New York: Bloomsbury USA, 2008), 45.

77 *The unscientific treatise offered:* Reva Seth, *First Comes Marriage: Modern Relationship Advice from the Wisdom of Arranged Marriages* (New York: Fireside, 2008).

79 *"What surprises me":* Anita Jain, *Marrying Anita: A Quest for Love in the New India*, 44.

4 How to Learn

88 *Yet as soon as they can:* Min Zhou and Susan S. Kim, "After-School Institutions in Chinese and Korean Immigrant Communities: A Model for Others?" *Migration Information Source*, May 2007. www.migrationinformation.org /Feature/display.cfm?id=598.

88 *Mostly nonprofits based in:* Cheong Huh (assistant director of the UCLA Equity and Access in Education Project), interview with author, July 2009.

88 *Today, according to a Los Angeles:* Zhou and Kim, "After-School Institutions in Chinese and Korean Immigrant Communities."

89 *Or worse, they are uncounted:* For a nuanced examination of the varied experiences of Korean students in this country, see Jamie Lew, *Asian Americans in Class: Charting the Achievement Gap Among Korean American Youth* (New York: Teachers College Press, 2006).

90 *In 2010, for the first time, they also:* www.miller-mccune.com/culture-society /asian-american-parenting-and-academic-success-26053.

90 *And in 2000, more than half:* Marybeth Shinn and Hirokazu Yoshikawa, eds., *Toward Positive Youth Development: Transforming Schools and Community Programs* (New York: Oxford University Press, 2008), 229–251.

92 *On most academic outcomes:* Susanne James-Burdumy, Mark Dynarski, Mary Moore, John Deke, Wendy Mansfield, and Carol Pistorino, *When Schools Stay Open Late: The National Evaluation of the 21st Century Community Learning Centers Program: Final Report* (U.S. Department of Education, Institute of Education Sciences, National Center for Education Evaluation and Regional Assistance, 2005). www.mathematica-mpr.com/publications/pdfs/21stfinal.pdf.

98 *The intellectual paradise:* Pyong Gap Min, *Changes and Conflicts: Korean Immigrant Families in New York* (Boston, Allyn and Bacon, 1998), 25–36.

98 *"Sleep five hours, fail":* Casey J. Lartigue, Jr., "You'll Never Guess What South Korea Frowns Upon," *Washington Post*, May 28, 2000.

98 *Seoul's Gimpo International Airport:* Valerie Reitman, "South Korea's Exam-Takers Have a Prayer," *Los Angeles Times*, November 15, 2000.

100 *Then, a few months before the girls:* Scott Kraft, "Calling India," *Los Angeles Times*, May 6, 2007.

5 How to Shelter

102 *Between 2001 and 2008, 60 percent:* These figures were calculated by David A. Cort, associate director of the Social and Demographic Research Institute, and assistant professor in the Department of Sociology, University of Massachusetts, Amherst, using data from the 5 percent sample of the Integrated Public Use Microdata Series and the American Community Survey (2001–2008), an ongoing statistical survey by the U.S. Census Bureau.

103 *Today, one-third of Jamaicans:* Mary C. Waters and Reed Ueda with Helen B. Marrow, eds., *The New Americans: A Guide to Immigration Since 1965* (Cambridge, MA: Harvard University Press, 2007), 479.

104 *The difference, she and her:* Philip Kasinitz, John H. Mollenkopf, Mary C. Waters, and Jennifer Holdaway, *Inheriting the City: The Children of Immigrants*

Come of Age (New York: Russell Sage Foundation; Cambridge, MA: Harvard University Press, 2008), 31.

105 *The more social support a mother:* Sarah Blaffer Hrdy, *Mothers and Others: The Evolutionary Origins of Mutual Understanding* (Cambridge, MA: Belknap Press of Harvard University Press, 2009), 103.

105 *Carefully tallying the calories:* Kristen Hawkes and Nicholas Blurton Jones, "Human Age Structures, Paleodemography, and the Grandmother Hypothesis," in Eckart Voland, Athanasios Chasiotis, and Wulf Schiefenhövel, eds., *Grandmotherhood: The Evolutionary Significance of the Second Half of Female Life* (New Brunswick, NJ: Rutgers University Press, 2005), 120.

105 *Just as we evolved to depend:* Kristen Hawkes, "The Grandmother Effect," *Nature* no. 428 (March 11, 2004): 128–29.

107 *From the 1920s to the 1960s:* Stephanie Coontz, *Marriage, a History: From Obedience to Intimacy, or How Love Conquered Marriage* (New York: Viking, 2005), 207–208.

107 *The Greatest Generation "designed a social":* Sharon Graham Niederhaus and John L. Graham, "Back to the Nest: The Trend of Kids Moving Back in with Their Parents Is Bad for America and Will Damage the Family Unit, Right? Not Quite," *USA Today*, February 6, 2007.

108 *"Marriages, like all relationships":* Jacqueline Olds and Richard S. Schwartz, *The Lonely American: Drifting Apart in the Twenty-first Century* (Boston: Beacon Press, 2009), 123.

109 *In a provocative but unscientific:* Seth Roberts, "Self-Experimentation as a Source of New Ideas: Examples About Sleep, Mood, Health, and Weight," *Behavioral and Brain Sciences* 27 (2004): 227–262. Also see Stephen J. Dubner and Steven D. Levitt, "Does the Truth Lie Within?" *New York Times Magazine*, September 11, 2005. www.nytimes.com/2005/09/11/magazine/11FREAK.html.

112 *Though their language:* Milton Vickerman, "Jamaicans," in Waters and Ueda, eds., *The New Americans,* 658.

113 *In the New York area, Chinese Americans:* Kasinitz, Mollenkopf, Waters, and Holdaway, *Inheriting the City,* 213.

119 *But their kids must craft a:* Mary Waters (professor of sociology, Harvard University), interview with author, 2007.

120 *The Massachusetts Bay Puritans persecuted:* Winthrop S. Hudson, *Religion in America,* 3rd ed. (New York: Charles Scribner's Sons, 1981), 28. Hudson notes, "With freedom to pursue an independent course, the early settlers of Massachusetts Bay were in no mood to permit dissent from the 'due form' of ecclesiastical government which they established. Having forsaken their homes to establish a new Zion in the American wilderness, they saw no reason why their endeavor should be compromised by dissidence. Others, they contended, had full liberty to stay away; and they noted there was ample room elsewhere in America for them to establish settlements of their own."

120 *The closer the physical proximity:* Joyce Gladwell (author of *Brown Face, Big Master,* first published in 1969), interview with author, January 2010.

122 *Even before the 2008:* Pew Research Center, "The Return of the Multi-Generational Family Household," March 18, 2010. http://pewsocialtrends.org/2010/03/18/the-return-of-the-multigenerational-family-household.

123 *"At building trade shows this year":* Mireya Navarro, "Families Add Third Generation to Households," *New York Times,* May 25, 2006. www.nytimes.com/2006/05/25/us/25multi.html.

123 *Examining the same trend:* Ana Veciana-Suarez, "Multigenerational Households Are Making a Comeback Across a Varied Demographic Range," *Miami Herald,* July 16, 2006, H1.

123 *The goodwill continued to rise:* Anna Bahney, "High School Heroes: Mom and Dad," *New York Times,* May 16, 2004.

124 *Only 25 percent of parents:* Niederhaus and Graham, "Back to the Nest."

6 How to Be a Good Neighbor

126 *According to an influential 2007 study:* Kathleen A. Cagney, Christopher R. Browning, and Danielle M. Wallace, "The Latino Paradox in Neighborhood Context: The Case of Asthma and Other Respiratory Conditions," *American Journal of Public Health* 97, no. 5 (May 2007): 919–925.

126 *It's aggravated by poor primary care:* According to the Children's Defense Fund's March 2010 Asthma Health Fact Sheet, "In Texas, the cost for a child to visit a doctor in the early stages of an asthma attack is about $100, but going to the emergency room to treat full-blown asthma symptoms can result in a three-day hospital stay costing more than $7,300."

127 *Draw the poverty card:* Felton Earls, "Chicago," *ReVista: Harvard Review of Latin America* (Winter 2003).

127 *A complicated, enigmatic disease:* Rosalind Wright (assistant professor, Harvard Medical School, the Channing Laboratory; director of the Asthma Center on Community, Environment and Social Stress), interview with author, February 2010.

128 *From 1980 to 1994, its prevalence:* American Medical Association, "Childhood Asthma: Emerging Patters [*sic*] and Prospects for Novel Therapies," *Report 2 of the Council on Scientific Affairs* (June 2002). www.ama-assn.org/ama/no-index/about-ama/13547.shtml.

128 *Today, it's America's number one:* Ruchi S. Gupta, Xingyou Zhang, Lisa K. Sharp, John M. Shannon, and Kevin B. Weiss, "The Protective Effect of Community Factors on Childhood Asthma," *Journal of Allergy and Clinical Immunology* 123, no. 6 (June 2009): 1312–1319.

129 *The National Institutes of Health:* Pulmonologist Ruchi S. Gupta has also studied this link in Chicago. According to Gupta and her research colleagues, "Criminal activity was significantly higher in neighborhoods with a high asthma prevalence, especially drug abuse violations, which increased more than six-fold, and violent crimes, which increased more than threefold. After adjusting for community race/ethnicity, only violent crime continued to be significantly associated with neighborhood asthma prevalence. When considered alongside socio-demographic and individual characteristics, violence continued to con-

tribute significantly, explaining 15 percent of neighborhood variation in child-hood asthma." R. S. Gupta, X. Zhang, E. E. Springston, L. K. Sharp, L. M. Curtis, M. Shalowitz, J. J. Shannon, and K. B. Weiss, "The Association Between Community Crime and Childhood Asthma Prevalence in Chicago," *Annals of Allergy, Asthma & Immunology* 104, no. 4 (April 2010): 299–306.

130 *At the beginning of the last century:* Eric Klinenberg, *Heat Wave: A Social Autopsy of Disaster in Chicago* (Chicago: University of Chicago Press, 2002), 92.

130 *But in large part:* Beryl Satter, *Family Properties: Race, Real Estate, and the Exploitation of Black Urban America.* (New York: Henry Holt, 2009), 4.

131 *Today, more than 80 percent:* www.metroplanning.org/uploads/cms/documents /olympicslittlevillagedemographics.pdf.

131 *Or, to use another common socioeconomic:* Eyal Press, "Do Immigrants Make Us Safer?" *New York Times Magazine,* December 3, 2006.

133 *Some also probably enable them:* Mary Patillo-McCoy, *Black Picket Fences: Privilege and Peril Among the Black Middle Class* (Chicago: University of Chicago Press, 1998), 68.

135 *And, stunningly, an asthma sufferer:* Gupta, Zhang, Sharp, Shannon, and Weiss, "The Protective Effect of Community Factors on Childhood Asthma," 1312.

135 *For African Americans in Chicago:* Sandra D. Thomas and Steve Whitman, "Asthma Hospitalizations and Mortality in Chicago: An Epidemiologic Overview," *Chest* 116, no. 4, supplement 1 (October 1999): 135S–141S.

136 *How often, they asked, do you:* The study, titled the Project on Human Development in Chicago Neighborhoods, and its research team are described in detail by Robert J. Sampson in the forthcoming *Great American City: Chicago and the Enduring Neighborhood Effect* (Chicago: University of Chicago Press, 2011).

136 *What they found defied the classic:* Cagney, Browning, and Wallace, "The Latino Paradox in Neighborhood Context."

136 *In Chicago's white population, just:* Numbers from Gupta, Zhang, Sharp, Shannon, and Weiss, "The Protective Effect of Community Factors on Childhood Asthma," are even more shocking: up to 44 percent in predominantly black neighborhoods in Chicago versus down to 2 percent in predominantly white neighborhoods versus down to 0 percent in predominantly Hispanic neighborhoods.

138 *But, she said, "these findings suggest":* Pulmonologist Ruchi Gupta and her colleagues note that community vitality (33 percent of which was community amenities) was significantly higher in neighborhoods with low asthma prevalence. Overall, they say, positive factors explained 21 percent of asthma variation in their study. Their conclusion was that asthma prevalence in Chicago is strongly associated with socio-environmental factors thought to enrich community. Gupta, Zhang, Sharp, Shannon, and Weiss, "The Protective Effect of Community Factors on Childhood Asthma."

139 *Any less than that—for example:* Christopher R. Browning, "The Social Ecology of Public Space: Street Activity and Violent Crime in Urban Neighborhoods." Unpublished paper, Center for Family and Demographic Research Seminar Series, Bowling Green University, October 2007.

140 *In Little Village specifically:* Press, "Do Immigrants Make Us Safer?"

140 *And finally, the torrent:* Religious activity also enriches the community's well-

being, notes resident Yadira Montoya, a community outreach specialist. "Churches are very, very active in Little Village," she told me. "There are several small ones and two huge ones. They are incredibly politically active and play a big role in providing social services and health information." Interview with the author, June 20, 2011.

142 *"The plaza does about a million things":* Sam Quiñones (author of *Antonio's Gun and Delfino's Dream*), interview with author, March 2011.

145 *In Little Village, the heat wave:* Eric Klinenberg, *Heat Wave: A Social Autopsy of Disaster in Chicago* (Chicago: University of Chicago Press, 2002), 87.

149 *In Chicago, multiethnic, ultra-educated:* Sampson, *Great American City: Chicago and the Enduring Neighborhood Effect.*

7 How to Eat

158 *Only its logistics have changed:* An Lee (author, *The Little Saigon Cookbook*, Guilford, CT: Insiders Guide, 2006), interview with author, 2009.

162 *In the decades since:* For a thorough discussion of the many difficulties of creating family mealtimes in recent years, and the correlations between family time and positive health and behavior outcomes, see Miriam Weinstein, *The Surprising Power of Family Meals* (Hanover, NH: Steerforth Press, 2005).

163 *The quantity of mealtime that a family:* S. L. Hofferth, "Changes in American Children's Time, 1981–1997," University of Michigan's Institute for Social Research, *Center Survey* (January 1999), and S. L. Hofferth, "How American Children Spend Their Time," *Journal of Marriage and the Family* 63 (2001): 295–308.

163 *As she suggests in her subtitle:* Weinstein, *The Surprising Power of Family Meals.*

164 *They show how to keep:* S. J Wolin, L. A. Bennett, D. L. Noonan, and M. A. Teitelbaum, "Disrupted Family Rituals: A Factor in the Intergenerational Transmission of Alcoholism," *Journal of Studies on Alcohol* 41, no. 3 (1980): 199–214.

164 *But people with an internal locus:* Amber Lazarus, "Relationships Among Indicators of Child and Family Resilience and Adjustment Following the September 11, 2001 Tragedy," Working Paper No. 36, Emory Center for Myth and Ritual in American Life (2004).

164 *Hearing stories at mealtimes:* Marshall P. Duke, Robyn Feivish, Amber Lazarus, and Jennifer Bohanek, "Of Ketchup and Kin: Dinnertime Conversations as a Major Source of Family Knowledge, Family Adjustment, and Family Resilience," Working Paper No. 26, Emory Center for Myth and Ritual in American Life (2003), 3.

166 *Working women find that deadline:* Reed Larson, "Mother's Time in Two-Parent and One-Parent Families: The Daily Organization of Work, Time for Oneself, and Parenting of Adolescents," in Kerry J. Daly, ed., *Minding the Time in Family Experience: Emerging Perspectives and Issues*, Contemporary Perspectives in Family Research 3 (New York: JAI Press, 2001), 85–109.

Anchoring

200 *In 2011, Yale law professor:* Amy Chua, *Battle Hymn of the Tiger Mother* (New York: Penguin Press, 2011).

201 *Even teaching improves, because:* Katharine Mieszkowski, "Private-School Refugees," *Slate*, March 2, 2010. www.slate.com/id/2246417/.

203 *Incentivizing sidewalk-building:* Claudia H. Williams, Robert Wood Johnson Foundation, "The Built Environment and Physical Activity: What Is the Relationship?" Research Synthesis Report, no. 11 (April 2007).

206 *Joining a group that meets once:* Tina Rosenberg, *Join the Club: How Peer Pressure Can Transform the World* (New York: W.W. Norton, 2011), 181.

206 *Though native-born Americans:* Bill McKibben, "Old MacDonald Had a Farmers' Market—Total Self-Sufficiency Is a Noble, Misguided Ideal," *In Character*, Winter 2007, 25–26. incharacter.org/archives/self-reliance/old-mac-donald -had-a-farmers-market-total-self-sufficiency-is-a-noble-misguided-ideal/.

207 *In a 2002 study of 137 couples:* Kelly K. Bost, Martha J. Cox, and Chris Payne, "Structural and Supportive Changes in Couples' Family and Friendship Networks Across the Transition to Parenthood," *Journal of Marriage and Family* 64 (May 2002): 517–531.

208 *Not only had she just summed up:* The conference, titled "The Immigrant Paradox in Education and Behavior: Is Becoming American a Developmental Risk?" was hosted by the Child Development in Context research lab at Brown University, March 6–7, 2009.

208 *But even though:* While the foreign-born arrive with better health than the native-born, and tend to live longer, even they seem to experience a deterioration in health over time here. Convergence, as this phenomenon is called, may be linked to worsening health behaviors as newcomers become more Americanized; it may also result from years of physical labor, poverty, and poor medical care. Kyriakos S. Markides and Kerstin Gerst, "Immigration, Aging, and Health in the United States" in R. Setterson and J. Angel, eds., *Handbook of the Sociology of Aging* (New York: Springer, 2011).

208 *According to one study of:* Amy Kerivan Marks, Tristan Guarini, Cynthia Garcia Coll, and Flannery I. Patton, "Non-English Language Use at Home as a Mediator of the Immigrant Paradox in Adolescent Risk Behaviors," presentation at the Biennial Meeting of the Society for Research in Child Development, March 2011.

209 *As political scientist Francis:* Francis Fukuyama, "Identity Crisis: Why We Shouldn't Worry About Mexican Immigration," *Slate*, June 4, 2000. www .slate.com/id/2101756/.

209 *So it should be no surprise that:* National Governors Association Center for Best Practices, "Rising to the Immigrant Integration Challenge: What States Are Doing—And Can Do," Issue Brief, November 4, 2009. www.nga.org/Files /pdf/0911IMMIGRANTINTEGRATION.PDF.

209 *Between 1995 and 2005, one out of every:* Ibid.

209 *In research on both Hispanic and:* Marks et. al., "Non-English Language Use at Home as a Mediator of the Immigrant Paradox in Adolescent Risk Behaviors"; Natalia Palacios, Katarina Guttmannova, and P. Lindsay Chase-Lansdale, "Early Reading Achievement of Children in Immigrant Families: Is There an Immigrant Paradox?" *Developmental Psychology* 44 (5, Sept. 2008): 1381–1395.

209 *In their groundbreaking book:* Alejandro Portes and Rubén G. Rumbaut, *Legacies: The Story of the Immigrant Second Generation* (Berkeley and Los Angeles: University of California Press, 2001).

210 *English, so essential to join U.S. culture:* NGA Center for Best Practices, "Rising to the Immigrant Integration Challenge."

210 *"It's a bit of a twist," the director:* Nina Bernstein, "Study Shows Health Benefit for Immigrants," *New York Times*, October 6, 2006.

211 *You can get a glimpse of how:* Ifeoma Onyefulu, *Ogbo: Sharing Life in an African Village* (San Diego, New York: Gulliver Books, Harcourt Brace, 1996).

ACKNOWLEDGMENTS

Wʜᴇɴ I ᴇᴍʙᴀʀᴋᴇᴅ ᴏɴ this book, I could never have guessed the role friendship would play in its creation. From my pal Dana Calvo, who first urged me to follow a money club, to the reporter friends who critiqued my final drafts, the people who know me best ended up befriending this project as well.

First, though, it required faith. My agents Larry and Sascha Weissman gave it generously. Martin Beiser, my first editor, offered such unwavering reassurance that when I finished a chapter I rewarded myself with a phone call to him. Emily Loose, who took over editing duties from Martin, expertly shaped the final product. I'm indebted to her and to the always patient Alexandra Pisano.

Heather Lambert, Stephanie Chapman, and Eric Ronis swooped in at tense moments with clear heads and *calor humano*. Austen Furse, Jay and Nirja Aiyer, Karen Brucki, Karen Hill, and Julie Wolf all took the time to share detailed insights—then put up with the ensuing barrage of follow-up questions. Karen O'Neill, Libby Graves, Sarah Alexander, and Elizabeth Winkleman delivered healthy feedback early on. Robert Davis, Kris Axtman Tinkham, Jeff Tinkham, David and Zoe Thompson, Nina Andrews Karohl, Jun Lu, Allan Turner, Julie Mason, Paul Duke, Nanci Zhang, Carolyn Bliss Branson, Michael Hirschorn, Shannon Langrand, Matt Emal, and Byrlan Cass Shively all offered me shelter: emotionally, with their ongoing good cheer, or practically, in homes from L.A. to Lake Travis.

First drafts can resemble unwieldy infants. I'll forever be grateful to the friends who peered in the crib and tidied things up. Jane McPherson blended a social worker's compassion and an editor's precision. Peggy Grodinsky helped skim the fat from my musings on food. Ari Posner generously made time to help me parse South Asian marriage. Anne Applebaum breezily solved several vexations for me—much as she has since we were in seventh grade. And Vijay Vaitheeswaran lent his cheerful skepticism, for which I thank him eternally.

Junda Woo scrupulously filled many a pothole. Spike Gillespie tended my ideas as carefully as she'd tended my health when my daughters were born. One of my first bosses, Chris Shively, delivered the same no-nonsense feedback on which I've relied since I faxed him stories from San Salvador. My longtime friend and editor, Mitchell Shields, performed lifesaving structural realignments. And Sharon Meers reminded me of what I was trying to say, even though I hadn't quite said it.

Finally, three people accompanied me from the earliest days of this journey. Christopher McDougall championed my idea, endured my whining, and beat feeble lines into shape. John Beckham, beloved former researcher of the *Los Angeles Times,* quietly nourished me with facts and ideas. Most constant of all, Sarah Viren became this book's *madrina,* its godmother. She is a rare and luminous friend.

Because reporting, like romance, often benefits from a middleman, I relied enormously on many cultural intermediaries who understood me and also the immigrants I was trying to meet. I owe deep thanks to Biet Le, Dai Huynh, Lana Khuong, Ann Le, and Anh Do; Purva Patel, Ayesha Hakki, Asra Nomani, and Reva Seth; Sampson Oli and Chido Nwangwu; Shirley Perez, Joyce Gladwell, Paulette Longmore, and Sharon Spence; and the extraordinary Esperanza Fonseca.

Numerous scholars, meanwhile, helped me understand the science or history behind what I saw. It was a joy to reap the intellectual generosity of Kyriakos Markides, Stephen Klineberg, Stephan Thernstrom, Robert Sampson, Rubén Rumbaut, Daniel Smith, Laurence Kruckman, Stephanie Coontz, Nestor Rodriguez, Suzanne Model, Katherine Masley, Kathleen Cagney, Christopher Browning, David Cort, Ruchi Gupta, Jeffrey Capizzano, Susan Kim, Eric Klinenberg, Sarah Blaffer Hrdy, Philip Kasinitz, Richard Rothstein, and Tomás Jiménez.

And sometimes what I needed appeared from on high. "I think you'll enjoy my new neighbors," my mother, Marielena, said one summer. How right she was. Nikki Greenspan, her husband Sven Schuessler, and their buddy Sandra Davis—all airline pilots—became dear friends. They were also literal *dei ex machinas*, helping me crisscross the country for research on standby.

If my feet nevertheless remained on solid ground, it's thanks to mentors who nurtured my interest in immigrants many years before this project started. Great thanks for this to John Kling, Darlene Stinson, James Gibbons, and Steve Jetton of the *Houston Chronicle*; and Scott Kraft and Bret Israel of the *Los Angeles Times*.

Networks and institutions enriched my work too: Caroline Collective; Las Comadres and the magnificent Nora Comstock; the Jamaica Organization of New Jersey; the Institute for Agulu Development; Becker Early Childhood Center; Rotary International; Janice Ford Griffin and Robert Wood Johnson Foundation Community Health Leaders; and The Harris Foundation. Then there's the literal embodiment of an enriching network: the hui. I still can't get over the gumption and goodwill of those first players, among them Carlos Puig, Yissel Ibarra, Bill Maxey, Kirste Reimers, Barbara Karkabi, Mike Snyder, Elena Vega, Maru Garcia, and Jack Richmond.

A few months ago, a bee in my bonnet sent me to Baltimore. I wanted to introduce my daughters to my cousin Gloria, one of the relatives who so inspired me as a child. Queenly and whip smart at eighty, she did not disappoint. As Anna and Elena listened astounded, Gloria told about her sister's car ride with Albert Einstein, her brother's passion for rescuing Soviet Jews, and her late father's insistence on being "Americanski."

Back in Houston a few weeks later, I was dumbfounded to hear the girls repeat with astonishing relish and accuracy every word of Gloria's family stories. "No," Elena said. "*Our* family stories."

What families do and say, in other words, tends to stick. I'm ardently grateful, then, to my siblings and best friends Luisa, Adam, and Jason Kolker for a lifetime of encouragement—and to my parents, Jonas and Marielena Kolker, who showed that love will cross any border. More recently, I am indebted to the liveliest and most loving in-laws of all time: Dean and Susan Stravato, Claudia Stravato, and Selden Hale.

I also give thanks to my merry, stouthearted daughters, Anna and Elena. Your help made putting this book together a fandango. Finally, and from the bottom of my heart, I thank Michael Stravato, who is my hero.

INDEX

Adams Morgan (D.C. neighborhood), 6
Adriana (cuarentena), 50–51
African Americans, 8, 104
    asthma prevalence in, 128, 135, 136
    in Chicago neighborhoods, 130, 131, 140
    health of, 5, 48
    money clubs and, 34–35
African immigrants, 5, 6, 11
Afterschools, 15–16, 87–101, 200–202
    evolution of, 201
    historical influences on, 97–98
    Korean term for (hagwon), 87
    public school programs compared with, 92–93
    reasons for success of, 92–95, 201
    stress caused by, 98–99
Agulu immigrants, 195–97, 210–14
Akron, Ohio, 15, 40, 45
Alcohol use, 6, 48
Alvarez, Anarosa, 40–42, 43, 44–46, 48, 49
American Journal of Public Health, 5, 126
American money club, 35–37, 176–93
    behavior modification via, 178, 204–5
    counting the money, 183–86, 187
    feedback from participants, 188–89
    money bottle and, 181–83, 186, 192
    reasons for participation in, 178–80
    reasons for refusals to join, 177–78
    rules of, 176
A Plus Math, 91–92
Appalachia, 14, 120

Aristide, Jean-Bertrand, 8
Arranged marriage, 63, 66–67, 70–71, 74, 199. *See also* Assisted marriage
Asian immigrants, 8, 10. *See also* South Asian immigrants
    academic performance of, 89–90, 209
    characteristics of newly arrived, 11
    East Asians, 5
    health of, 5
    model minority stereotype, 89, 90
    as percentage of U.S. population, 89
Assisted marriage, 15, 61–86, 198–99
    American customs compared with, 62, 67, 69
    auntie system in, 63, 83
    biodata in, 66, 84
    characteristics of participants, 63
    consideration toward contenders in, 73–74
    dating compared with, 61, 63–64, 69–70, 73–74
    "love" marriages compared with, 71
    for non-Indians, 82–85
Asthma, 126–29, 134–38, 139, 140, 144, 148, 202
    crime and, 129, 223–24n
    outcomes in Chicago residents, 135
    research breakthrough, 135–38
    rise in, 127, 128
    stress and, 126, 129
    symptoms and triggers of, 126
Asthma Center on Community, Environment, and Social Stress, 129
Astro Dry Clean, 27, 186

CPSIA information can be obtained at www.ICGtesting.com
Printed in the USA
BVOW05s0513040515

398699BV00003B/208/P

9 781416 586838